ST. IRENAEUS

PROOF
OF
THE APOSTOLIC PREACHING

Ancient Christian Writers

THE WORKS OF THE FATHERS IN TRANSLATION

EDITED BY

JOHANNES QUASTEN, S. T. D.
*Professor of Ancient Church History
and Christian Archaeology*

JOSEPH C. PLUMPE, Ph. D.
*Professor of Patristic Greek
and Ecclesiastical Latin*

The Catholic University of America
Washington, D. C.

No. 16

ST. IRENAEUS
PROOF OF THE
APOSTOLIC PREACHING

TRANSLATED AND ANNOTATED

BY

JOSEPH P. SMITH, S. J.

Professor in
The Pontifical Biblical Institute, Rome

NEWMAN PRESS

New York, N.Y./Ramsey, N.J.

De Licentia Superioris Ordinis
  Nihil Obstat
          J. Quasten
              Censor Deputatus

Imprimatur:
              Patricius A. O'Boyle, D.D.
                  Archiepiscopus Washingtonensis
                      die 19 Maii 1952

Library of Congress
Catalog Card Number: 78-62503

ISBN: 0-8091-0254-4

PUBLISHED BY PAULIST PRESS
Editorial Office: 1865 Broadway, New York, N.Y. 10023
Business Office: 545 Island Road, Ramsey, N.J. 07446

PRINTED AND BOUND IN THE UNITED STATES OF AMERICA

CONTENTS

V

CONTENTS

vii

C. CHRIST IN THE OLD LAW 75

42. The Prophecies. — 43. The Son in the Beginning. — 44. The Son and Abraham. Sodom and Gomorrha. — 45. The Son and Jacob. Theophanies are of the Son. — 46. The Son and Moses in the Desert. — 47. The Trinity and Creatures. — 48. *The Lord saith to my Lord . . .* (Ps. 109). — 49. The Son Anointed King. God speaks in the Prophets. — 50-51. The Son Pre-existent. Saviour of All. — 52. The Message of Scripture. — 53. *The Virgin shall conceive.* "Christ Jesus." — 54. "Emmanuel." Virgin Birth. — 54-55. "Wonderful Counsellor." — 56. *They shall wish that they had been burnt with fire.* — 57. "A Ruler from Juda." "Blood of the Grape." — 58. Star of Jacob. — 59. Rod and Flower from the Roots of Jesse. — 60. "Just Judgement to the Lowly." — 61. *The wolf shall feed with the lamb.* — 62. *I will raise up the tabernacle of David.* — 63. Bethlehem of Judaea. — 64. The Son of David for evermore. — 65. Entry into Jerusalem. — 66. Christ in the Prophets. — 67. Christ's Miracles. — 68-69. The Passion. — 69 The Taking of Judgement. — 70. *Who shall declare His generation?* —. 71. *Under Thy shadow shall we live.* — 72. The Death of the Just Man. — 73. The Resurrection. — 74. Herod and Pilate. — 75. The Passion (by the Will of the Father). — 76. The Arrest of Christ. — 77. Christ before Herod. — 78. Descent into Hell. — 79. Crucifixion. — 80. The Parting of the Garments. — 81. The Thirty Pieces of Silver. — 82. Gall and Vinegar. — 83. The Ascension. — 84. The Entry into Heaven. — 85. Awaiting the Judgement.

D. CHRIST IN THE NEW LAW 100

86. The Prophets and the Apostolic Preaching. — 87. Charity supersedes the Law. — 88. Christ in Glory. He Himself redeemed us. — 89. The Spirit supersedes the Law. — 90. Newness of Spirit. The New Covenant. — 91-92. The Gentiles Heirs to the Promises. — 93. The Gentiles to be a Holy People. — 94. Church more fruitful than Synagogue. — 95. The Gentiles supplant Israel. — 96. We have no need of the Law. — 97. Nearness of Almighty Aid. — 98. Conclusion. — 99. Error against the Persons of the Trinity. — 100. Beware of Heretics!

Contents

ST. IRENAEUS

PROOF
OF
THE APOSTOLIC PREACHING

INTRODUCTION.

A. AUTHOR AND WORKS. PUBLICATIONS OF THE *PROOF*.

1. THE AUTHOR. St. Irenaeus (end of second century) comes in the history of patrology after the " Apostolic Fathers," and the " Apologists," and in some ways constitutes a link between the latter and the Alexandrians. He may be said to belong to the third generation of Christian teachers, for in his youth in Asia Minor he had known the celebrated Polycarp, and the latter had himself known our Lord's own disciples, in particular the apostle St. John, who made him bishop of Smyrna.[1] In the reign of Marcus Aurelius, when persecution was raging at Lyons, Irenaeus was a presbyter in that city, and about the years 177-8 succeeded the martyr St. Pothinus as its bishop.[2] The year of Irenaeus's death is unknown; it is commonly put at about 202, at the time of the renewed persecution under Septimius Severus, and he is venerated as a martyr; but the evidence for his martyrdom is unsatisfactory.[3]

2. HIS WORKS. Eusebius of Caesarea, to whom we are ultimately indebted for all we know about Irenaeus (apart of course from what may be gathered of him from his own writings), mentions as his works a treatise against Marcion, various letters, of which the most celebrated is the one written to Victor of Rome on the Paschal controversy, sundry other treatises, including one " for the proof of the apostolic preaching " (the one here translated: hereafter referred to as " the *Proof* "), and — his principal work — the five books

3

of his treatise against the Gnostics, commonly known under the title *Adversus haereses*, "Against the heresies." [4] This work, as we shall see later, is of especial importance for the understanding of several passages of the *Proof*. Irenaeus wrote in Greek, but his works have not come down to us, as such, in the original.[5] We have, however, in addition to numerous fragments in various languages, much of the original Greek as quoted by later writers, and the complete text, in an early Latin version, of *Adversus haereses*, and also an Armenian version of the last two of the five books of that work, and of the *Proof*. This last-named version is the one here translated into English; with the exception of a few fragments textually of little help and also in Armenian, it is our only source for the text of the *Proof*.

3. ARMENIAN TEXT. The *Proof* was for long supposed to have been irretrievably lost, but in 1904 an Armenian version of it was found, in a manuscript belonging to the church of Our Lady at Erevan (now the capital of Soviet Armenia) by the Most Rev. Archimandrite (of Etschmiadzin) Karapet Ter Mekerttschian, who was at the time acting as Vicar to the Catholicos, and later became bishop of Azerbaidjan.[6] In addition to the *Proof*, the same manuscript contained several other items, including the Armenian version, referred to in the previous paragraph, of books 4 and 5 of *Adversus haereses*, which is in the same peculiarly distinctive Armenian style as that of the *Proof*. The Armenian text of the *Proof* was first published, by the finder of the manuscript, in 1907, along with a German translation, and with annotations by Adolf von Harnack, who also divided the text into a hundred "chapters." [7] It was republished in 1919 in Graffin and Nau's *Patrologia Orientalis*.[8]

4. TRANSLATIONS. The German translation of the *editio*

princeps appeared in a revised edition in 1908; meanwhile a Russian version had been published by Professor Sagarda.[9] In 1912 Professor Simon Weber published a new German translation, and in 1917, after a controversy as to the accuracy of the rival German versions, the same scholar published a Latin one whose aim was to reproduce the Armenian text, so far as possible, word for word.[10] In the meantime a French version, made by the Rev. J. Barthoulot, S. J., had been published by Professor Tixeront.[11] This was reprinted as an appendix to the *Patrologia Orientalis* republication of the text (1919), which was itself accompanied with an English version made by the finder and others. In 1920 another English version was published by J. Armitage Robinson, and a Dutch one by H. U. Meyboom; and in 1923 an Italian one, by Ubaldo Faldati.[12] The present translation was made from the text of the *editio princeps* (attention being paid to various emendations since suggested) and collated with the text as republished in the *Patrologia Orientalis*. All the other translations mentioned above, except the Dutch one and the second edition of the first German one, were glanced through, and are occasionally mentioned in the notes to this version, but no attempt was made to collate them exhaustively. The chapter-division of the *editio princeps*, though open to certain criticisms, has of course been retained.

B. TEXTUAL HISTORY.

5. AUTHENTICITY. That the work here presented to us is really, as the manuscript describes it, the "Proof of the Apostolic Preaching" of Irenaeus, is certain on internal grounds. The title and the name (chapter 1) of the addressee agree with the information given us by Eusebius;[13] the work reflects the conditions of the end of the second

century,[14] and its matter and manner and many of its turns of expression agree with Irenaeus's known writings, and with his views and preoccupations; the parallels with *Adversus haereses* are many and striking; in chapter 74, to mention a particular example, we have the erroneous statement that Pontius Pilate was procurator under Claudius, a peculiar error which agrees with what we know to have been Irenaeus's opinion;[15] and in chapter 99 the author refers to his work against heretics, using the longer title which is given by Eusebius as that of *Adversus haereses*.[16]

6. DATE AND PLACE OF COMPOSITION. This reference in the *Proof* to the author's *Adversus haereses* enables us to date the former work approximately, since it must be posterior to at least the earlier part of *Adversus haereses*. In book three of this work there is a list of the bishops of Rome, which concludes with the mention of Eleutherus as then reigning.[17] Since Eleutherus became bishop of Rome about the year 174, and Irenaeus became bishop of Lyons about 177-8 and died early in the following century, we may say that he composed the *Proof* at Lyons, when bishop of that city, in the last two decades of the second century, or possibly in the early years of the third. Certain indications have been taken to favour a later rather than an earlier date within that period, and it has even been suggested that the work belongs to the last years of its author's life; but this is all pure conjecture.[18]

7. DATE OF THE MANUSCRIPT. TEXTUAL TRADITION. Our manuscript bears, at the end of the *Proof*, a scribal postscript naming as its owner the " Lord Archbishop John . . . brother of the holy king." This can be none other than the well-known " John Arkhayeghbayrn (= ' king's-brother ')," for his learning also called " Rabbun," younger brother of

King Hethum I of Cilicia (1226-1270). John, who died in 1289, was consecrated bishop in 1259 and only some years later is given the title "archbishop." Hence one may date the manuscript around the middle of the second half of the thirteenth century, say between the years 1265 and 1289. The translation itself was certainly made long before that date, and is in a style which lends itself to certain corruptions; exactly to what extent corruption has taken place we have no external means of judging; as has already been said, our only sources for the text of the *Proof* are this manuscript and a few Armenian fragments. The latter exhibit certain differences from the text of the manuscript, and these differences are most likely to be accounted for by "editing" of a text more faithfully copied in our manuscript.[19] Two questions, however, we are now able to answer with a certain degree of confidence: at what date was the Armenian translation made, and was it made directly from the Greek. As will be seen from the following paragraphs, it was almost certainly made in the sixth century, and most probably between the years 570 and 590, and was made directly from the Greek.

8. DATE OF TRANSLATION: EXTERNAL EVIDENCE. In previous editions of the *Proof*, or of the Armenian version of *Adversus haereses* 4-5, the dating has been based on quotations from those works found in earlier manuscripts than ours. Both versions are in the same peculiar style, and were assumed to be the work of the same translator and so of the same approximate date. When the two versions were first published, earlier quotations were known from " Stephen the Philosopher," who was identified with the eighth-century Stephen of Siunikh, and from the " Catholicos Sahak," who was identified as Sahak (Isaac) III, who died about the end

of the seventh century.[20] Hence the translations were said to be not later than the seventh century.[21] Later, however, quotations were found which were datable to the beginning of that century.[22] The quotations are but slight, and show certain differences from our text, so that one might suspect them to be the result of independent translation, and so far from proving that our translation already existed, rather to suggest the contrary. There is, however, sufficient evidence of the peculiar style of our version to allow us to account for the differences by supposing editorial revision and the corruption to which the style lends itself, and conclude, with Jordan, that our version must have been made before the year 600.[23]

9. DATE OF TRANSLATION: INTERNAL EVIDENCE. As soon as the Armenian text of the two works in our manuscript was published, Conybeare pointed out its stylistic resemblance to the Armenian version of Philo, and maintained that it must be from the same pen, and hence of the early fifth century, since the version of Philo was then assigned to that period.[24] Subsequent research has established beyond a doubt that our text does in fact belong, if not necessarily to the same pen, at least to the same school and to the same short period as the Armenian Philo and certain other translations from the Greek; but the dating of this school has been matter of dispute.[25] The Armenian Philo was known to Moses of Khoren, who used to be assigned to the mid-fifth century. Considerable doubt has been thrown on this dating, most scholars now maintaining that Moses of Khoren must be assigned to the eighth or ninth century. Conybeare controverted this view, and so do other scholars.[26] Failing Moses of Khoren, the earliest witness to the Armenian Philo is the historian Elisaeus; he also used

to be assigned — and by many still is assigned — to the mid-fifth century; but it has been maintained that he wrote subsequently to 570.[27] What may be regarded as certain is that the translation of the *Proof*, along with that of Philo and others, belongs to the earliest phase of the so-called " Hellenising " school of Armenian. It has been maintained that this school cannot be earlier than the sixth century: it has seemed necessary to allow for a considerable lapse of time between the " golden age " of Armenian (first half of fifth century) and this strange style; and the school seems to have been unknown to the philhellene historian Lazar of Pharp, who wrote at the beginning of the sixth century. If we accept the beginning of the sixth century as the earliest date, and the end of the same century as the latest, both because of the evidence mentioned in the previous paragraph and because of Elisaeus, we are left with the sixth century as the period within which our translation was made. The extraordinary style, however, of the versions in question can scarcely be accounted for except by supposing them to have been intended as " keys " to the Greek text, and the most probable dating of the rise of the Hellenising school is that of Akinean, who places it among the Armenian exiles at Byzantium after 570.[28] That was the period at which Armenian students had need of such keys. The early phase in question cannot have lasted long, and in any case many of the exiles returned after 590, so that one may say that our version was most probably made at Byzantium between the years 570 and 590. In deference, however, to the views of a number of scholars, it should be pointed out that this is the latest dating, that the reasons for denying that the Hellenising school can have existed before the sixth century are by no means cogent, and that if those scholars are right in maintaining the traditional date for Moses of Khoren or Elisaeus, our translation may be put into the first half of the fifth century. This, however, seems to the present writer unlikely.

10. TRANSLATION DIRECTLY FROM GREEK. In the case of an Armenian translation of an early Greek work, one has to take into account the possibility that the translation was made not directly from the Greek, but from a Syriac version. In the *editio princeps* of the *Proof* attention was drawn to certain peculiarities in the text of the *Proof* and of *Adversus haereses* which seemed to indicate such a Syriac intermediary, but in view of the counter-indications the question was left open, and in republishing the text in *Patrologia Orientalis* Bishop Karapet mentions the general agreement that the version had been made directly from the Greek (though indeed in the meantime it had even been suggested that the translation had been made from a Latin version).[29] In fact, the indications of Syriac transmission were with one exception utterly negligible, and even that exception is inconclusive, while the indications of translation directly from the Greek were very strong.[30] One may now assert with confidence that our version, like the other products of the Hellenising school, is based immediately on the Greek text; one may even go further and say that it seems to have been made with a view to providing those insufficiently acquainted with Greek with a key to a text they were studying in the original.

11. STATE OF TEXT. From what has just been said, the reader will be able to form an idea of the style of Armenian in which the version is cast.[31] At its worst it approaches the type "The hand-shoes, which on the table were, have I in the pocket put." A particular feature of this early period of

the Hellenising school is the use of doublets or expanded expressions to render Greek compound words or "bracket" the exact meaning of single Greek words.[32] This does not as a rule occasion any difficulty, as the resulting expressions, though often awkward, are fairly intelligible. The attempt, however, to reproduce the syntactical features of the original in a language which has its own different syntax results inevitably in passages whose meaning is most obscure, even when one knows the language whose syntax is so reproduced, and which are not infrequently quite unintelligible to the average scribe and so give rise to corruptions in the text which increase the difficulty of reconstructing the original.[33] The text presented to us by our manuscript is no doubt fairly faithful, and is on the whole not unsatisfactory, but it is too often obscure, and in several places is manifestly corrupt.[34] It may however be said that there is no doubt in any matter of importance as to the general sense, and one can confidently accept the version as being on the whole a faithful rendering of Irenaeus's work.

12. PRINCIPLES OF THIS TRANSLATION. In making the present version, the translator has aimed at producing a readable English text which should represent not the peculiarities of the text of our manuscript, but Irenaeus's work, while still remaining a translation of our manuscript, not a paraphrase. Accordingly, where the Armenian text seemed certainly at fault, the necessary emendation has been rendered in the text of this version, the meaning of the manuscript's text being relegated to the notes. Other emendations, while not so accepted into the text, have been mentioned in the notes. Where the exact sense of the Armenian was uncertain, the present version has sometimes aimed at reproducing in English the same ambiguity; at other times a likely version

has been given in the text, and alternatives in the notes; in one or two places, where the general sense was clear enough, but the expression obscure or corrupt, a paraphrase has been given, representing what seemed most likely to have been the original expression. In all such cases the reading of the manuscript is given and briefly discussed in the notes, as also in cases in which it might be useful to readers to know the origin — and the degree of probability or possibility — of variant renderings in other versions. Such textual notes, however, have been kept as brief as might be, this series not being the place for philological discussions. The punctuation of the Armenian text is not invariably felicitous, and has been departed from without acknowledgement of such departure in the notes, except once or twice where the change of punctuation has induced a notable change of sense. In the Scriptural quotations the wording of the Douay version has been used as a rule wherever the Armenian seemed to rest on the same reading of the Scriptural original. In dealing with the peculiarities of the Armenian style (use of doublets and expansions) there is perhaps a certain inconsistency. Such doublets are not seldom desirable in English, and they have occasionally been retained for that reason; in general, however, expanded expressions have been reduced where English usage normally requires such a reduction (for example, the constantly recurring " it is right and necessary " is regularly rendered by use of the verb " must "); moreover, in several places a wordy expression of the text has been kept even though in all probability it represents an expansion of the original.

C. TITLE, ADDRESSEE, FORM AND STYLE.

13. TITLE. Eusebius refers to the work as (λόγος) . . . εἰς τὴν ἐπίδειξιν τοῦ ἀποστολικοῦ κηρύγματος, "(a treatise) for the demonstration of the apostolic preaching."[35] The word here rendered "demonstration" is in Greek *epídeixis*, and the treatise is therefore sometimes referred to as "the Epideixis." This word means, more or less, "demonstration," since it connotes not only "proof" but also "display, exposition," and J. Armitage Robinson used for his English version the title "Demonstration of the Apostolic Preaching."[36] The present version retains the title "Proof . . . ," both because it has some claim to be regarded as the traditional English title, and because it goes better in English, and because it represents in fact the scope of the treatise. The academic question has been raised, whether Irenaeus's title was (Λόγος) εἰς τὴν ἐπίδειξιν . . . , "(A treatise) for the proof . . . ," as we read in Eusebius, or simply Ἐπίδειξις . . . , "Proof . . . ," the rest being merely the turn of phrase used by Eusebius in order to work the title into his sentence. In any case, the Armenian manuscript bears the shorter form: "Proof of the Apostolic Preaching."

14. ADDRESSEE. The treatise is addressed, in chapter 1, to "my dear Marcianus," and Eusebius tells us that Irenaeus wrote it ἀδελφῷ Μαρκιανῷ, "to brother Marcianus."[37] The use of this expression does not necessarily mean that Marcianus was the writer's brother according to the flesh, though this is a natural interpretation of it, and there seems to be no reason why that should not be the meaning. If Marcianus was Irenaeus's brother, he was presumably some years his junior. A "brother Marcianus" is also named as author of the *Martyrium Polycarpi*, and some have sought to identify

him with the addressee of the *Proof*; but the reading " Marcion " is regarded as more likely than " Marcianus " in the *Martyrium*.[38] Others have thought our Marcianus must have been a recent convert from Judaism, in view of Irenaeus's repeated insistence, in the *Proof*, that the Old Law has been abrogated.[39] This insistence is indeed remarkable, and calls for an explanation, but as we shall see, it is not necessary to seek such an explanation in any judaising tendency of the addressee. He must have been a former companion of Irenaeus, for in chapter 1 we read: " Would that it were possible for us to be always together. . . . As it is, as we are at the present time distant in body from each other . . ."; and he may perhaps have been a bishop, or at least a priest, for in the same chapter he is told that the treatise will help him to confound heretics and preach the truth, and it seems to be suggested — though the rendering here is uncertain — that he has the " care of souls." [40] It seems clear at least that he was not a mere catechumen.

15. LITERARY FORM. The *Proof*, then, is written in the form of a letter, as indeed all of Irenaeus's writings seem to have been, not only the " letters " more properly so called, but his other treatises also being cast in letter form; even *Adversus haereses* is addressed, in the prefaces to the individual books, to an unnamed " dearly beloved " (in the singular). It is, however, evident that the *Proof*, like *Adversus haereses*, is a planned composition, and destined for the general public, so that though it was doubtless addressed to a real Marcianus, we may regard the letter-form as being in effect a literary artifice; it was at that time a common one. The construction is on the whole clear and logical enough in the arrangement of the matter, though in this, as we shall see later, Irenaeus was probably simply following his source;

and precisely in the earlier chapters, where he is himself responsible for the arrangement of the matter, there is a little of the confusion and repetitiveness which seems to have been characteristic of Irenaeus.[41] If one has at times the impression of a string of quotations introduced by nearly identical formulas, this is only to be expected in view of the nature of the work; and in other places the quotations are led up to or followed in a more artistic manner.

16. STYLE. In the preface to the first book of *Adversus haereses* Irenaeus says that niceness of language is not to be expected of him, since he was living "among Celts" and speaking for most of his time a foreign tongue; nor artistic elegance, since he had never learnt it; but he adds that he writes with affection and expects to be read with affection. The style of the *Proof*, like that of *Adversus haereses*, is frequently confused — in fairness to the men who translated Irenaeus into often enigmatic Latin and Armenian, it should be remarked that not all of the obscurity is due to the fault of the translators — and at times repetitive and diffuse; and here, in fairness to Irenaeus, it may be said that the failure of his translators to see their author's point has led to not a little false phrasing and lost emphasis which have made the style seem even more repetitive. The very sentence, in the first chapter, in which the author promises to be brief, is itself a model of rhetorical prolixity. So indeed is the whole chapter, and the following section, and it seems clear that, as is normally the case, the introductory portion of the work was aiming deliberately at literary effect.

D. DIVISION AND CONTENTS.

17. DIVISION. Harnack, as has already been said, divided the text into a hundred numbered "chapters," and this

division is retained in the present translation. In addition, for convenience of reference, headings have been added, which do not always coincide with the chapter-division, and the treatise has been divided into four main sections. There is a fairly clear distinction of topic in the course of the treatise, which serves as a basis for this division, but it is not so easy to choose the exact spot at which to divide, and the division here adopted makes no claim to being better than others. The treatise may be first divided into two parts, corresponding to the " moments " before and after Christ, and each of these parts may be further divided into two sections. After a short introduction on the need of orthodox faith and good works, there follows a section on the Trinity, creation, and the fall of man. This constitutes the first section of the " pre-Christian " part; the second section recounts the development of God's plan for the undoing of the evil wrought by the fall, in the course of Old Testament history, culminating in the Incarnation. The first section of the " Christian " part deals with Christ as seen in the Old Testament; and the second section with the New Law. There is a short conclusion, warning once more against heretics. The thesis of each of the four sections may be summarised as follows.

18. GOD AND CREATURES; THE FALL. (Chapters 1-16): the way of life is that of the orthodox faith and good works. Faith tells us we are baptised for the remission of sins in the name of one God almighty, Father, Son (who became man and died and was raised), and Holy Spirit (who spoke through the prophets and is poured out upon the faithful). God is supreme ruler over all things, for they are His own creation; with His Word (the Son) and Wisdom (the Holy Spirit) He made all things. The Father is invisible and incomprehensible, the Son appears as a link with man, the

Holy Spirit is given by the Son to man, and leads him to the Son, who brings him to the Father, who gives incorruptibility; God has made us His sons. There are seven heavens in which dwell angels. God is glorified by His Word and Spirit and by their angels. He made man as His own image, from earth and His own Spirit, free and lord of the world, including its angels, and set him in Paradise, giving him a help like himself. Adam and Eve were children, innocent and guileless, and were deceived by the jealous angel into disobeying God's prohibition of the tree of knowledge, imposed on them as a sign of subjection and a condition of immortality; so man was cast out of Paradise and became subject to death, the angel and the serpent being cursed for their part in his fall.

19. HISTORY OF REDEMPTION. (Chapters 17-mid. 42): The devil brought about the first death through Cain, and man went from bad to worse, especially through marriage with angels, who corrupted him with wicked knowledge, until man was destroyed by the Flood. God saved Noe and his sons; of the latter, Cham was cursed and the curse worked itself out in his descendants, while first Sem and then Japheth were blessed, the blessings being inherited in the same order by their descendants. That of Sem came to Abraham, who found God and was justified by faith, and to his seed, whom God rescued from Egypt through Moses, and to whom He gave the Old Law. Through Jesus son of Nun (to whom He had given that holy name) He brought them into the promised land, which they took from the descendants of Cham, and where they had a kingdom and were taught by the prophets, until God's promises were fulfilled in the virgin birth of Christ of the seed of Abraham and of David; so man was brought into contact with God,

by a repetition of creation and by obedience which restored
man to the likeness of God and undid the primal disobedience. Christ's birth, death, and resurrection are real, so we
are really saved. His apostles founded the Church and gave
the Holy Spirit to the faithful, and in the calling of the
Gentiles through the Church the blessing of Japheth is
inherited by his descendants.

20. CHRIST IN THE OLD LAW. (Chapters mid. 42-85):
All this is foretold in the Old Testament. Christ is there as
the " Son in the beginning " in creation; He appeared to
Abraham and to Jacob, and spoke with Moses, and spoke
through the prophets. The prophets foretold His eternal
kingdom, His incarnation, the virgin birth, and told where
and of what stock He would be born, and foretold His kingdom of peace in the Church. They prophesied His entry
into Jerusalem, His miracles, His sufferings and crucifixion,
His descent into hell, His resurrection and His ascension
into glory, where He now reigns at the right hand of the
Father, till He judge in triumph. (This section, though it
may so be resumed in brief space, is the largest of the four.)

21. CHRIST IN THE NEW LAW. (Chapters 86-100): The
fulfilment of the prophecies confirms our faith, showing the
truth of the mission of the apostles. The abrogation of the
Old Law was foretold; it is superseded by the Law of
Charity. Christ's exaltation was foretold, and the establishment of the New Covenant, as the inheritance of the Gentiles, who were to become a holy people. So is brought about
a change of heart in man, and the Church is more fruitful
than the Synagogue; the old chosen people has given place
to the new, and we have no need of the Law. Man is
restored to his lost innocence and is virtuous without the
Law. He is saved by the invocation of the name of Christ;

God accomplishes what is impossible to man. This is the preaching of the truth, which is that of the Church and must be sincerely accepted. Heretics sin against Father or Son or Holy Spirit; we must avoid their ways if we hope to be saved.

22. PROBLEMS PRESENTED. Certain problems cannot fail to present themselves to the reader of the *Proof*. In the first place, the title suggests that the work is an exposition of the preaching of Christianity; but though the theology is of course Christian, the argument is drawn practically entirely from the Old Testament, and there is no mention for instance of the Eucharist, or of several other points essential to Christianity. On the other hand, there are certain curious emphases, and in particular the repeated insistence on the abolition of the Old Law. These and similar problems find an answer in the following sections in this Introduction.[42]

E. SCOPE AND IMPORTANCE.

23. APPARENT AIM: CATECHETIC. The aim of the treatise is stated in its first chapter: to give Marcianus " in brief the proof (*or* exposition) of the things of God," or, as we would put it nowadays, " a compendium of theology," which should serve both to guide him to salvation and to enable him to refute heretics and expound the faith with confidence " in its integrity and purity." This description suffices to show the importance, as a Christian document, of the *Proof*; it seems to correspond to the title understood in the sense " exposition of the apostolic preaching," and to promise to be the earliest summary of Christian doctrine we have, and at that, from the pen of a bishop separated by only one intervening generation of teachers from the apostles themselves. It has in fact been called a catechetical

work, representing Christianity as then expounded by the bishops to the faithful.[43] Nevertheless, this estimate must be accepted with reserve. Beyond a doubt, we have here in fact an exposition of much of what was preached by the apostles; but a perusal of the *Proof* suffices to show that it cannot be regarded as a complete exposition of their preaching, or of what Irenaeus regarded as "Christianity."

24. REAL AIM: APOLOGETIC. Though Marcianus is told that by means of the treatise he may "comprehend all the members of the body of truth," this is to be "in a few details"; the treatise is "in the form of notes on the main points," and its aim is to confirm the faith of Marcianus and enable him to confound heretics.[44] The real thesis of the work is seen from the passage in chapter 42 in which we are told that God caused our redemption to be prophesied in order that when it came we might believe, and from the passage in chapter 86 in which we are told that the realisation in Christ of the prophecies is the proof that the witness of the apostles is the truth, and from the author's preoccupation especially at the beginning and end of the work to insist on the need for orthodoxy and the avoidance of heresy.[45] The author wishes to prove that what the apostles preached was true rather than to give an exposition of their preaching, and is concerned for the "integrity" of the faith not so much in the sense of its "exhaustiveness" as in the sense of its "soundness."[46] The points on which he repeatedly insists are those which were denied by the heretics. Hence the work has been said to be apologetic rather than catechetical;[47] and while its catechetical aspect cannot be denied, it is certainly apologetic in aim, though not in quite the same sense as the works of the earlier "apologists." It is rather "apologetics" in the modern sense, aiming not so much at the

defence of Christianity against paganism or Judaism, as at the positive establishment of the credentials of the orthodox Church. It is, in fact, a " proof of the apostolic preaching," that is, a proof of the divine mission of the Church founded by the apostles. It may indeed be called a " compendium of theology," but, as Weber puts it, it is " fundamental theology." [48] It has the practical aim of establishing the truths whose acceptance means acceptance of the orthodox Church — the rest will follow from that.

25. METHOD. EXEGESIS. This proof is drawn mainly from the Old Testament, and the treatise is important for its use of Scripture; indeed it has been called a Biblical manual.[49] It passes in review practically the whole of the Old Testament, showing how it prepares the way for the New. Irenaeus's exegesis is characterised by that development of " typical " senses which was so much in accord with the spirit of the times, the method employed by the apologists, developed still further by Irenaeus and Clement of Alexandria, and carried to its greatest heights by the latter's successors. The exegesis of the *Proof*, as befits a work written not for edification alone, but to bring conviction, is comparatively sober. Inevitably it is at times arbitrary or based on mere associations, but it is free from the wilder flights of fancy found elsewhere, and there is no cabbalistic juggling with letters or numbers.[50]

26. IMPORTANCE. The importance of the *Proof* as a " manual of theology," although not in the same sense as might have been hoped, is clear enough from what has been said in the preceding paragraphs; it should be pointed out, however, that the finding of this lost work has in fact added little to what was already known. The *Proof* contains little that was not already to be found in even earlier documents;

in particular, little that is not in *Adversus haereses*. There
are, it is true, one or two points which may be regarded as
an advance on that work, but the real importance of the
Proof, as compared with *Adversus haereses*, is due to its
manner of presentation, its brevity and coherence. One may
say that it is important not so much for its theology, as for
being precisely a *manual* of theology.

F. THEOLOGY OF THE *PROOF*.

27. IRENAEUS'S PREOCCUPATIONS. For an account of
Irenaeus's theology in general, or of that of the *Proof* in
particular, or of the systems of his Gnostic adversaries, the
reader must be referred to the existing treatises on those
subjects. There are certain points, however, which should
be touched on here, because some acquaintance with them
is necessary to the proper understanding of the author's expressions in the *Proof*. Irenaeus has certain definite ideas
to which he constantly returns, and his allusions are not
seldom difficult to interpret without knowledge of the idea
underlying them. Moreover there are in the *Proof* several
statements of which one risks missing the point unless one
knows what prompted the author to make them, namely his
preoccupation with the errors — now long forgotten — of his
opponents, the Gnostics in general, and Marcion in particular. It will not be out of place, therefore, to give here a
brief account of such points of Irenaeus's theology, and of
Gnosticism, as are relevant to the understanding of the *Proof*.

28. GNOSTICISM; MARCION. The proper title of Irenaeus's principal work, commonly known as *Adversus
haereses*, was "Exposure and Overthrowal of Knowledge
falsely so called"; and the "knowledge falsely so called"
was Gnosticism, which may be roughly described as belief

in various systems of esoteric doctrine, whose knowledge was supposed to bring salvation to the initiate.[51] In the broad sense Gnosticism is fairly universal both in time and in space, but in the strict sense the word is applied to certain forms current in the Greco-Roman world from some time before the birth of Christ until several centuries later. In Irenaeus's time such "fancy religions" were rife, and constituted an especial danger to Christian orthodoxy. Gnosticism is not, of course, a specifically Christian heresy, but then, as ever since, Gnostic sects drew largely from Biblical and Christian sources; several of their leaders, and many of their adherents, were ex-Christians, or regarded themselves as being Christians, as having the true interpretation of Christian revelation. Marcion, against whom Irenaeus wrote a special treatise, was the son of a bishop, and seems to have been a bishop himself, and was one of the most prominent of the pseudo-Christian leaders, numbered by Irenaeus and others along with the Gnostics, though his system differed considerably from the general run of Gnosticism.[52] Though all Gnosticism was distinguished by certain fundamental peculiarities, the various sects differed considerably in their views; not all sects held all the views attributed in the following paragraphs to "the Gnostics," as is clear enough from the fact that several of them are mutually exclusive.

29. GOD AND THE WORLD. The perpetual problem of theology is to reconcile the transcendence and goodness of God with this world's dependence on Him and with the existence of evil. For the Gnostics, the supreme God was unknowable, entirely aloof from matter, and matter was the root of evil. The void between God and the world was filled by a number of spiritual beings produced by "emanation" from God and by multiplication among themselves, and

called Aeons.[53] Matter was eternal, or the abortive product of a fallen Aeon; material things and the spiritual principle in the world were not of like nature, matter being foreign to God and the root of corruption and beyond salvation, but spirit being (ultimately) from God, and immortal. This world was created, or formed from chaotic matter, by a being, who himself owed his origin to God or to the Aeons, known as the demiurge; [54] for some sects, the angels were creators. Though, as has been said, the origin of evil was seen in matter, an evil principle was commonly posited as a third member of a triad: God — demiurge — " devil." From this account there arise several particular points which have their repercussions on the *Proof*, and which will be considered in greater detail in the following paragraphs. Irenaeus's own outlook naturally resembles that of the Gnostics in certain respects; both were the product of the same intellectual milieu, and both were ultimately based on the same sound philosophy. For Irenaeus too, as we shall see, the gulf between God and the world had to be filled in; but it was filled in not by intermediate "emanated" beings, but by God's own Word and Spirit; matter was of itself incapable of salvation or incorruption, but was nevertheless good, created by God, and part of man, and so, by the redemption, brought into touch with incorruptibility; evil is due not to any essentially evil principle but to the misuse of godlike free will.

30. GOD THE FATHER. The "God the Father" of the New Testament is the supreme God. In that, Irenaeus and the "Christian" Gnostics are in agreement. For Irenaeus, as for the Gnostics, He is invisible, incomprehensible, not to be circumscribed in space; yet it is He who "contains" all things; He is unknowable and unapproachable — save through His Son and the Holy Spirit.[55] The "God" of the

Old Testament is, as He Himself says, the creator. Hence, for the Gnostics, He was *not* the supreme God, the Father-God of the New Testament, but the demiurge; some of them even represented Him as the enemy of God, and the source of evil. Marcion in particular elaborated the distinction between the God of the Old Testament and the God of the New; the former was the demiurge, the "God" of the Law, just but severe, jealous and violent, having for his favourite people the Jews, and intent on bringing about a Messianic Jewish empire, and the source of strife and evil; whereas the God of the New Testament is kind and merciful, a God of peace, and wishes to save men from evil, by making use of the demiurge's Messianic plans and turning them to His own ends. In all these views, God's intervention to save mankind could be described as the interference, by an "other God" with the creatures of the demiurge. Hence the importance for Irenaeus of the line of argument adopted in the *Proof*, showing the continuity between the Old Law and the New; and hence the special emphasis on the identity of God the Father with the creator, on the fact that He — the creator — is Lord of all men, Jews and Gentiles alike, both just judge and loving Father.[56]

31. GOD THE SON. As "God the Father" is the supreme God, so Christ is His Son. Here too Irenaeus is at least in verbal agreement with the Gnostics. For Irenaeus, He is the Word of God; God created through Him, it is He who gives matter its solidity, and He is immanent in the universe as the Platonic world-soul.[57] He was ever with man, and is the link whereby we have access to the transcendent Father.[58] He is "the Son" because He is the "reproduction" of the Father, His image, expressed on the plane of possible contact with creation; He was always with the Father; the manner of

His " generation " is inscrutable.[59] Because He is the visible image of the invisible Father, it was He who manifested Himself materially in the theophanies of the Old Testament (to Adam, to Abraham and Jacob and Moses).[60] So too man is made in His image;[61] and in His incarnation He reproduced the original creation of man in order to " recapitulate " all things.[62] It is He who confers the Holy Spirit. For the Gnostics, Christ the Saviour was an Aeon. In consequence of their view of matter as essentially evil, they maintained that he did not really assume a human body. According to Marcion and others he took only a " seeming " body, and that not through the Virgin, but by a special act; Marcion represented him as appearing for the first time in the synagogue at Capharnaum; according to others, he came " through " the Virgin, but " took nothing from her." [63] According to others, the child born of Mary was not Christ but only Jesus, the son of Joseph, or of the demiurge, or a man prepared to act as the " vehicle " of Christ; Christ descended upon him in the form of a dove at his baptism, and left him before his passion. In all these views " Christ " was not really born, nor did he really die or rise again. These errors also find their reactions in the *Proof*.[64]

32. THE HOLY SPIRIT. The Holy Spirit, for Irenaeus, is the Wisdom of God; in creation, He is associated with the Word; it is He who speaks through the prophets, and in Scripture, but it is the Word who communicates Him to men.[65] At man's creation, God breathed into him His own Spirit, which is free from evil and so kept man innocent until man rejected Him by the fall.[66] Man's likeness to God was given by the Spirit, and restored by the pouring out of the Spirit on the faithful, which gives man back his lost innocence, rendering him virtuous without the law; it is the

Spirit who leads man to Christ.[67] Irenaeus does not state explicitly the divinity or personality of the Holy Spirit, but that is no reason for speaking of his "binitarianism." He enumerates Father, Son, and Holy Spirit as the three "articles" of the faith; he says the Spirit is the Wisdom of God, and he constantly associates Him with the Word, whose divinity and personality he does expressly declare; so that his view is clearly perfectly orthodox: the Holy Spirit is a divine Person, proceeding from the Father (though Irenaeus does not of course use that expression), and conferred on creatures through the Son.[68] Marcion and others rejected the sending of the Holy Spirit, and His gifts, especially that of prophecy; for which they are taken to task, without being named, in the *Proof*.[69]

33. MAN. God made man with His own hands, that is, with the Word and the Spirit; He made him from earth, giving him an outward form to His own "image" (that is, to that of the Son), and gave him "likeness" to God by breathing into him His own Spirit.[70] Man was created free like God, and lord of the world, including its angels, and immortal; he was intended to develop a more and more perfect likeness to God, but the very freedom of will which likened him to God proved his undoing, since he misused it and so lost his high estate and his "likeness" to God (though the "image" was in his outward form and not lost) and his immortality.[71] Man is composed of body, soul, and spirit; in *Adversus haereses* Irenaeus gives an account of this composition, with the soul drawn between the attractions of spirit and body, resembling the description of the charioteer in the *Phaedrus*.[72] All three elements are necessary to man as God made him and meant him to be, but whereas body and soul are the constituents of man as an animal forming part of

creation as a whole, the spirit is a special "godlikeness." [73]
For the Gnostics, matter was evil and incapable of salvation;
only the soul and spirit could be saved. Irenaeus insists
that the body too is part of man, and that everything is
equally the creation of the one God, not only angels and
the (spiritual) heavens, but also this world and man, body
as well as soul and spirit. [74]

34. "SPIRITUAL MAN" AND GOOD WORKS. For the
Gnostics, all men were not alike; fundamental to Gnosticism
was a special interpretation of the trinity body — soul — spirit.
As has already been said, the body was for them beyond
salvation. The soul might be saved, the spirit could not but
be saved. A current characterisation of men (not peculiarly
Gnostic; it is found for example in the New Testament)
divided mankind into three classes; according to his "spiritual
level" a man might be described as "material" (or "earthly"
or "carnal"); or as "sensual" (to use the translation adopted
in the Douay version); or as "spiritual." [75] For the Gnostics
this represented a division of the human race into three
classes with respect to salvation. The "material" man — the
unbeliever — would not be saved in any case; the "sensual"
man — the ordinary run of believers; for the "Christian"
Gnostics, orthodox Christians — could attain a measure of
salvation, by reason of his faith, but must supplement it by
good works; the "spiritual" man — the Gnostic initiate —
was saved as such, by virtue of his superior knowledge, quite
apart from "good works." [76] Irenaeus interprets quite differ-
ently from the Gnostics the statement that *flesh and blood
cannot possess the kingdom of God;* [77] and if he agrees with
them not only that the "sensual man" needs good works as
well as faith, but also that he who has the spirit is thereby
saved and is superior to the law, which *is not made for the*

just man; [78] this is because the spirit knows no evil, and he who has it is virtuous by reason of the "change of heart" which it produces, and abounds in good works without needing to be admonished by the formulated word of the law. [79] The Spirit is offered to all men and necessary to all men; the man who does evil loses the spirit and ceases to be a "spiritual man." Instead of being distributed between three classes, belonging as it were to the devil, to the demiurge, and to God, all men alike — believers, Jews, or Gentiles — are the creatures of the one God, though He does not stand in the same relation to all of them. [80]

35. THE TRINITY AND MAN. Particularly clear and striking in Irenaeus is the account of the persons of the Trinity in their dealings with man. Reference has already been made to the distinction between the "image" of God (the Son) and the "likeness" (in the Spirit), and to the representation of the Son and the Spirit as the "hands" of God. [81] The rôles of the persons of the Trinity are expressed in the exegesis of Eph. 4. 6: here it is the transcendent Lord, the Father, who is *above all*, the creative Word, the "world-soul," who is *with all*, and the vivifying Spirit in man's constitution who is *in us all*. [82] The Father reveals Himself in His "reproduction," the Son, and the Son gives the Spirit to the prophets, who convey the revelation to man. In the process of redemption there are two chains of action, from God to man and from man to God. In the former, God the Father sends the Son, who becomes incarnate, and who confers the Spirit, who enables man to live as he should; in the latter, the Spirit leads man to the Son, who presents him to the Father, and the Father confers "rebirth" and incorruptibility. [83] "The Son is knowledge of the Father, and knowledge of the Son is through the Holy Spirit." [84]

36. RECAPITULATION; COMMUNION; INCORRUPTIBILITY.
Mention should also be made of certain other ideas to which
Irenaeus often makes reference: the "recapitulation" of all
things in Christ, man's "communion" with God, and his
reception of "incorruptibility" as the fruit of the redemption. The idea of "recapitulation" ("summing up," "re-
storing") is a central theme in Irenaeus; the word is of course
taken from St. Paul, but the idea has been worked out by
Irenaeus in his own way.[85] For him the "recapitulation" is
a "fresh start," accomplished in the manner of the incarnation; a taking up again and restitution of God's original plan
for man by the reproduction in the incarnation of the features
of the original creation, and the reversal of the features of the
fall. The immediate effect of this "fresh start" is to bring
about, or rather, to restore, a "communion" between God
and man. The reference is not merely to the two natures in
the person of Christ, for the "communion" is between the
human race and God the Father. It is more than a mere
"reconciliation" in the sense of the putting off of wrath; the
expression implies friendly intercourse, a readmission in some
degree to the privileged position held by Adam as the companion of God. By it we are enabled to be "adopted" by
God, and to approach the Father and so receive the ultimate
fruit of the redemption, "incorruptibility."[86] For the Gnostics, as has been said, incorruptibility, the immortality of the
body, was a contradiction in terms, matter being essentially
corruptible; only the soul or spirit could be immortal. For
Irenaeus too, incorruptibility was bound up with the transcendence and unattainability of God, not "natural" to
matter, but a special favour, granted originally under condition, and after the fall unattainable to man, had it not been
for the visible coming of Christ. Soul or spirit, however, is

part of man but not man; the whole man is saved, body included; thanks to the coming of Christ, to the "fresh start" or recapitulation accomplished in His incarnation, and the restored communion with the Father, man is enabled to receive from the Father that incorruptibility which will finally restore him to the state to which the first, immortal, man was destined before the fall.[87]

G. LITERARY AFFINITIES OF THE *PROOF*.

37. IRENAEUS AND HIS SOURCES; *Contra Iudaeos*. It has been suggested that Irenaeus is rather a reporter or compiler than either an original thinker or even a systematiser; and it is true that investigation of his works reveals much that parallels or echoes the works of earlier writers, and that if one amplify the echoes, almost the whole of Christian literature up to his time might seem to have been drawn upon by him; he can hardly, however, be called an uncritical compiler, and his system, though often confusedly expressed, is — *pace* Loofs — coherent enough.[88] Moreover, many parallels between Irenaeus and earlier writers are doubtless to be explained not so much by direct borrowing as by a common source in the catechetical tradition, or by independent exploitation of a common work of reference. In the case of the *Proof*, it was suggested by J. Rendel Harris, as soon as the text was published, that the source of the main body of the work was probably a collection — since lost — of "Testimonies against the Jews," that is to say, of Scriptural texts grouped under argument-headings, intended to convince the Jews out of the Old Testament itself that the Old Law was abolished, that its abolition was foreseen in the Old Testament, and that its purpose had been to prepare and prefigure the New Law of Christ.[89] Such "testimonies"

have come down to us from later times, and it seems not improbable that such a collection of Scriptural "ammunition" existed already before the time of the apologists, perhaps even before the New Testament was written. The "apostolic preaching" itself must have relied largely on such arguments (witness the examples in the New Testament), and that not only as addressed to the Jews. Such a hypothesis explains not only the almost exclusive use, in the *Proof*, of the Old Testament, and that in an ordered series of texts, and the insistence on the abolition of the Old Law, and such arguments as the greater fruitfulness of the Church as compared with the Synagogue, but also several points of detail, which will be mentioned briefly in the following paragraphs.

38. SCRIPTURE. It would seem, from the *Proof*, that Irenaeus was not acquainted with the whole of the Old Testament — not that there is anything very remarkable in that. Both Harnack and Tixeront remark that he restricts his Old Testament history within the limits which are traditionally those of such a catechesis.[90] This is but natural; but in the course of his review of the historical books, Irenaeus has inserted, in the appropriate places, what seems to be intended as a description of the book of Leviticus, and what is expressly put forward as a description of the book of Deuteronomy, though neither of these books is of great use for the end in view; and both the descriptions leave one with the impression that Irenaeus knew little of the books in question, beyond their names, although he has quotations from both of them.[91] He must, of course, have been acquainted with such portions of the Old Testament as were in "liturgical" use, for reading at Christian assemblies; and no doubt for him, as for most other Christian writers and speakers, the liturgical text with which he was acquainted

was often the immediate source of his quotations. For the *Proof*, however, he seems, as has been said, to have used a collection of texts grouped under argument-headings, rather than the original text or even such selections from it as were used liturgically. Certain of the texts cited by him as if they were continuous and taken *en bloc* from the book of the Old Testament which he names as their source are in fact formed out of the relevant portions of a longer continuous passage, or simply composite, consisting of phrases taken from quite different parts of the same book (though at other times he separates such phrases and says explicitly that they are from different places).[92] It would seem here that Irenaeus has simply transcribed what was grouped together in his source, rather than sought his matter in the text of the Scripture itself. The occasional false attribution of quotations is easily explained by supposing that Irenaeus has attributed a text to the author named in his source for a preceding text, but harder to explain if he looked up the original text; the same may perhaps apply to one or two apparently apocryphal quotations; Irenaeus may have mistaken a headline or gloss for a quotation.[93] Moreover, though he is as a rule careful to name the sources of his quotations, he leaves some of them attributed to an unnamed " prophet " or " the prophets," or " the book of the twelve prophets." [94] Had he taken the quotation directly from the source he could easily have ascertained who was the author; but perhaps his secondary source did not distinguish them; though it is of course possible that he was citing from memory or from his own notes and had simply forgotten or not noted the author. The quotation, in the *Proof*, of Isa. 5. 9 in two different forms, in close succession and apparently without realisation that the same passage was in question, shows that the passage was not simply taken from a copy of Isaias.[95] It may also be remarked here that where an Old Testament passage has been quoted in slightly different form in the New Testament, Irenaeus, while attributing the passage to its Old Testament source, and making no mention of the New, quotes nevertheless in the form used in the New Testament.[96] So too he quotes simply as " Jeremias " the passage attributed to that prophet in Matt. 27, 9-10, although it is not found in our Old Testament text.[97] Moreover, in one place he attributes to " the Law " not only the expression which is in fact from " the Law," namely *the God of Abraham and the God of Isaac and the God of Jacob*, but also the words *the God of the living*, which occur in the argument with which the New Testament follows up the quotation from the Law.[98] Apart from this circumstance, the actual text of the New Testament is little used in the *Proof*, though both St. Paul and St. John are quoted, and there are of course echoes of the New Testament and statements based on it, and a parallellism of argument — more likely due to Irenaeus's immediate source than to the New Testament itself — especially with the epistle to the Romans, and with the Acts. In *Adversus haereses* Irenaeus makes it clear that for him the Septuagint version represents the genuine Old Testament in Greek; [99] but his quotations occasionally depart from the standard " Septuagint," and that not only when they are in the form given in the New Testament. This may well be another indication of a collection of " Testimonies " as an immediate source; indeed the agreement with the New Testament forms seems to be accounted for in this manner rather than by use of the New Testament as the immediate source.[100]

39. APOCRYPHA. Not only canonical Scripture, but also

apocryphal books have evidently served, directly or indirectly, as sources. They are rarely, however, quoted as "Scripture." In addition to the quotation attributed to Jeremias in the New Testament, of which mention has already been made, there is in the *Proof* another quotation attributed to Jeremias, which is not to be found in our Old Testament text, and one attributed to David which is likewise not to be found.[101] There are several other statements or expressions, some of them apparently quotations, which may perhaps have an apocryphal source.[102] Under this heading it may be remarked here that the quotation from the *Shepherd* of Hermas which is found (unacknowledged) in the *Proof* is also found in *Adversus haereses*, and is there cited as "Scripture."[103] Apart however from direct quotation, there are several dependences upon apocryphal literature. The account of the corruption of humanity before the flood is evidently taken from an apocryphal source, almost certainly the book of Enoch.[104] The "seven heavens" are more likely to have been taken from such a source than from the Gnostics, whom Irenaeus would scarcely have copied; he may have taken them from the Testament of Levi, or from the *Ascensio Isaiae*, of which there seem to be some echoes in other places of the *Proof*; or he may have been influenced by the apologist Aristo.[105] The account of the behaviour of the star at Bethlehem, and of Abraham's search for God, are also doubtless of apocryphal origin.[106]

40. TRADITION; PLATO; THE "ELDERS." As has already been remarked, much of what is common to Irenaeus and other writers may well represent not so much influence of one on another as the common stock. So too the influence of philosophical systems, especially Platonism, is to be accounted for not so much by direct influence of the authors of those

systems, as by the intellectual common stock of educated men
of the time. The influence of Platonism on Irenaeus's theology, as on that of his fellows, is evident; Christian theology
was formulated against a background of Platonism, and the
Platonic tradition passed into the Christian one. It is natural
that Irenaeus, who was so proud of his connection, through
Polycarp, with the apostles, should appeal to tradition in
the form of the declarations of men of the apostolic age. He
refers in several places (twice in the *Proof*) to the "elders,"
by which he means "the disciples of the Apostles," as evidence for what he says; but it is worthy of notice that one of
the references in the *Proof* merely records as a tradition of
the "elders" the chiliastic interpretation of Isa. 11. 1-10
which Irenaeus defended in *Adversus haereses* against the
one which he gives in the *Proof*.[107] The erroneous view,
which reappears in the *Proof*, that Christ was crucified under
Claudius, is said in *Adversus haereses* to have been the
tradition of the "elders."[108] Irenaeus's source for what he
attributes to the "elders" was no doubt, to a certain extent,
Polycarp. For chiliasm in particular, however, though it is
also found in Justin, and for other matters also, his source
was that indefatigable and uncritical collector of "apostolic
gossip," Papias.[109] Whether he had any other written source
is doubtful. No doubt much of the Johannine and Pauline
character of Irenaeus's thought is to be attributed to the influence of Polycarp, who had known St. John personally,
and who repeatedly quotes St. Paul in his own epistle to
the Philippians.

41. APOSTOLIC FATHERS. In addition to Papias, whose
chiliasm is represented in the *Proof* by the brief reference
to the tradition of the "elders," and to Polycarp, who is
quoted by name in *Adversus haereses*, and of whose epistle

to the Philippians there may be an echo in the *Proof*, and to
whom Irenaeus doubtless owed much that he had assimilated
in youth and no longer consciously referred to any source,
Irenaeus is indebted to others of the apostolic age.[110] Mention has already been made of the quotation in the *Proof* of
the *Shepherd* of Hermas, and of the fact that in *Adversus
haereses* the same quotation is attributed to "Scripture."
There are also perhaps other echoes of the *Shepherd* in the
Proof, and there is what may be a reminiscence of the
Didache, though it is not likely that the expression "the
teaching of the twelve apostles" in chapter 46 is an allusion
to the title of that work; and there are echoes of the Epistle
of Barnabas, and perhaps of Clement of Rome. All these
"echoes" however are but echoes, some of them very faint,
and do not prove any real dependence on those works.[111]

42. JUSTIN. The most considerable of the apologists, and
a man who enjoyed a great reputation for his learning, was
St. Justin "philosopher and martyr." It seems not improbable that Irenaeus knew Justin personally at Rome, and it
is certain that he knew his works and was influenced by
them. The dependence of Irenaeus on Justin has commonly
been regarded as evident and extensive. Whole passages of
Irenaeus can be parallelled in the works of Justin; Irenaeus's
Scriptural repertoire, and his readings of the text, agree to
a large extent with Justin's; Irenaeus often repeats not merely
the exegesis or argument of Justin, but even some of the
actual wording used by Justin.[112] On the other hand, there
are certain notable differences, and the community of Scriptural repertoire and exegesis may well be due to a common
use of a source book rather than to dependence of Irenaeus
on Justin.[113] The hypothesis put forward above, of a book of
texts against the Jews, would account for the choice of texts

and the order and nature of arguments of both writers, and would better account for the differences of treatment, since such a source book would give simply the headings and the texts and glosses, not a detailed working out of the argument; while the occasional echoes of the wording used are, as Harris has pointed out, much better accounted for by supposing that both authors echo a gloss or a headline or an adjacent text of a source book, than by supposing that Irenaeus had gone to the works of Justin for his quotations and echoed some chance phrase in Justin's further argument.[114] In *Adversus haereses*, Irenaeus names Justin as the author of a treatise against Marcion; otherwise he does not refer to him, and Loofs, in his posthumously published article on the sources of Irenaeus, went so far as to say that there is no demonstrable borrowing on the part of Irenaeus from the extant works of Justin.[115] This statement, like several others in the same article, will scarcely meet with general approval; but it may well be admitted that direct dependence of Irenaeus on Justin cannot be shown to have been so extensive as it has been thought to be.

43. THEOPHILUS; OTHER APOLOGISTS. In the work just referred to, Loofs endeavoured to show that one of Irenaeus's principal sources was the lost work of Theophilus of Antioch against Marcion. However that may be, it seems certain enough that Irenaeus owed something to Theophilus. There are not a few echoes in Irenaeus of Theophilus's extant work *Ad Autolycum*. The most striking of these to be found in the *Proof* is the representation of Adam and Eve as children, used to explain both their innocence and the ease with which they were misled into sin.[116] There are also in the *Proof* a couple of points of resemblance to Melito of Sardis, and perhaps an echo of the *Epistola ad Diognetum*; and in

one or two points there may be dependence on Aristo: mention has already been made of the fact that belief in " seven heavens " is said to have been found in Aristo. The account given by Origen of Aristo's lost " Discussion between Jason and Papiscus " shows it to have been a sort of " Summa contra Iudaeos," but though such a work may well have influenced both Justin and Irenaeus, it is not likely that it is to be identified with the lost " Testimonies " supposed as a common source for the latter; more likely it too was an elaboration of that source.[117]

44. CLEMENT OF ALEXANDRIA? That there are parallels between the works of Irenaeus and those of Clement of Alexandria is undeniable. It seems however more likely that such parallels are to be attributed to a common source, or that if there was any borrowing, it was Clement who borrowed from Irenaeus rather than vice versa. The literary activity of Irenaeus falls in the last quarter of the second century, until his death perhaps about 202; that of Clement extends from about the eighties of the second century until his death about 215. Hence the two were contemporaries, and influence in both directions is possible. Clement, however, probably started writing later than Irenaeus, and certainly continued after the latter's death. Moreover, book three of *Adversus haereses* can be dated by the reference to Eleutherus as the reigning pontiff to between the years 174 and 189.[118] Clement was already writing before the death of Eleutherus, but of his extant writings only the *Protrepticus* can be assigned with any likelihood to that early period; while both *Stromata* and *Paedagogus* were produced after the date commonly assigned for the death of Irenaeus.

H. SOME REMARKS ON THE MATTER OF THE *PROOF*.

45. OMISSIONS AND INCLUSIONS. What has been said in the preceding sections supplies an answer to some of the problems mentioned in § 21. The almost exclusive use of the Old Testament, the silence (apart from the mention of baptism) on ecclesiastical, liturgical, or sacramental discipline, and the insistence, on the contrary, on the abrogation of the Old Law, may be explained both by the scope of the work — to induce acceptance of the orthodox Church, which will ensure all the rest — and by the hypothesis that the source used was a book of "Testimonies against the Jews," a source suitable for a work with such a scope. The comparative silence on eschatological questions may be accounted for in the same way; this was not a point of importance for the question of orthodoxy, except in so far as Gnostic views on the possibility of bodily resurrection were concerned, and this point is dealt with. Various other emphases and repetitions are likewise due to the need to set orthodox theology against the views of the Gnostics. Thus in treating of the Trinity Irenaeus naturally does not concern himself with points that only later took on special importance, such as the divinity of the Holy Spirit or the Person and natures of Christ; but he does insist on the divinity of the Creator, and His identity with God the Father, and on the genuineness of Christ's birth, and on the charism of prophecy given by the Holy Spirit, because these points, little as it may now seem necessary to dwell on them, were the ones denied by the "trinitarian heretics" of the time. The curious insertion, as if it were fundamental to Christianity, of the "seven heavens" may perhaps be due to the desire to set this "orthodox Gnosticism" against the more extravagant Gnostic cosmologies.

46. SOME NOTABLE POINTS. From what has been said of the contents of the *Proof* and of the theology of Irenaeus, it will be clear that the work contains much that is of interest to theologians: the theology of the Trinity, the Soteriology, and especially the development of the parallelism between creation — fall and incarnation — redemption; and the exposition of Old-Testament history as leading up to the Church. Among minor particular points may be mentioned the attribution of Scripture to the Holy Spirit, and of the fourth gospel to Christ's " disciple John," and the testimony to the use of the trinitarian formula in baptism.[119] The resemblance between the account of Christianity given at the end of the *Proof* and that given by the " Reformers " has been remarked on by several writers; [120] lest this resemblance be regarded as having any polemical value it should perhaps be pointed out that it is purely negative and due to the scope of the work, which is clearly not the exposition of Christian institutions; and that Irenaeus does insist on the insufficiency of faith without good works, and that the faith which he demands is clearly " dogmatic faith," that is, orthodoxy; and that redeemed man undergoes a " change of heart," and by virtue of the Spirit is not " still a sinner." [121]

47. SOME PECULIARITIES. Mention may be made of several points in the *Proof* which are striking not because of their importance, but because of their comparative rarity, at least in an account of the fundamentals of Christianity. Thus the reading of Gen 1. 1, whence Irenaeus derives his interpretation " a Son in the beginning . . . ," is not extant elsewhere than in the *Proof*, though similar interpretations are found elsewhere.[122] The other points are none of them uniquely Irenaean, and some of them are not very uncommon, but they may still be remarked upon; some of them

are certainly erroneous. Thus he includes, as if it were essential to orthodoxy, the doctrine that there are seven concentric heavens; and he says Pontius Pilate was procurator of Claudius.[123] There is also a reference to the Millenarian tradition, so phrased however that it cannot be concluded with certainty that Irenaeus still upheld the truth of that tradition.[124] Other points more or less "peculiar" are the representation of Adam and Eve as children, and of man as lord of the world, including the angels in it; the attribution to the Word of God's walking with man in Paradise, and of the theophanies of the Old Testament, and of the punishment of Sodom and Gomorrha; and the statement that the decalogue was abolished along with the rest of the Old Law.[125] Remarkable also is the exegesis of the blessings of Sem and Japheth, the latter being realised in the calling of the Gentiles through the Church; and the detailed parallelism between the creation of Adam, from virgin soil and the Spirit of God, and the incarnation of Christ, from the Virgin and the Holy Spirit; and the identification of the Holy Spirit, instead of the Word, with divine Wisdom; and the distinction between the Persons of the Trinity founded on their activity *ad extra*.[126]

48. LEADING IDEAS. It may be said that the main points of the doctrine of the *Proof* are, as Irenaeus says, the three "articles" of the baptismal "rule of faith": Father (Creator, transcendent but accessible giver of incorruptibility), Son (the Word with the Father from the beginning, immanent in the universe and always with man, linking him with the Father, and in His incarnation "recapitulating" the creation and reversing the fall), and the Holy Spirit (in man, giving him likeness to God and leading him to the Son, speaking through the prophets, making man sinless and superior to

the Law, by abiding Charity). The framework of the various
"Creeds" is here already clearly discernible.[127] The historical section is of course ruled by the Christian outlook on
the history of the world as a history of redemption, with the
incarnation as its culmination. In the working out of the
argument one may perhaps, by a useful but not rigorously
accurate generalisation, distinguish what may be called the
"Johannine" and the "Pauline" trains of thought: the
Johannine insistence on "the Word from the beginning"
and His rôle as our link with the Father, and the primacy
and sinlessness of Charity in the Spirit; and the Pauline argument from the helplessness of fallen man and the reversal
of the fall by Christ, and the abrogation of the Old Law, as
the culmination of God's calling first of Israel and then of
the Gentiles to be the heirs of Abraham's justification by
faith. Regarded precisely as a "proof," the *Proof* has for its
basis the fact that the old dispensation was but the prepara-
tion and prophecy of the new, and that the realisation of
that prophecy is the proof of the genuineness of the message
brought by the Gospel.

I. CONCLUSION (SUMMARY).

49. IRENAEUS AND THE *Proof*. To resume, by way of
conclusion, in the form of an appreciation of the work: it is
certain that the thirteenth-century Armenian manuscript
here translated is a version, made almost certainly in the sixth
century, and from the Greek original, of the "Proof of the
Apostolic Preaching" written by St. Irenaeus, bishop of
Lyons, in that city towards the end of the second century.
Only one intervening generation of tradition separated its
author from the apostles themselves, and its value lies in
the fact that, invested as it is with the authority of so early

a successor to the apostolic ministry, it is the earliest document we have that professes to give an exposition of the basis on which the apostolic preaching rests. It is important as a catechetic-apologetic document, and for its exegesis; though it adds little new matter to what we already knew from *Adversus haereses*, its value, as compared with that work, lies in its compendiousness.

50. THE MESSAGE OF THE *Proof*. The *Proof* must not be supposed to contain a full exposition of what its author regarded as essential to Christian theology and behaviour; its scope is to prove the Church's credentials. It is addressed to a fellow-Christian, Marcianus, who may have been the author's brother, and who may have been a bishop. It expounds the " rule of faith " in the formula of baptism (the mysteries of the Trinity and of the Incarnation), and the history in the Old Testament of the creation and fall of man and the unfolding of God's design for his restoration, showing also how the details of the Incarnation, Ministry, Passion, Resurrection, Ascension and universal Kingdom of Christ were foretold, and thereby proves the truth of the mission of the apostles, and so of the Church which they founded. In the calling of all nations through the Church God's plan reaches its term; as was also foreseen and foretold, the Old Law is superseded by the Law of Charity; we are saved through the name of Christ, by good works and the faith of the orthodox Church.

ST. IRENAEUS

PROOF OF THE APOSTOLIC PREACHING

Translated from the unique Armenian manuscript as edited
by Bishop Karapet Ter Mekerttschian.

N. B.: The headings are not in the manuscript.

What is enclosed within angular brackets ⟨ ⟩ is not
in the manuscript, but has been supplied by the present
translator as a restoration of the original.

Empty square brackets [ ] indicate the omission of
what is to be found in the manuscript, but certainly
not in the original.

Words preceded by an asterisk * are corrections
which depart notably from the manuscript.

The translation does not always follow the punctuation of the manuscript.

45

PROOF OF THE APOSTOLIC PREACHING.

A. GOD AND CREATURES. THE FALL.

THE WAY OF LIFE.

1. Knowing, my dear Marcianus, your inclination to walk the path of God's service (which alone brings man to eternal life), I both congratulate you, and pray that you may keep the faith in its purity and so be well-pleasing to God your Maker.[1] Would it were possible for us to be always together, to help each other, and to relieve the preoccupations of earthly life by daily conference on profitable themes. As it is, since we are at the present time distant in body from each other, we have not delayed, so far as may be, to commune with you a little in writing, and to set forth in brief the preaching of the truth, to confirm your faith.[2] What we are sending you is in the form of notes on the main points, so that you may find much matter in short space, comprehending in a few details all the members of the body of truth, and receiving in brief the proof of the things of God.[3] In this way, not only will it bear fruit in your own salvation, but also you may confound all those who hold false views, and to all who wish to hear, you may with all confidence expound what we have to say in its integrity and purity.[4] For the road of all those who see is a single upward path, lit by heavenly light; but the ways of those who see not are many and dark and divergent. The former road leads to the kingdom of heaven by uniting man with God, but the others bring down to death by severing man from God.[5] Therefore

47

must both you, and all those who look after the salvation of souls,[6] make your way by faith, without deviation, with courage and determination, lest through lack of tenacity or perseverance you remain at a standstill in material passions, or even be led astray and turn aside from the straight path.[7]

FAITH AND GOOD WORKS.

2. And since man is an animal made up of soul and body, that must come about through the instrumentality of both of these;[8] and since occasions of stumbling follow from both of them, there is both bodily holiness, the safeguard of abstinence from all shameful things and all wicked deeds, and holiness of soul, the preservation in its integrity of faith in God, adding nothing and subtracting nothing from it. For piety is clouded and loses its lustre by contamination, by impurity of body, and is broken and stained and loses its integrity when falsehood enters the soul; but it will be preserved in beauty and measure by the constant abiding of truth in the mind and of holiness in the body.[9] For what is the use of knowing the truth in word, while defiling the body and accomplishing the works of evil? Or what real good at all can bodily holiness do, if truth be not in the soul?[10] For these two rejoice in each other's company, and agree together and fight side by side to set man in the presence of God.[11] Therefore the Holy Spirit says through David: *Blessed is the man who hath not walked in the counsel of the ungodly*,[12] that is, the counsel of the peoples that know not God; for those are "ungodly" who do not worship Him who IS, essentially, God.[13] Therefore the Word says to Moses: *I am He-who-IS*;[14] so those who do not worship the God who really IS are the "ungodly." *Nor stood in the way of sinners;* and "sinners" are they who have knowledge of God, and do

not keep His commandments; that is, scornful, disdainful folk.[15] *Nor sat in the chair of the pestilential*; and " pestilential " are they who with wicked and perverse doctrine corrupt not only themselves but also others; for " the chair " is a symbol of the school; and such are all heretics. *In the chair of the pestilential* sit and are brought to corruption those who take the poison of their doctrine.[16]

THE RULE OF FAITH.

3. So, lest the like befall us, we must keep strictly, without deviation, the rule of faith, and carry out the commands of God, believing in God, and fearing Him, because He is Lord, and loving Him, because He is Father.[17] Action, then, is preserved by faith, because *unless you believe*, says Isaias, *you shall not *continue*; and faith is given by truth, since faith rests upon reality: for we shall believe what really is, as it is, and, believing what really is, as it is for ever, keep a firm hold on our assent to it.[18] Since, then, it is faith that maintains our salvation, one must take great care of this sustenance, to have a true perception of reality.[19] Now, this is what faith does for us, as the elders, the disciples of the apostles, have handed down to us.[20] First of all, it admonishes us to remember that we have received baptism for remission of sins in the name of God the Father, and in the name of Jesus Christ, the Son of God, who became incarnate and died and was raised, and in the Holy Spirit of God; [21] and that this baptism is the seal of eternal life and is rebirth unto God, that we be no more children of mortal men, but of the eternal and everlasting God; [22] and that the eternal and everlasting One *is* God, and is above all creatures, and that all things whatsoever are subject to Him; [23] and that what is subject to Him was all made by Him,[24] so that God is not

ruler and Lord of what is another's, but of His own,[25] and all things are God's; that God, therefore, is the Almighty,[26] and all things whatsoever are from God.

ORIGIN OF CREATURES.

4. For creatures must have the origin of their being from some great cause; and the Origin of all is God, since It Itself was not made by anyone, but by It were made all things whatsoever.[27] Therefore, first, one must believe that there is one God, the Father, who made and fashioned everything, and brought being out of nothing, and, while holding all things, is alone beyond grasp.[28] But in "all things" is included this world of ours, with man in it; so this world too was created by God.[29]

THE TRINITY AND CREATURES.

5. In this way, then, there is declared one God, the Father, uncreated, invisible, maker of all things, above whom is no other God whatever, and after whom there is no other God.[30] And God is rational, and therefore produced creatures by His Word, and God is a spirit, and so fashioned everything by His Spirit, as the prophet also says: *by the word of the Lord the heavens were established, and all the power of them by His Spirit.*[31] Hence, since the Word "establishes," that is, works bodily and consolidates being,[32] while the Spirit disposes and shapes the various "powers," so the Word is fitly and properly called the Son, but the Spirit the Wisdom of God.[33] Hence too His apostle Paul well says: *one God, the Father, who is above all and with all and in us all;*[34] for "above all" is the Father, but "with all" is the Word, since it is through Him that everything was made by the Father, and "in us all" is the Spirit, *who cries: Abba, Father,*[35] and

has formed man to the likeness of God.[36] So the Spirit manifests the Word, and therefore the prophets announced the Son of God, but the Word articulates the Spirit, and therefore it is Himself who gives their message to the prophets, and takes up man and brings him to the Father.[37]

THE THREE ARTICLES OF THE FAITH.

6. And this is the drawing-up of our faith, the foundation of the building, and the consolidation of a way of life.[38] God, the Father, uncreated, beyond grasp, invisible, one God the maker of all; this is the first and foremost article of our faith.[39] But the second article is the Word of God, the Son of God, Christ Jesus our Lord, who was shown forth by the prophets according to the design of their prophecy and according to the manner in which the Father disposed; and through Him were made all things whatsoever.[40] He also, *in the end of times*,[41] for the recapitulation of all things, is become a man among men, visible and tangible, in order to abolish death and bring to light life, and bring about the communion of God and man.[42] And the third article is the Holy Spirit, through whom the prophets prophesied and the patriarchs were taught about God and the just were led in the path of justice, and who *in the end of times* has been poured forth in a new manner upon humanity over all the earth renewing man to God.[43]

THE TRINITY AND OUR REBIRTH.

7. Therefore the baptism of our rebirth comes through these three articles, granting us rebirth unto God the Father, through His Son, by the Holy Spirit.[44] For those who are bearers of the Spirit of God are led to the Word, that is, to the Son; but the Son takes them and presents them to the Father; and the Father confers incorruptibility.[45] So without

the Spirit there is no seeing the Word of God, and without
the Son there is no approaching the Father; for the Son is
knowledge of the Father, and knowledge of the Son is
through the Holy Spirit.[46] But the Son, according to the
Father's good-pleasure, administers the Spirit charismatically [47] as the Father will, to those to whom He will.[48]

GOD THE FATHER AND MANKIND.

8. And the Father is called by the Spirit *Most High*, and
Almighty, and *Lord of Hosts*,[49] that we may learn that God
is indeed such, that is, creator of heaven and earth and the
whole world, and maker of angels and men, and Lord of all,
who upholds all things, and by whom everything is sus-
tained; merciful, compassionate and most tender, good, just,
God of all, both of Jews and of Gentiles and of the faithful.[50]
But to the faithful He is as a Father, for *in the end of times*
He has opened the testament of adoption of sons.[51] But to
the Jews He was as Lord and Lawgiver, for when in the
mean time mankind had forgotten and fallen away and
rebelled against God, He brought them into subjection
through the Law,[52] that they might learn that they had a
Lord who was author and maker, who grants the breath of
life; and to Him we must return homage by day and by night.
But to the Gentiles He is as Maker and Creator and Almighty. But for all alike He is sustainer and nourisher and
king and judge — for none shall escape immune from His
judgement, neither Jew nor Gentile nor sinner among the
faithful, nor angel.[53] But those who are now sceptical of
His kindness will know His power in the judgement, as the
blessed apostle says: *knowing not, that the benignity of God
leadeth thee to penance, but according to thy hardness and
impenitent heart, thou treasurest up for thyself wrath, in the*

*day of wrath, and revelation of the just judgement of God,
who will render forth to every man according to his works.*[54]
This is He, who is called in the Law *the God of Abraham
and the God of Isaac and the God of Jacob, the God of the
living.*[55] Yet is the sublimity and greatness of this same God
beyond the power of expression.[56]

SEVEN HEAVENS.

9. But the earth is encompassed by seven heavens, in
which dwell Powers and Angels and Archangels, giving
homage to the Almighty God who created all things, not
as to one having need of anything, but lest they too be idle
and useless and accursed.[57] Therefore the Spirit of God in
His indwelling is manifold, and is enumerated by Isaias the
prophet in the seven charismata [58] resting on the Son of God,
that is, the Word, in His coming as man. For he says: *the
spirit of God shall rest upon him, the spirit of wisdom and
of understanding, the spirit of counsel and of fortitude, ⟨the
spirit of knowledge⟩ and of godliness; the spirit of the fear
of God shall fill him.*[59] Hence the first heaven from the top,
which encloses the others, is wisdom; and the one after it,
that of understanding; but the third is that of counsel, and
the fourth, counting from the top downwards, that of fortitude, and the fifth that of knowledge, and the sixth that of
godliness; and the seventh, this firmament of ours, full of
the fear of this Spirit, who lights up the heavens.[60] For after
this pattern Moses received the seven-branched candlestick
always burning in the sanctuary; since it was on the pattern
of the heavens that he received the liturgy, as the Word says
to him: *Thou shalt do according to all the pattern of what
thou hast seen on the mount.*[61]

GOD SUPREME RULER.

10. This God, then, is glorified by His Word, who is His Son for ever, and by the Holy Spirit, who is the Wisdom of the Father of all. And their Powers (those of the Word and of Wisdom), which are called Cherubim and Seraphim, with unfailing voice glorify God, and the entire establishment of heaven gives glory to God, the Father of all.[62] He has established with the Word the whole world, and angels too are included in the world; and to the whole world He has given laws, that each one keep to his place and overstep not the bound laid down by God, each accomplishing the work marked out for him.[63]

CREATION OF MAN.

11. But man He fashioned with His own hands, taking of the purest and finest of earth, in measured wise mingling with the earth His own power;[64] for He gave his frame the outline of His own form, that the visible appearance too should be godlike — for it was as an image of God that man was fashioned and set on earth — and that he might come to life, He *breathed into his face the breath of life*, so that the man became like God in inspiration as well as in frame.[65] So he was free, and his own master, having been made by God in order to be master of everything on earth.[66] And this world of creation, prepared by God before He fashioned man, was given to the man as his domain, with all things whatsoever in it.[67] In the domain were also, with their tasks, the servants of that God who fashioned all, and this domain was in the keeping of the administrator-in-chief, who was set over his fellow-servants; and the servants were angels, but administrator-in-chief the archangel.[68]

PARADISE.

12. So, having made the man lord of the earth and every-thing in it, He made him in secret lord also of the servants in it.[69] They, however, were in their full development, while the lord, that is, the man, was a little one; for he was a child and had need to grow so as to come to his full per-fection.[70] And so that he might have nourishment and grow up in luxury, a place was prepared for him better than this world, well-favoured in climate, beauty, light, things good to eat, plants, fruit, water, and all other things needful to life; and its name is the Garden.[71] And so fair and goodly was the Garden, the Word of God was constantly walking in it; He would walk round and talk with the man, prefiguring what was to come to pass in the future, how He would become man's fellow, and talk with him, and come among mankind, teaching them justice.[72] But the man was a little one, and his discretion still undeveloped, wherefore also he was easily misled by the deceiver.

EVE.

13. God, then, in Paradise, while the man was walking around, brought before him all living things and bade him give names to them all; and *whatever Adam called each living being, *this was its name.*[73] And He decided also to make a help for the man; for *God said: it is not good for the man to be alone; let us make him a help like unto himself.*[74] For among all other living things there was not to be found a helper equal and the peer and the like of Adam.[75] But God Himself *brought a trance upon Adam, and put him to sleep,*[76] and, that one work be accomplished out of another, as sleep had not been brought into being in the Garden, it was brought upon Adam by the will of God.[77] And God *took*

*one of Adam's ribs, and filled up flesh for it, and built up the
rib which He took into a woman, and brought in this wise to
Adam.*[78] But he, on seeing this, said: *This now is bone of
my bone and flesh of my flesh; she shall be called woman,
because she was taken out of her man.*[79]

PRIMAL INNOCENCE.

14. And Adam and Eve (for this is the name of the
woman) *were naked and were not ashamed,*[80] for their
thoughts were innocent and childlike, and they had no conception or imagination of the sort that is engendered in the
soul by evil, through concupiscence, and by lust.[81] For they
were then in their integrity, preserving their natural state,
for what had been breathed into their frame was the spirit
of life; [82] now, so long as the spirit still remains in proper
order and vigour, it is without imagination or conception
of what is shameful.[83] For this reason they *were not ashamed*,
as they kissed each other and embraced with the innocence
of childhood.[84]

TREE OF KNOWLEDGE. IMMORTALITY.

15. But so that the man should not have thoughts of
grandeur, and become lifted up, as if he had no lord, because
of the dominion that had been given to him, and the freedom,
fall into sin against God his creator, overstepping his bounds,
and take up an attitude of self-conceited arrogance towards
God, a law was given him by God, that he might know that
he had for lord the Lord of all.[85] And He laid down for
him certain conditions: so that, if he kept the command of
God, then he would always remain as he was, that is, immortal; but if he did not, he would become mortal, melting
into earth, whence his frame had been taken.[86] And the

commandment was this: *Of every tree within the Garden eating thou shalt eat; but only of the tree whence is knowledge of good and evil, you shall not eat; for in what day you eat, you shall die the death.*[87]

THE FALL.

16. This commandment the man did not keep, but disobeyed God, being misled by the angel, who, becoming jealous of the man and looking on him with envy because of God's many favours which He had bestowed on the man, both ruined himself and made the man a sinner, persuading him to disobey God's command.[88] So the angel, having become by falsehood the head and fount of sin, both was himself stricken, having offended against God, and caused the man to be cast forth out of Paradise.[89] And because, at the prompting of his nature, he had rebelled and fallen away from God, he was called in Hebrew Satan, that is, rebel; but the same one is also called the slanderer.[90] So God rebuked the serpent, who had been the bearer of the slanderer, and this curse fell upon both the animal itself, and the angel, Satan, lurking hidden within it; and the man He put away from His face, and sent away to dwell by the road into the Garden, since the Garden does not admit a sinner.[91]

B. HISTORY OF REDEMPTION.

CAIN AND ABEL.

17. Expelled from the Garden, Adam and his wife Eve fell into many miseries of mind and body, walking in this world with sadness and toil and sighs.[92] For under the rays of our sun the man tilled the earth, and the earth brought forth thorns and thistles, the punishment of sin.[93] Then came

to pass also what is written: *Adam knew his wife, and she conceived and brought forth Cain, and after him she bore Abel.*[94] But the rebel angel, the same who had brought the man into disobedience, and made him a sinner, and been the cause of his being cast out of the Garden, not content with this first evil, brought about in the brothers a second one; for, filling Cain with his own spirit, he made him a slayer of his brother.[95] And thus Abel died, slain by his brother, a sign for the future, that some would be persecuted and straitened and slain, but the unjust would slay and persecute the just. Whereupon God became exceedingly angry and cursed Cain; and it came to pass, that every generation in the line of succession from him became like its forefather.[96] And God raised up another son to Adam in place of Abel who was slain.[97]

THE GIANTS.

18. And wickedness very long-continued and widespread pervaded all the race of men, until very little seed of justice was in them. For *unlawful unions [98] came about on earth, as angels linked themselves with offspring of the daughters of men, who bore to them sons, who on account of their exceeding great size were called Giants.[99] The angels, then, brought to their wives as gifts teachings of evil, for they taught them the virtues of roots and herbs, and dyeing and cosmetics and discoveries of precious materials, love-philtres, hatreds, amours, passions, constraints of love, the bonds of witchcraft, every sorcery and idolatry, hateful to God; and when this was come into the world, the affairs of wickedness were propagated to overflowing, and those of justice dwindled to very little.[100]

THE FLOOD.

19. At last, when a judgement came upon the world from God, by means of a flood, in the tenth generation from the first man, Noe alone was found just, and because of his justice both he himself was saved, and his wife and his three sons and the three wives of his sons, shut up in the ark with all animals which God ordered Noe to bring into the ark.[101] And when all who were on earth, both mankind and other living things too, were brought to destruction, what was preserved in the ark was saved. And the three sons of Noe were Sem, Cham, and Japheth; and his stock was multiplied again; for these were the beginning of mankind since the flood.[102]

THE CURSE OF CHAM.

20. But of these, one fell under a curse, and two inherited a blessing, for their deeds; for the youngest of them, who is called Cham, mocked their father, and, reprobated for the sin of impiety because of the affront and offence against his father, received a curse, and brought a share of the curse upon all his offspring, whence it came about that every generation after him was accursed, increased and multiplied in sin. But Sem and Japheth, his brothers, won a blessing for their dutifulness towards their father.[103] Now the curse of Cham, with which his father Noe cursed him, is this: *Cursed be the child Cham; a slave shall he be of his brethren;* [104] and when this came upon his stock, he had much offspring upon earth, growing as it were into a forest in fourteen generations, and then his race was delivered unto judgement and mown down by God.[105] For the Chanaanites and the Hittites and the Pherezites and the Hevites and the Amorrhites and the Jebusites and the Gergesites and the

Sodomites, the Arabs and the dwellers in Phoenicia, all the Egyptians and the Lydians are of the stock of Cham, who fell under the curse, and for long was the curse extended over the ungodly.[106]

THE BLESSINGS OF SEM AND JAPHETH.

21. And in the same way as the curse, so too the blessing came down to the posterity of him who was blessed, each in his turn; and the first of them to be blessed was Sem, in these words: *Blessed be the Lord, God of Sem; be Cham his servant.*[107] The force of the blessing is this: that God, the Lord of all, was to be for Sem a peculiar possession of worship; and this blessing burgeoned when it reached Abraham, descended from the stock of Sem, assigned by the genealogy to the tenth generation.[108] And therefore the Father and God of all was pleased to be called *the God of Abraham and the God of Isaac and the God of Jacob;* [109] for Sem's blessing was carried over to Abraham.[110] But the blessing of Japheth was as follows: *May God enlarge Japheth, and let him *dwell in the house of Sem, and Cham be his servant;* [111] and *this blossomed forth in the end of this age, *in the manifestation of the Lord to the Gentiles of the calling, when God extended to them His call,[112] and *their sound went forth into all the earth, and their words unto the ends of the world.*[113] So " enlarge " refers to the calling from the Gentiles, that is to say, the Church, and he " dwells in the house of Sem," that is to say, in the heritage of the patriarchs, in Christ Jesus receiving the birthright.[114] So, according to the order in which each was blessed, in the same degree does he receive in his posterity the fruit of the blessing.

THE COVENANT WITH NOE.

22. But after the flood God established a covenant for the whole world, and for all living beasts, and for men, that He would no more destroy with a flood all the new life of the earth; and He appointed them a sign: *When the sky is covered with clouds, a bow shall appear in the cloud, and I will remember my covenant, and no more destroy with water every living thing that moves on the earth.*[115] And He made a change in the food of mankind, bidding them eat flesh; for from the first man, Adam, until the flood, men had been nourished only on the seeds and fruits of trees, but flesh food was not allowed them. And because the sons of Noe were a beginning of the race of men, God blessed them for multiplication and growth, saying: *Increase and multiply, and fill the earth, and be its lord; and let the fear and dread of you be upon all living beasts and upon all the birds of heaven; and they shall be food for you, even as green herbs; save only you shall not eat the flesh of the blood of life; for I will require your blood at the hand of every beast, and at the hand of man; whoever shall shed man's blood, it shall be shed in return for his blood; for as the image of God hath He made man;* [116] and the " image " is the Son of God, in whose image man was made.[117] And therefore, He was *manifested in the last times,*[118] to show the image like unto Himself. After this covenant the race of men was multiplied, arising from the offspring of the three; and *there was one lip on earth,*[119] that is, one tongue.

BABEL.

23. So they arose and made their way from the land of the East; and in their passage over the earth they came into the vast land of Senaar, where they undertook the building of a tower, and were planning by this means to mount to the

heavens, being able to leave their work as a memorial to mankind after them. And the building was being made of baked brick and bitumen, and the boldness of their temerity was making great strides, they being of one mind and heart, and through the medium of a single language carrying out their tasks in conformity with what was in their intention.[120] So, lest their work advance further, God divided their tongues, so that they might no longer be able to understand one another.[121] Thus they were split up and dispersed, and occupied countries and dwelt distributed in groups according to their respective languages; hence all the various peoples and different languages on earth. So three races of men occupied the earth, and one of them was under a curse, two under a blessing; and the blessing came first to Sem, whose progeny dwelt in the East and held the land of the Chaldees.[122]

ABRAHAM, ISAAC, AND JACOB.

24. And with the passage of time, that is, in the tenth generation after the flood, we have Abraham seeking the God who was his rightful due by the blessing of his progenitor.[123] And since, following the bent and prompting of his heart, he was going all about the earth, seeking where was God, and was growing faint and beginning to desist from the discovery, God, having pity on him who alone quietly sought Him, appeared to Abraham, manifesting Himself through the Word as through a ray of light.[124] For He spoke to him from the heavens, and said to him: *Go forth out of thy country, and from thy kindred, and out of thy father's house, and go over into a land which I will show thee,*[125] and dwell there; and he trusted the voice from heaven, and, *while he was seventy years old, and had a wife, *and while she herself was of a ripe age, he rose up with her and went

forth from Mesopotamia, taking with him Lot, the son of his dead brother.[126] And when he came into the land which is now called Judaea, which at that time was inhabited by seven nations, descended from Cham, God appeared to him in a vision and said: *to thee will I give this land, and to thy seed after thee, as a possession for ever;* [127] and that his seed would be a stranger in a land not their own, and there be molested, ill-treated and enslaved for four hundred years; and in the fourth generation return to the place promised to Abraham, and God would judge the people that had enslaved his seed.[128] And that Abraham might know not only the great number but also the splendour of his seed, God led him forth by night and said to him: *Look up to heaven, and see if thou canst number the stars in heaven; so shall be thy seed.*[129] And when God saw the faith and resolution of his spirit, He testified to him, saying through the Holy Spirit in the Scriptures: *and Abraham believed God; and it was reputed to him unto justice.*[130] And he was not circumcised, when he received that testimonial; and that the excellence of his faith might be marked by a sign, He gave him circumcision, *a seal of the *justice of his faith in uncircumcision.*[131] And after this there was born to him a son, Isaac, of Sara, the barren, according to God's promise; and he circumcised him, in accordance with God's covenant with him; and of Isaac was born Jacob.[132] And in this way the original blessing given in the beginning to Sem came to Abraham, and from Abraham to Isaac, and from Isaac to Jacob, the Spirit assigning to them the inheritance, for He was called *the God of Abraham and the God of Isaac and the God of Jacob.*[133] And there were born to Jacob twelve sons, after whom the twelve tribes of Israel are named.[134]

EGYPT. THE PASSOVER.

25. And when all the earth was in the grip of a famine, it happened that in Egypt alone there was food; so Jacob migrated along with all his progeny into Egypt.[135] And the number of all those who migrated was seventy-five souls; and in four hundred years, as the oracle had said in the beginning, they became six hundred and sixty thousand.[136] And since they were greatly afflicted and oppressed by cruel servitude, and turned with sighs and tears to God, the God of the patriarchs, Abraham and Isaac and Jacob, led them forth from Egypt at the hand of Moses and Aaron, striking the Egyptians with ten plagues, in the tenth of which He sent a killer angel, destroying their firstborn, from man to brute.[137] From this He saved the children of Israel, showing forth in a mystery the Passion of Christ, by the immolation of a spotless lamb, and by its blood, given as a guarantee of immunity to be smeared on the houses of the Hebrews; and the name of this mystery is the Passover,[138] source of freedom. And He divided the Red Sea and brought the children of Israel with all care into the desert; and the pursuing Egyptians, who came after them into the sea, all perished; this was God's judgement on those who had unjustly afflicted Abraham's seed.[139]

THE LAW.

26. And in the desert Moses received from God laws, ten sentences on *tablets of stone, written with the finger of God;* and " finger of God " is that which is put forth by the Father in the Holy Spirit, and the commandments and laws which He committed to the children of Israel to be kept.[140] He also constructed at God's command the tabernacle of the testimony, a visible construction on earth of what is spiritual and

invisible in heaven, and a figure of the form of the Church, and a prophecy of things to be; and in it both vessels and altars and an ark, in which he put the tablets.[141] And he also appointed as priests Aaron and his sons, giving the priesthood to them and to all their stock; and they were of the tribe of Levi; but he also summoned at God's word the whole of that tribe, to work in the service of the temple of God, and also gave them the levitical law, for the character and behaviour of those whose occupation it was to carry on constantly the work of the service of God's temple.[142]

THE SPIES. THE WANDERING IN THE DESERT.

27. And when they were near to the land which God had promised to Abraham and his seed, Moses chose one man out of each tribe and sent them to spy the land and the cities in it and the inhabitants of the cities.[143] At that time God revealed to him the name which alone has power to save him who believes in it, and Moses changed the name of Osee, son of Nun, one of the envoys, and named him Jesus, and so sent him with the power of the Name, confident that he would receive them safe back, under the conduct of the Name; and so it came to pass.[144] They did return, after their journey and spying and reconnaissance, bearing a cluster of grapes; but some of the twelve envoys cast the whole people into a timidity of apprehension, saying that the cities were huge, and fortified, and the inhabitants giants, sons of the Titans, so that they could hold the land; and upon this all the people fell to weeping, losing trust in God who was lending them strength and bringing all into subjection.[145] And they also spoke disparagingly of the land, as if it were not a good one, and as if it were not worth taking risks for the sake of such a land.[146] But two of the twelve,

Jesus, son of Nun, and Caleb, son of Jephone, rent their garments at the misdeed, and begged the people not to let their spirits be discouraged or their hearts cast down, for God had given everything into their hands, and the land was very good indeed.[147] And since the people did not believe, but still remained in the same state of mistrust, God diverted and changed their course, to lead them astray, punishing [148] and afflicting them in the desert. And, counting a year for each day of all the days spent on the journey there and back of those who had spied out and reconnoitred the land — and that was forty days — He kept them for forty years in the desert; not one of those who were fully grown and had full use of reason did He judge worthy to enter the land, because of their unbelief, but only the two who had spoken in favour of the inheritance, Jesus son of Nun and Caleb son of Jephone, and such as were babes not knowing their right hand from their left.[149] So all the unbelieving people gradually came to an end and died out in the desert, suffering as their unbelief merited; but the children who grew up during the forty years filled and made up the number of the dead.

DEUTERONOMY.

28. When the forty years were completed, the people came near to the Jordan, and were assembled and drawn up over against Jericho.[150] Here Moses assembled the people and again summed everything up, recounting the great works of God even to that day, preparing and disposing those who had grown up in the desert to fear God and obey His commandments, and imposing on them as it were a new code of laws, in addition to the one made before. And this was called Deuteronomy, and in it also many prophecies are written

about our Lord Jesus Christ and about the people and about the calling of the Gentiles and about the kingdom.[151]

THE PROMISED LAND.

29. And Moses, having finished his course, is told by God: *Mount on high onto the mountain, and die*,[152] for thou shalt not bring my people into the land. And *he died, according to the word of the Lord*, and was succeeded by Jesus, son of Nun.[153] This man, dividing the Jordan, brought the people across into the land; and overthrowing and destroying the seven nations that dwelt in it, distributed it among the people; here is Jerusalem, where was King David, and his son Solomon, who built the temple to the name of God, after the likeness of the tabernacle which Moses had made on the pattern of heavenly and spiritual things.[154]

THE PROPHETS.

30. Hither were sent by God the prophets, through the Holy Spirit; they admonished the people and brought it back to the God of the patriarchs, the Almighty, and were the heralds of the revelation of our Lord Jesus Christ, the Son of God, announcing that His flesh would blossom forth from the seed of David, that He would be according to the flesh a son of David, who was the son of Abraham through a long line of succession; but according to the Spirit, Son of God, pre-existent with the Father, born before all the building of the world, and appearing to the whole world in the end of this age as man, the Word of God, *resuming anew* in Himself *all things in heaven and on earth*.[155]

INCORRUPTIBILITY.

31. So He united man with God and brought about a communion of God and man, we being unable in any other

wise to have part in incorruptibility, had it not been for His coming to us.[156] For incorruptibility, while invisible and imperceptible, would not help us; so He became visible, that we might be taken into full communication with incorruptibility.[157] And because, being all implicated in the first *formation of Adam, we were bound to death through disobedience, the bonds of death had necessarily to be loosed through the obedience of Him who was made man for us; [158] because death ruled in the body, it was necessarily through the body that it should be done away with and let man go free from its oppression.[159] So *the Word was made flesh*,[160] in order that sin, destroyed by means of that same flesh through which it had gained the mastery and taken hold and lorded it, should no longer be in us; and therefore our Lord took up the same first *formation for an Incarnation, that so He might join battle on behalf of His forefathers, and overcome through Adam what had stricken us through Adam.[161]

ADAM AND CHRIST.

32. Whence, then, comes the substance of the first man? From God's Will and Wisdom, and from virgin earth. For *God had not rained*, says the Scripture, before man was made, *and there was no man to till the earth*.[162] From this earth, then, while it was still virgin, God took dust and fashioned the man, the beginning of humanity. So the Lord, summing up afresh this man, reproduced the scheme of his incarnation, being born of a virgin by the Will and Wisdom of God, that He too might copy the incarnation of Adam, and man might be made, as was written in the beginning, *according to the image and likeness* of God.[163]

EVE AND THE MOTHER OF GOD.

33. And just as it was through a virgin who disobeyed that man was stricken and fell and died, so too it was through the Virgin, who obeyed the word of God, that man resuscitated by life received life.[164] For the Lord came to seek back the lost sheep, and it was man who was lost;[165] and therefore He did not become some other formation, but He likewise, of her that was descended from Adam, preserved the likeness of formation;[166] for Adam had necessarily to be restored in Christ, that mortality be absorbed in immortality, and Eve in Mary, that a virgin, become the advocate of a virgin, should undo and destroy virginal disobedience by virginal obedience.[167]

THE TREE OF KNOWLEDGE AND THE CROSS.

34. And the sin that was wrought through the tree was undone by the obedience of the tree, obedience to God whereby the Son of man was nailed to the tree, destroying the knowledge of evil, and bringing in and conferring the knowledge of good; and evil is disobedience to God, as obedience to God is good.[168] And therefore the Word says through Isaias the prophet, foretelling what was to come to pass in the future — for it was because they told the future that they were " prophets " — the Word says through him as follows: *I refuse not, and do not gainsay, my back have I delivered to blows and my cheeks to buffets, and I have not turned away my face from the contumely of them that spat.*[169] So by the obedience, whereby He obeyed unto death, hanging on the tree, He undid the old disobedience wrought in the tree.[170] And because He is Himself the Word of God Almighty, who in His invisible form pervades us universally in the whole world, and encompasses both its length and

breadth and height and depth — for by God's Word everything is disposed and administered — the Son of God was
also crucified in these, imprinted in the form of a cross on
the universe; [171] for He had necessarily, in becoming visible,
to bring to light the universality of His cross, in order to show
openly through His visible form that activity of His: [172] that
it is He who makes bright the height, that is, what is in
heaven, and holds the deep, which is in the bowels of the
earth, and stretches forth and extends the length from East
to West, navigating also the Northern parts and the breadth
of the South, and calling in all the dispersed from all sides
to the knowledge of the Father.[173]

PROMISE TO ABRAHAM FULFILLED. JUSTIFICATION BY FAITH.

35. So He fulfilled the promise made to Abraham by
God, that He would make his seed like the stars of heaven;
for Christ did this by being born of the Virgin who came of
Abraham's seed, and setting up as lights in the world those
who believe in Him, justifying the Gentiles through the same
faith with Abraham.[174] For *Abraham believed God, and it
was reputed to him unto justice;* [175] in like manner we too
are justified by believing God, for *a just man shall live by
faith.*[176] So *not through the law was the promise to Abraham,
but through faith.*[177] For Abraham was justified by faith, and
the law is not made for the just man.[178] So too are we
justified not through the law, but through the faith of Him
to whom witness was borne by the law and the prophets
whom the Word of God brought to us.[179]

PROMISE TO DAVID FULFILLED: VIRGIN BIRTH.

36. And He fulfilled the promise made to David, for God
had promised him to raise up from the *fruit of his bowels

an everlasting king, of whose reign there would be no end.[180] And this king is Christ the Son of God, made Son of man, that is to say, made fruitfulness from the Virgin, who came of the seed of David; and therefore the promise was in the form " from the *fruit of the bowels," which is birth taken separately and specially of conception by a woman, and not " from the fruit of the loins," or " from the fruit of the reins," which is birth taken separately and specially *of a man; [181] in order to declare as unique and separate and special this fruitfulness of the virginal womb sprung from David, who was everlasting King over the house of David, and of whose reign there shall be no end.[182]

THE TRIUMPH OF THE REDEMPTION.

37. In such wise, then, was His trumph of our redemption,[183] and His fulfilment of the promise to the patriarchs, and His doing away with the primal disobedience: the Son of God became a son of David and a son of Abraham; for in the accomplishment of these things, and in their summing up in Himself, in order to give us His own life, the Word of God was made flesh through the instrumentality of the Virgin, to undo death and work life in man; for we were in the bonds of sin, and were to be born through sinfulness and to live with death.[184]

GENUINE BIRTH, DEATH, AND RESURRECTION.

38. Great, then, was the mercy of God the Father: He sent the creative Word, who, when He came to save us, put Himself in our position, and in the same situation in which we lost life; [185] and He loosed the prison-bonds, and His light appeared and dispelled the darkness in the prison, and He sanctified our birth and abolished death, loosing those

same bonds by which we were held. And He showed forth the resurrection, becoming Himself *the first-born from the dead*,[186] and raised in Himself prostrate man, being lifted up to the heights of heaven, at the right hand of the glory of the Father, as God had promised through the prophet, saying: *I will raise up the tabernacle of David, that is fallen*,[187] that is, the body sprung from David; and this was in truth accomplished by our Lord Jesus Christ, in the triumph of our redemption, that He raise us in truth, setting us free to the Father.[188] And if anyone accept not His virgin birth, how shall he accept His resurrection from the dead? For it is nothing marvellous, nothing astonishing, nothing unheard-of, if one who was not born rose from the dead — but we can not even speak of the "resurrection" of one who came into being without birth, for he who is not born is also immortal; and he who was not subject to birth will not be subject to death either; for how can one who did not take on man's beginning receive his end? [189]

39. So, if He was not born, neither did He die; and if He did not die, neither was He raised from the dead; and if He was not raised from the dead, He has not conquered death, nor is its reign abolished; and if death is not conquered, how are we to mount on high into life, being subject from the beginning to death? [190]

THE PRIMACY OF CHRIST.

So those who exclude redemption from man, and do not believe God will raise them from the dead, despise also our Lord's birth, which the Word of God underwent for our sake, to be made flesh, that He might manifest the resurrection of the flesh, and take the lead of all in heaven: [191] as the first-born, first-begotten of the thought of the Father,

the Word, Himself in the world making all things perfect by
His guidance and legislation; as the first-born of the Virgin,
a just and holy man, a servant of God, good, pleasing to God,
perfect in all things, freeing those who follow Him from
Hell; as the first-born of the dead, head and source also of
the life unto God.[192]

40. Thus, then, does the Word of God *in all things hold
the primacy*,[193] for He is true man and *Wonderful Counsellor
and God the Mighty*,[194] calling man back again into communion with God, that by communion with Him we may
have part in incorruptibility.[195]

REVIEW: MOSES TO THE APOSTLES.

So, He who was preached by the law through Moses and
the prophets of the Most High and Almighty God, Son of
the Father of all, Source of all things, He who spoke with
Moses — He came into Judaea, begotten by God through the
Holy Spirit, and born of the Virgin Mary, of her who was
of the seed of David and of Abraham: Jesus, God's anointed,
showing Himself to be the one who had been preached in
advance through the prophets.[196]

41. And as precursor there went before Him John the
Baptist, preparing in advance and disposing the people to
receive the Word of life, declaring that He was the Christ,
on whom rested the Spirit of God, united with His body.[197]
Taught by Him, and witnesses of all His good works and of
His teaching and of His passion and death and resurrection
and ascent into heaven after the bodily resurrection, were
the apostles, who after ⟨the descent of⟩ the power of the Holy
Spirit were sent by Him into the whole world and carried
out the calling of the Gentiles, showing mankind the way of
life, turning them back from idols and from fornication and

from selfish pride, purifying their souls and their bodies through the baptism of water and of the Holy Spirit; dispensing and administering to the faithful the Holy Spirit they had received from the Lord.[198]

APOSTOLIC PREACHING.

And by these dispositions they established the churches.[199] By faith and charity and hope they realised that calling of the Gentiles, according to the mercy extended to them by God, which was heralded by the prophets, making it known through the work of their ministry, and receiving them into the promise made to the patriarchs, that so, to those who believed and loved the Lord, and in return for holiness and justice and patience, the God of all would bring, through resurrection from the dead, the life everlasting which He had promised, through Him who died and was raised, Jesus Christ; to whom He has committed the kingship of all that is, and the principality of the living and the dead, and the judgement. And they gave counsel, with the word of truth, to keep the body unstained unto resurrection, and the soul incorruptible.

42. For so (they said) do the faithful keep when there abides constantly in them the Holy Spirit, who is given by Him in baptism, and is kept by him who has received Him by the practice of truth and holiness and justice and patience; [200] for it is resurrection of this spirit that comes to the faithful, when the body receives once more the soul, and along with it is raised by the power of the Holy Spirit and brought into the kingdom of God.[201] This is the fruit of the blessing of Japheth, in the calling of the Gentiles, revealed through the Church, in constant obedience to receive the " dwelling in the house of Sem " according to God's promise.[202]

C. CHRIST IN THE OLD LAW.

THE PROPHECIES.

That all these things would come to pass was foretold by the Spirit of God through the prophets, that those who served God in truth might believe firmly in them; for what was quite impossible to our nature, and therefore like to be little believed in by men, God caused to be announced in advance by the prophets, that from the prediction made long beforehand, when at last the event took place just as had been foretold, we might know that it was God, who had revealed to us in advance our redemption.[203]

THE SON IN THE BEGINNING.

43. But we must necessarily believe God in all things, for God is in all things truthful.[204] And that there was born a Son of God, that is, not only before His appearance in the world, but also before the world was made, Moses, who was the first to prophesy, says in Hebrew: BARESITh BARA ELOVIM BASAN BENUAM SAMENThARES, of which the translation [ ] is: *A Son in the beginning God established then heaven and earth.*[205] Witness to this is borne also by Jeremias the prophet, saying as follows: *Before the daystar I begot Thee, Thy name is before the sun,*[206] that is, before the world was made, for at the same time as the world the stars also were made. And again he says: *blessed is He who existed before He was made man;* [207] for the Son was as a beginning for God before the world was made, but for us, at the time of His appearance, but before that He did not exist for us, in that we knew Him not.[208] To this purpose also His disciple John, telling us who God's Son is, who was with the Father before the world was made, says also, that

it was through Him that all creatures were made, as follows: *In the beginning was the Word, and the Word was with God, and the Word was God; the same was in the beginning with God; all things were made by Him, and without Him was made nothing;* [209] most plainly declaring, that all things were made by the Word who was in the beginning with the Father, and that is His Son.[210]

THE SON AND ABRAHAM. SODOM AND GOMORRHA.

44. And again Moses says that the Son of God drew near to exchange speech with Abraham: *and God appeared to him at the oak of Mambre at midday, and lifting up his eyes, he saw, and behold, three men were standing over him; and he prostrated himself to the ground and said: Lord, if I have truly found favour before thee;* [211] and all the rest of his speech is with the Lord, and the Lord speaks to him. Two, then, of the three, were angels, but one the Son of God; and with Him Abraham also spoke pleading for the men of Sodom, that they might not perish, if at least ten just men were found there.[212] And while they were speaking, the two angels go down to Sodom, and Lot receives them; and then the Scripture says: *and the Lord rained upon Sodom and Gomorrha brimstone and fire from the Lord out of heaven;* [213] that is, the Son, the same who spoke with Abraham, being " the Lord," received power to punish the men of Sodom " from the Lord out of heaven," from the Father, who is Lord over all.[214] So Abraham was a prophet, and saw what was to come to pass in the future, the Son of God in human form, that He was to speak with men, and eat food with them, and then to bring down judgement from the Father, having received from Him, who is Lord over all, power to punish the men of Sodom.[215]

THE SON AND JACOB: THEOPHANIES ARE
OF THE SON.

45. Jacob also, while journeying into Mesopotamia, sees Him, in a dream, standing at the ladder, that is, the tree, set up from *earth even to heaven; [216] for by it those who believe in Him mount to heaven, for His passion is our raising on high. And all visions of this kind signify the Son of God, in His speaking with men and being with them; for it is not the Father of all, who is not seen by the world, the Creator of all, who said: *Heaven is my throne, and the earth my footstool; what manner of house will you build for me, or what is the place of my rest?* [217] and who *holds the land in His fist and the heavens in His span* [218] — it is not He who would stand circumscribed in space and speak with Abraham, but the Word of God, who was always with mankind, and foretold what was to come to pass in the future, and acquainted man with God. [219]

THE SON AND MOSES IN THE DESERT.

46. He it was, who spoke with Moses in the bush, and said: *I have indeed seen the affliction of my people in Egypt, and I am come down to deliver them.* [220] He it was, who was mounting and descending for the deliverance of the afflicted, taking us out of the domination of the Egyptians, that is, out of every idolatry and impiety, and freeing us from the Red Sea, that is, liberating us from the deadly turbulence of the Gentiles and from the bitter current of their blasphemy; [221] for in these things our affairs were being rehearsed, the Word of God at that time prefiguring what was to be; but now, bringing us in reality out of the bitter servitude of the Gentiles, He has both caused to gush forth in abundance in the desert a stream of water from a rock — and the rock is

Himself — and given twelve springs — that is, the teaching
of the twelve apostles — and let the recalcitrant and unbelieving die out and be consumed in the desert, but brought
those who believed in Him and those who were children in
malice into the heritage of the patriarchs, which not Moses
but Jesus inherited and distributed by lot; and He too frees
us from Amalec by the stretching forth of His hands, and
takes us and bears us into the kingdom of the Father.[222]

THE TRINITY AND CREATURES.

47. Therefore the Father is Lord, and the Son is Lord,
and the Father is God and the Son is God; for He who is
born of God is God.[223] And thus God is shown to be one
according to the essence of His being and power; but at
the same time, as the administrator of the economy of our
redemption, He is both Father and Son: since the Father
of all is invisible and inaccessible to creatures, it is through
the Son that those who are to approach God must have
access to the Father.[224] Moreover David speaks clearly and
most manifestly of the Father and the Son, as follows: *Thy
throne, O God, is for ever and ever; Thou hast loved justice,
and hated iniquity, therefore God hath anointed Thee with
the oil of gladness above Thy fellows.*[225] For this means
that the Son, being God, receives from the Father, that is,
from God, the throne of the everlasting kingdom, and the oil
of anointing above His fellows. And "oil of anointing" is
the Spirit, through whom He is the Anointed, and "His
fellows" are the prophets and the just and the apostles, and
all who receive fellowship of His kingdom, that is, His
disciples.[226]

THE LORD SAITH TO MY LORD . . . (Ps. 109).

48. And again David says: *The Lord saith to my Lord: sit at my right hand, until I make Thy enemies Thy footstool; the Lord will sent forth a sceptre of power out of Sion; and Thou, rule amidst Thy enemies. With Thee in the beginning in the day of Thy strength, in the brightness of the saints, from the womb before the daystar I begot Thee. The Lord hath sworn, and He will not repent: Thou art a priest for ever according to the order of Melchisedech, and the Lord at Thy right hand. He hath broken kings in the day of wrath; He shall judge among nations, He shall fill ruins and shall crush the heads of many upon earth. He shall drink of the torrent in the way; therefore shall He lift up the head.*[227] By this, then, He declared that He came into being long before, and that He rules over nations, and judges all men, and the kings, who now hate Him and persecute His name, for these are His enemies; and when God called Him a priest for ever, He declared His immortality.[228] And this is why He said: *He shall drink of the torrent in the way; therefore shall He lift up the head*: He is referring to the exaltation with glory, after His human nature, and after humiliation and ingloriousness.[229]

THE SON ANOINTED KING. GOD SPEAKS IN THE PROPHETS.

49. And again Isaias the prophet says: *Thus saith the Lord to my anointed Lord: whose right hand I have taken hold of: that the nations hearken before Him;* [230] and as for how the Son of God is called both the *"anointed" and king of nations, that is, of all men, David also says that He both is called and is Son of God and king of all, as follows: *The Lord hath said to me: Thou art my Son, this day have I

begotten Thee; ask of me and I will give Thee the nations for Thy inheritance, and the whole earth for Thy posses-sion.[231] These things were not said to David, for he did not have dominion over "the nations," nor over "the whole earth," but only over the Jews.[232] So it is clear, the promise to the *"anointed," that he should be king over the whole earth, is made to the Son of God, whom David himself acknowledges his Lord, saying: *The Lord saith to my Lord: sit at my right hand,* and so on, as we said before.[233] For he means that the Father is speaking with the Son as we showed a little earlier, of Isaias, for he said: *Thus saith the Lord to my anointed Lord: that the nations hearken before Him;* because the promise is the same through both the prophets, that He would be king, so consequently God is addressing one and the same person, that is, I say, Christ the Son of God.[234] Since David says: *The Lord hath said to me,* one must say that it is not David who is speaking; nor does any other at all of the prophets speak in his own name, for it is not a man who utters the prophecy; but the Spirit of God, taking form and shape in the likeness of the person con-cerned, spoke in the prophets; sometimes He spoke on the part of Christ, sometimes on that of the Father.[235]

THE SON PRE-EXISTENT. SAVIOUR OF ALL.

50. So most properly does Christ report in the first person, through David, the Father's speech with Him; and most properly also does He say the other things too through the prophets in the first person, as *for example through Isaias as follows: [236] *And now thus saith the Lord, who formed me as His servant from the womb, to assemble Jacob, and to assemble Israel to Him; and I shall be magnified before the Lord, and my God shall be a strength to me. And He said:*

it shall be a great thing for Thee to be called my servant, to raise up and sustain the tribes of Jacob and turn back the dispersed of Israel; and I have set Thee as a light to the Gentiles, that Thou mayest be for salvation unto the farthest part of the earth.[237]

51. For here, in the first place, we have that the Son of God was pre-existent, from the fact that the Father spoke with Him, and caused Him to be revealed to men before His birth; and next, that He had to become a man, born of mankind, and that the very God Himself forms Him from the womb, that is, that He would be born of the Spirit of God; and that He is Lord of all men, and Saviour of those who believe in Him, Jews and others; for " Israel " is the name of the Jewish people in the Hebrew language, from the patriarch Jacob, who was also the first to be called " Israel "; and " Gentile " he calls all men; and that the Son calls Himself the Father's servant, because of His obedience to the Father, every son being a servant of his father among men too.[238]

THE MESSAGE OF SCRIPTURE.

52. That Christ, then, being Son of God before all the world, is with the Father, both being with the Father and being with men in a close and intimate communion, and king of all, for the Father has made all subject to Him, and Saviour of those who believe in Him — such is the message of similar passages of Scripture. Since it is beyond our scope and power to draw up an ordered list of all the Scriptures, you will comprehend from these passages the others also, that speak in like manner, believing Christ and seeking from God wisdom and understanding to understand what was said by the prophets.

"THE VIRGIN SHALL CONCEIVE." "CHRIST JESUS."

53. And that this Christ, who was with the Father, being the Word of the Father, was to take flesh and become man and undergo the coming into being through birth and be born of a virgin and walk with men, the Father of all effecting also His incarnation, Isaias so says: *Therefore the Lord Himself shall give thee a sign. Behold, the virgin shall conceive, and bear a son, and you shall call Him Emmanuel. He shall eat butter and honey; before He know or even distinguish evil, He chooses the good. For before the child know good or evil, He shall refuse evil things, to choose the good.*[239] He both announced that He was to be born of a virgin, and points out beforehand that He is truly man, by the fact of His eating, and by calling Him a child, but also by setting Him a name. For this is an error even of the one that is born.[240] And He has a double name in the Hebrew tongue, Messias — Christ ⟨(Anointed)⟩ — and [   ] Jesus — Saviour — and both names are names of certain deeds performed.[241] For He is named Christ ⟨(Anointed)⟩, because through Him the Father anointed and arrayed all things, and according to His coming as man, because He was the Anointed by the Spirit of God His Father, as He also says speaking of Himself through Isaias: *The Spirit of the Lord is upon me, wherefore He hath anointed me to bring good tidings to the poor;*[242] and Saviour from the fact that He became the cause of salvation to those who were at that time freed by Him from all manner of ills and from death, and to those to be, who believed after them, and the conferrer of eternal salvation.[243]

"EMMANUEL." VIRGIN BIRTH.

54. So therefore " Saviour "; " Emmanuel," however, is translated " God with *us," or, as an expression of desire uttered by the prophet, the equivalent of " God be with us "; and thus it is the explanation and manifestation of the " good tidings." [244] For " behold," he says, " the Virgin shall conceive and bear a Son, and the latter, being God, is to be with us "; and while as it were marvelling at these things, he at the same time tells the future, that God will be with us.[245] Also, concerning His birth, the same prophet says in another place: *Before she who was in labour brought forth, and before the pains of labour came, there came forth delivered a man child;* [246] he proclaimed His unlooked-for and extraordinary birth of the Virgin.

"WONDERFUL COUNSELLOR."

And again the same prophet says: *A son is born to us and a child is given to us, and His name has been called, Wonderful Counsellor, God the Mighty.*[247]

55. And he calls Him " Wonderful Counsellor," even of the Father; whereby it is pointed out that it is with Him that the Father works all things whatsoever, as we have in the first of the Mosaic books, which is entitled " Genesis ": *And God said: let us make man according to our image and likeness.*[248] For He is here seen clearly, the Father addressing the Son, as Wonderful Counsellor of the Father.[249] Now He is also our Counsellor, giving counsel — not constraining, as God, and nonetheless being " God the Mighty," he says — and giving counsel to leave off our ignorance and receive knowledge, and to go forth from error and come to truth, and to cast forth corruptibility and receive incorruptibility.[250]

"THEY SHALL WISH THAT THEY HAD BEEN BURNT WITH FIRE."

56. And again Isaias says: *And they shall wish that they had been burnt with fire; for a child is born to us, and a son is given to us, whose government is set upon His shoulders; and His name is called Messenger of Great Counsel. For I will bring peace upon the princes, again peace and health to Him. Great is His empire, and of His peace there is no end, upon the throne of David and upon his kingdom, to guide and to uphold with justice and right, from henceforth and for ever.*[251] For thereby it is proclaimed that the Son of God both is to be born and is to be everlasting king. But the words *they shall wish that they had been burnt with fire* refer to those who do not believe Him, and who have done to Him all they have done; for they will say in the judgement: " Oh that we had rather been burnt with fire before the Son of God was born, than not to have believed Him when born! " For those who died before the appearance of Christ have hope of attaining salvation in the judgement of the risen Christ; [252] whoever feared God and died in justice and had the Spirit of God within them, such as the patriarchs and the prophets and the just. But for those who after the manifestation of Christ have not believed Him, there is in the judgement inexorable vengeance. But the words *whose government is set upon His shoulders* mean allegorically the Cross, on which He held His back when He was crucified; for what was and is an ignominy for Him, and because of Him, for us, the Cross, that, he says, is His government, that is, a sign of His empire.[253] And he says *Messenger of Great Counsel*: messenger of the Father, whom he announced to us.

"A RULER FROM JUDA." "BLOOD OF THE GRAPE."

57. And from what has been said it is clear, how it was made known beforehand through the prophets, that the Son of God was to become subject to birth, and to what manner of birth, and that He would be manifested as Christ.[254] And after that, it was foretold also in what land and among what men He was to appear through birth. Thus Moses in Genesis speaks as follows: *There shall not lack a ruler from Juda, nor a leader from his loins, till He come, for whom it lies in store; and He shall be the expectation of the nations; washing His robe in wine, and His garment in the blood of the grape.*[255] But Juda, a son of Jacob, was ancestor of the Jews, who also take their name from him; and a ruler did not lack among them, or a leader, until the coming of Christ; [256] but from the time of His coming, the forces of the quiver were taken,[257] the land of the Jews was given over into the dominion of the Romans, and they had no more their ruler or leader on their own. For He had come to His destination [258] *for whom lies in store* a kingship in heaven, and who washed *His robe in wine, and His garment in the blood of the grape.* And "His robe," as also "His garment," are those who believe in Him, and whom He has cleansed, redeeming us with His blood. And His blood was called "the blood of the grape" because, just as no man makes the blood of the grape, but God makes it and gladdens those who drink it, so too His nature of flesh and His blood were not the work of man, but made by God; [259] *the Lord Himself gave the sign* of the Virgin, that is, Emmanuel, who came of the Virgin, and who also gladdens those who drink Him, that is, who receive His Spirit, an everlasting gladness.[260] Therefore is He also *the expectation of the nations*, of those who hope in Him,[261] because we expect Him to re-establish the kingdom.

STAR OF JACOB.

58. And again Moses says: *A star shall rise out of Jacob, and a leader shall spring up from Israel,*[262] clearly announcing that the dispensation of His coming into being according to the flesh would be among the Jews; and from Jacob and the Jewish race He who was born, coming down from heaven, took up the dispensation so laid down.[263] For a star appears in heaven; and "leader" means king, for He is king of all the saved. But the star appeared at His birth to those men, the magi, who dwelt in the East, and through it they learned that Christ was born; and led by the star they came to Judaea, till the star reached Bethlehem, where Christ was born, and having entered the house where the boy lay wrapped in swaddling clothes, stood above His head, showing the magi the Son of God, Christ.[264]

ROD AND FLOWER FROM THE ROOTS OF JESSE.

59. Then again, the same Isaias also says: *And there shall come forth a rod from the roots of Jesse, and a flower shall go forth from the root. And the spirit of the Lord shall rest upon Him, the spirit of wisdom, and of understanding, the spirit of counsel, and of fortitude, the spirit of knowledge, and of godliness. The spirit of the fear of the Lord shall fill Him. He shall not judge according to appearances, nor reprove according to report, but He shall give just judgement to the lowly, and shall have pity on the lowly of the earth. And He shall strike the earth with the speech of His mouth, and with the breath of His lips he shall slay the ungodly. And His loins shall be girded with justice, and His flanks clad in truth. And the wolf shall feed with the lamb, and the leopard with the kid, and the calf and the lion shall pasture together. And a little child shall thrust His hand into the*

vipers' hole, and into the den of the brood of vipers, and they shall not hurt Him. And it shall be in that day: the root of Jesse, and He who riseth to rule over the nations, in Him shall the nations hope; and His rising shall be honour; [265] thereby he says that it is of her, who is descended from David and from Abraham that He is born. For Jesse was a descendant of Abraham, and father of David; the descendant who conceived Christ, the Virgin, is thus become the " rod "; [266] and therefore Moses too worked his miracles before Pharaoh with a rod, and among others too of mankind, the rod is a sign of empire.[267] And the " flower " refers to His body, for it was made to bud forth by the Spirit, as we have already said.

"JUST JUDGEMENT TO THE LOWLY."

60. But the words He shall not judge according to appearances, nor reprove according to report, but He shall give just judgement to the lowly and have pity on the lowly of the earth [268] show His divinity more strongly. For to judge without acceptance of persons or partiality, not favouring the noble, but rendering to the lowly what is right and equitable and fair, corresponds to the exaltation and sublimity of God's justice, for God is not subject to influence, and favours none but the just man; and to have pity is especially proper to God, to Him, who can also save out of pity. And also he shall strike the earth with a word and slay the ungodly by a word alone; this is proper to God, who works all things whatsoever by His Word. But in saying His loins shall be girded with justice, and His flanks clad in truth, he announces His outward human form, and His inward supreme justice.[269]

"THE WOLF SHALL FEED WITH THE LAMB."

61. But as regards the union and concord and tranquillity of the animals of different kinds, and by nature mutually hostile and inimical, the elders say, that it will really be even so at the coming of Christ, when He is to be king of all.[270] For he now tells in parable the gathering together in peaceful concord, through the name of Christ, of men of different nations and like character; for the assembly of the just, who are likened to calves and lambs and kids and children, will not be hurt at all by those, both men and women, who at an earlier time had become brutal and beast-like because of selfish pride, till some of them took on the likeness of wolves and lions, ravaging the weaker, and waged war on their like, and the women ⟨took on the likeness⟩ of leopards and of vipers, as like as not to bring down even friends with their deadly venom, or out of cupidity . . . , these gathered together in *one name will be possessed by the grace of God in justice of conduct, changing their wild and untamed nature.[271] And this has already come to pass, for those who were before most perverse, to the extent of omitting no work of ungodliness, coming to know Christ, and believing Him, no sooner believed than they were changed to the extent of omitting no superabundance, even, of justice; so great is the change wrought by faith in Christ, the Son of God, in those who believe in Him. And he says *who riseth to rule over the nations,*[272] because having died He is to rise, and to be acknowledged and believed as Son of God and king; therefore he says *and His rising shall be honour,*[273] that is, glory, for it was when He was raised that He was glorified as God.

"I WILL RAISE UP THE TABERNACLE OF DAVID."

62. Therefore again the prophet says: *In that day I will raise up the tabernacle of David, that is fallen;* [274] clearly he is declaring the body of Christ — born, as we said before, of David — as raised after death from the dead; for the body is called a " tabernacle." [275] For in these passages, both that He who according to the flesh was of the seed of David, the *anointed,[276] would be Son of God, and that after His death He would rise again, and that He would be in figure man, but in power God, and that He would be judge of the whole world, and sole worker of justice and redeemer — all has been declared by the Scripture.

BETHLEHEM OF JUDAEA.

63. And again the prophet Micheas also tells that the place where Christ was to be born was Bethlehem of Judaea, saying as follows: *And thou, Bethlehem of Judaea, art not the least among the leaders of Juda; for out of thee shall come forth a leader, who shall shepherd my people Israel.*[277] But Bethlehem is also David's country, so that He is of the seed of David not only through the Virgin, who bore Him, but also by the fact that He was born in David's country, Bethlehem.[278]

THE SON OF DAVID FOR EVERMORE.

64. And again David says that Christ is to be born of his seed, as follows: *For Thy servant David's sake, turn not away the face of Thy *anointed. The Lord hath sworn truth to David, and will not lie to him: of the *fruit of thy bowels I will set upon thy throne, if thy children keep my covenant, and my testimonies, which I have covenanted with them; and their son for evermore.*[279] But none of David's sons reigned

" for evermore " — and even their kingdom was not " for evermore," for it is destroyed — but that king who was born of David, that is, Christ. All these testimonies concerning His descent according to the flesh tell explicitly and clearly both His race, and the place where He was going to be born, so that men should not seek Him who was born Son of God among the Gentiles, or anywhere else, but in Bethlehem of Judaea, from Abraham and from the seed of David.

ENTRY INTO JERUSALEM.

65. And His manner of entry into Jerusalem, which was the metropolis of Judaea, and where were His palace and the temple of God, is told by the prophet Isaias: *Say to the daughter of Sion: behold, a king cometh to thee, meek, and seated upon an ass, a colt, the foal of an ass.*[280] For He entered Jerusalem so seated on an ass's colt, the multitudes spreading their garments for Him to ride upon; [281] and " daughter of Sion " is what he calls Jerusalem.

CHRIST IN THE PROPHETS.

66. Thus, then, did the prophets announce that the Son of God was to be born, and by what manner of birth, and where He was to be born, and that He is Christ, the sole eternal king. And now, how they foretold that when He came He would heal men (and He did heal them), and raise the dead (and He did raise them), and be hated and despised and undergo sufferings and be slain by crucifixion — as He was hated and despised and slain.[282]

CHRIST'S MIRACLES.

67. Let us now speak of His healings. Isaias says as follows: *He hath taken our infirmities and carried our ills;* [283] that is, " will take " and " will carry," for sometimes the Spirit

of God relates through the prophets as a past event what is to come to pass in the future; for with God, what is approved and determined and decreed to be done is already accounted as done, and the Spirit uses expressions having in view the time in which the outcome of the prophecy is realised.[284] And as for the kinds of cure, he *recorded them in these words: *In that day the deaf shall hear the words of the book, and in darkness and obscurity the eyes of the blind shall see.*[285] And again, the same prophet says: *Be strengthened, feeble hands, and palsied knees; be consoled, ye dispirited in mind; be strengthened, fear not; behold our God will render judgement, He will come Himself and save us. Then shall the eyes of the blind be opened, and the ears of the deaf shall hear, then shall the lame man leap as a hart, and the tongue of the stammerer shall be free.*[286] And concerning the raising of the dead he says: *So shall the dead rise again, and those shall rise again who are in the tombs*; and by doing these things He will be believed to be Son of God.[287]

THE PASSION.

68. And that He would be despised and tormented and finally slain, Isaias says as follows: *Behold, my son shall *understand, and be exalted and extolled greatly; as many shall be astonished at Thee, so shall Thy visage be inglorious among men. And many peoples shall be astonished, and kings shall shut their mouths; for they to whom it was not told of Him shall see, and they who heard not shall take notice. Lord, who hath believed our report? and to whom is the arm of the Lord revealed? We have told our tale before His face, like a child, as a root in thirsty ground; and He had no comeliness, and no glory. And we have seen Him, and He had no comeliness, and no beauty. But His look was*

inglorious, made less than other men, a man in bruises and acquainted with the bearing of torments; because His face was turned away, He was despised and not esteemed. He beareth our sins, and for our sake suffereth pains, and we esteemed Him to be in pains and in bruises and in torments. But He was wounded because of our iniquities, and was tormented because of our sins. The chastisement of our peace is upon Him, by His wounds we are healed.[288] And thereby it is also declared that He was tormented, as David says too: *and I was tormented.*[289] But David was never tormented, but Christ, when order was given that He be crucified.[290] And again *the Word says through Isaias: *I have given my back to blows, and my cheeks to buffets, and I have not turned away my face from the contumely of spitting.*[291] And the prophet Jeremias says the same thing, as follows: *He shall give His cheek to him that striketh, He shall be filled with reproaches.*[292] All these things Christ underwent.

69. Isaias, then, goes on as follows: *By His wounds we are healed. All we like sheep have gone astray, man hath gone astray in his way; and the Lord hath delivered Him unto our sins;* [293] so it is clear that it came about by the will of the Father that these things happened to Him, for the sake of our salvation. Then he says: *And through His suffering He opened not the mouth; He was led as a sheep to the slaughter, mute as a lamb before the shearer.*[294] See how he declares His voluntary coming to death.[295]

THE TAKING OF JUDGEMENT.

But when the prophet says that *in humility His judgement was taken away,*[296] he is speaking of the appearance of His humility: the taking of the judgement was according to the form of abasement.[297] And the taking of the judgement is for some unto salvation, and for others unto torments of perdition; for there is taking *to* a person, and taking *from* a person.[298] So too the judgement has been taken *on* some, and they have it in the torments of their perdition; but *off* others, and they are thereby saved. But those men took judgement on themselves, who crucified Him, and, having thus treated Him, did not believe Him, so that they be brought to perdition with torments through the judgement which was taken by them.[299] And judgement has been taken off those who believe in Him, and they are no more subject to it; and the judgement, which is to come by fire, will be the perdition of those who did not believe, towards the end of this world.

" WHO SHALL DECLARE HIS GENERATION? "

70. Then he says: *Who shall declare His generation?* [300] Lest we despise Him as a man insignificant and of little account, because of His foes and because of the pains of His sufferings, this was said to put us right; for He who underwent all these things has a generation that cannot be declared, for " generation " means His lineage, and that is, His Father is beyond declaration and expression.[301] Recognise, therefore, even this as the lineage of Him who underwent all these sufferings, and despise Him not for the sufferings which He deliberately underwent for thy sake; but fear Him for His lineage.

"UNDER THY SHADOW SHALL WE LIVE."

71. And in another place Jeremias says: *The spirit of our face is the Lord Christ; and how He was taken in their toils, of whom we said: under Thy shadow shall we live among the Gentiles.*[302] Scripture both tells that Christ, being Spirit of God, was to become a man subject to suffering, and

as it were is struck with astonishment and wonder over His Passion, that He was thus to undergo sufferings, " under whose shadow we said we would live ";[303] and " shadow " means His body, for as a shadow is made by a body, so too Christ's body is made by His Spirit. But by " shadow " he also alludes to the lowliness and abjection of His body, for as the shadow even of bodies which are standing erect is on the ground and is trodden underfoot, so too the body of Christ was cast to the ground and trodden underfoot by His Passion, as it were.[304] He also named the body of Christ a " shadow " as having become a shade of the glory of the Spirit, covering Him.[305] But also, many a time, when the Lord was passing by, they laid beside the way those in the grip of divers sicknesses, and those whom His shadow touched were delivered.[306]

THE DEATH OF THE JUST MAN.

72. And again the same prophet speaks as follows concerning the sufferings of Christ: *Lo, how the just perisheth, and no man layeth it to heart; and just men are taken away, and no man understandeth; for the just man is taken away from before the face of iniquity. His burial shall be peace, He hath been taken away from the midst.*[307] And who else is " the just man " to perfection, but the Son of God, who perfects by justifying those who believe in Him, who, like Him, are persecuted and slain?[308] But in saying: *His burial shall be peace*, he tells how He died for the sake of our salvation — for " in peace " means, in that of salvation [309] — and that by His death, those who were before mutually hostile and opposed, believing with one accord in Him, will have peace with one another, made well-disposed and friendly because of common faith in Him; as also happens. But the

words: *He hath been taken away from the midst* refer to
His resurrection from the dead — for He was no more seen
as one dead, after His burial.[310] That by dying and rising
again He was to be permanently immortal, the prophet says
thus: *He sought life of Thee and thou hast given Him even
length of days for ever and ever.*[311] What, then, is the point
of "he sought life," since He was to die? He is therefore
proclaiming His resurrection from the dead, and that having
risen from the dead, He is immortal; for He received "life"
that He might rise again, and "length of days for ever and
ever," that He might be incorruptible.

THE RESURRECTION.

73. And again David speaks as follows concerning the
death and resurrection of Christ: *I have slumbered and slept;
and I have awakened, because the Lord hath taken me.*[312]
David was not saying this of himself, for he did not rise when
he died, but the Spirit of Christ, who also spoke in the other
prophets about Him, now also through David says: *I have
slumbered and slept; and I have awakened, because the Lord
hath taken me.* He calls death "sleep" because He rose.

HEROD AND PILATE.

74. And again David speaks as follows about the Passion
of Christ: *Why have the Gentiles raged, and the peoples
devised vain things? Kings on earth stood by and princes met
together, about the Lord and about His anointed one.*[313] For
Herod, king of the Jews, and Pontius Pilate, procurator of
Claudius Caesar,[314] came together and condemned Him to
be crucified; for Herod was frightened lest he be ousted by
Him from the kingship, as if He were going to be some
earthly king, while Pilate was constrained by Herod and by

the Jews around him to deliver Him, unwillingly, to death, on the grounds that not to do so would be to go against Caesar by liberating a man who was given the title of king.[315]

THE PASSION (BY THE WILL OF THE FATHER).

75. And concerning the passion of Christ, moreover, the same prophet says: *Thou hast rejected and despised us, Thou hast cast forth Thy anointed, Thou hast made void the covenant of my servant, Thou hast cast down His sanctuary. Thou hast broken down all His hedge, Thou hast cast His stronghold into trembling. Those who passed by the way have robbed Him, He is become a reproach to His neighbours. Thou hast exalted the right hand of His oppressors, Thou hast made His enemies to rejoice over Him. Thou hast turned away the help of His sword, and hast not assisted Him in battle; Thou hast cut Him off from purification, Thou hast cast His throne down to the ground. Thou hast shortened the days of His time; Thou hast covered Him with confusion.*[316] He plainly declared both that He would undergo these things, and that it would be by the will of the Father; for it was by the will of the Father that He was to undergo the Passion.

THE ARREST OF CHRIST.

76. And Zachary says as follows: *Awake, O sword, against my shepherd, and against the man that cleaveth to me; strike the shepherd, and the sheep of the flock shall be scattered.*[317] And this took place when He was arrested by the Jews; for all His disciples left Him, fearing lest perchance they die with Him. For even still not even they believed firmly in Him, till they saw Him risen from the dead.

CHRIST BEFORE HEROD.

77. Again, He says in the twelve prophets: *and they brought Him bound as a present to the king.*[318] For Pontius Pilate was procurator of Judaea, and was at that time on bad terms with Herod, king of the Jews. Now therefore Pilate sent Christ, who was brought to him, bound, to Herod, bidding him ascertain by questioning whatever he wished concerning Him; [319] having found in Christ an apt occasion for reconciliation with the king.

DESCENT INTO HELL.

78. And in Jeremias He thus announces His death and descent into hell, in the words: *And the Lord the Holy One of Israel bethought Him of His dead, who in the past had slept in the dust of the earth, and went down unto them, to bring the good news of salvation, to deliver them.*[320] Here He also gives the reason for His death; for His descent into hell was salvation for the departed.

CRUCIFIXION.

79. And again, concerning His Cross, Isaias says as follows: *I have stretched forth my hands all the day to a stubborn and contrary people;* [321] for this is a figure of the Cross. And also, more plainly, David says: *Hounds have encompassed me on all sides, the council of the malignant hath surrounded me; they have dug my hands and feet.*[322] And again he says: *My heart is become like wax melting in the midst of my bowels; and they have scattered my bones.*[323] And again he says: *Deliver my soul from the sword, and my body from the nailing; for the council of the malignant is risen up over me.*[324] In this He clearly and plainly signifies His own crucifixion. But Moses too says the same thing to

the people, as follows: *And thy life shall be hanging before thy eyes, and thou shalt fear night and day, neither shalt thou trust thy life.*[325]

THE PARTING OF THE GARMENTS.

80. Again David says: *They have looked upon me, they parted my garments among them; and upon my coat they cast lots.*[326] For when they crucified Him the soldiers divided His garments, according to their custom, and tore the garments to share them out. But as for the coat, because it was woven throughout without a seam, they cast lots, that he who won should take it.[327]

THE THIRTY PIECES OF SILVER.

81. And again Jeremias the prophet says: *And they took the thirty pieces of silver, the price of Him whom they bought of the children of Israel, and they gave them unto the potter's field, as the Lord appointed unto me.*[328] For Judas, who was one of the disciples of Christ, having come to terms with the Jews and contracted with them — since he saw that they wished to kill Him — because he had been reproved by Him, taking the thirty staters *of the Law,[329] delivered Christ to them, and then, repenting of what he had done, gave up the silver back again to the leaders of the Jews, and hanged himself.[330] But they, judging it not proper to cast it into their treasury, because it was the price of blood, bought with it the field of a certain potter, for the burial of strangers.[331]

GALL AND VINEGAR.

82. And when they raised Him on the Cross, as He asked for drink, they gave Him to drink vinegar mixed with gall.[332]

And this very thing was told by David: *They gave me gall for my food, and in my thirst they gave me vinegar to drink.*[333]

THE ASCENSION.

83. And that when raised from the dead He was to be taken up into heaven, David says as follows: *The chariot of God is myriadfold, thousands of charioteers; the Lord among them in Sina, in the holy place, hath ascended on high, He hath led captivity capitive. He hath taken, hath given gifts to men.*[334] And " captivity " refers to the destruction of the dominion of the rebel angels. And he announced also the place whence He was to mount to heaven from earth; for *the Lord*, he says, *in Sion hath ascended on high.*[335] For it was on the mountain which is called that of Olives, over against Jerusalem, after His resurrection from the dead, that, having assembled His disciples and having instructed them concerning the kingdom of heaven, He was lifted up in their sight, and they saw how the heavens opened and received Him.[336]

THE ENTRY INTO HEAVEN.

84. Again David says this very thing: *Take up your gates, O ye princes, and be lifted up, O eternal gates; and the king of glory shall enter in;*[337] for the " eternal gates " are the heavens. But because the Word came down invisible to creatures, He was not known to them in His descent; since the Word had become incarnate, He was also visible, in His ascension; and when the principalities saw Him, the angels underneath called to those who were on the firmament: *Take up your gates, and be lifted up, O ye eternal gates, that the king of glory enter in.*[338] And when these wondered and said: *Who is this?*[339] those who have already

seen Him testify a second time: *the Lord strong and mighty,*
He is the king of glory.[340]

AWAITING THE JUDGEMENT.

85. And as He is risen and ascended, He awaits ever at
the Father's right hand the time appointed by the Father
for the judgement, when all His enemies are made subject to
Him; and His enemies are all those who are found in rebellion, angels and archangels and principalities and thrones,
who spurned the truth.[341] Indeed, the same prophet, David,
says as follows: *The Lord said to my Lord: sit at my right*
hand, until I set Thy enemies beneath Thy feet.[342] And
David says that He ascended to the place whence He had
descended: *His going out is from the end of heaven, and*
His resting-place even to the end of heaven.[343] Then he
refers to His judgement, saying: *And there is none that*
shall hide himself from His heat.[344]

D. CHRIST IN THE NEW LAW

THE PROPHETS AND THE APOSTOLIC PREACHING.

86. So, if the prophets have prophesied that the Son
of God was to appear on earth, and have prophesied also
in what place on earth, and how, and as what manner of
man He should appear,[345] and the Lord took on Himself all
these prophecies, our belief in Him was well-grounded, and
true the tradition of the preaching, that is, the witness of
the apostles, who, sent by the Lord, preached to the whole
world that the Son of God was come unto sufferings, under-
gone for the destruction of death and the giving of life to the
flesh; that by casting out hostilities to God, that is, iniquities,
we should receive peace with Him, doing what is acceptable

to Him. And this was announced by the prophets in the words: *How beautiful are the feet of them that bring good tidings of peace, and that bring good tidings of good things.*[346] And that these were to come from Judaea and from Jerusalem to announce to us the word of God, which is also for us the law, Isaias says thus: *For the law shall come forth from Sion, and the word of the Lord from Jerusalem.*[347] And David says that it was to be preached to all the earth: *Their sound is gone forth into all the earth, and their words unto the ends of the earth.*[348]

CHARITY SUPERSEDES THE LAW.

87. And that men were to be saved not according to the wordiness of the law, but according to the brevity of faith and charity, Isaias says thus: *a word shortened and cut short in justice; because a short word shall God make upon all the earth.*[349] And therefore the apostle Paul says: *Love is the fulfilment of the law,*[350] for he who loves the Lord has fulfilled the law. But the Lord too, when He was asked, what was the first commandment, said: *Thou shalt love the Lord thy God with thy whole heart and with thy whole strength; and the second, like to it: thou shalt love thy neighbour as thyself. On these two commandments,* He says, *dependeth the whole law and the prophets.*[351] So He has increased, through our faith in Him, our love towards God and our neighbour, rendering us godly and just and good. And therefore He has made a *short word upon the earth.*

CHRIST IN GLORY. HE HIMSELF REDEEMED US.

88. And that after the ascension He was to be exalted above all, and that there would be none to be compared or likened to Him, Isaias says thus: *Who is there that is judged?*

Let him stand opposite. And who is there that is justified?
Let him draw near to the Son of the Lord. Woe to you, who
will all grow old like a garment, and the moth shall eat you
up. And all flesh shall be brought low to the ground and the
Lord alone shall be exalted among the exalted.[352] And Isaias
says that those who served God are in the end to be saved
through His name: *And those who served me shall be called*
by another name, which shall be blessed upon earth, and
they shall bless the true God.[353] And that He was Himself
to bring about these blessings in person, Isaias declared in
the words: *Not an intercessor, nor an angel, but the Lord*
Himself hath given them life, because He loves them and has
pity on them; He Himself redeemed them.[354]

THE SPIRIT SUPERSEDES THE LAW.

89. That He does not wish those who are to be redeemed
to be brought again under the Mosaic legislation — for the
law has been fulfilled by Christ — but to go free in newness
by the Word, through faith and love towards the Son of
God,[355] is said by Isaias: *Remember not former things and*
attend not to what is from the beginning; behold I do a new
thing, and now it shall spring forth, and you shall know it.
*I will make a way *in the desert, and rivers in dry land, to*
give drink to my chosen race and to my people, whom I have
made my own, to tell my prowesses.[356] And " desert " and
" dry land " is what the calling of the Gentiles was previously,
for the Word neither passed among them, nor *gave them
to drink the Holy Spirit,[357] who prepared the new way of
godliness and justice. And He has poured forth rivers in
abundance, to disseminate the Holy Spirit upon earth, as
He had promised through the prophets to pour forth the
Spirit on the face of the earth in the end of days.[358]

NEWNESS OF SPIRIT. THE NEW COVENANT.

90. So our calling is *in newness of spirit and not in the oldness* *of the letter,*[359] as Jeremias prophesied: *Behold, days come, saith the Lord, and I will perfect for the house of Israel and for the house of Juda* ⟨*a new covenant, not according to*⟩ *the covenant,*[360] *which I covenanted with their fathers, in the day that I took their hand to bring them out of the land of Egypt; for they did not remain firm in the covenant, and I regarded them not, saith the Lord. For this is the covenant, which I* *will covenant with the house of Israel after these days, saith the Lord: giving my law in their minds I will write it also in their heart; and I will be their God, and they shall be my people. And they shall no more teach every man his fellow citizen and every man his brother, saying: Know the Lord; for all shall know me, from the least of them even to the greatest; for I will be propitious to their iniquities, and I will remember their sins no more.*[361]

THE GENTILES HEIRS TO THE PROMISES.

91. And that these promises were to be inherited by the calling from the Gentiles, in whom also the new testament was opened,[362] Isaias thus says: *In that day man shall have hope in his maker, and his eyes shall look to the Holy One of Israel, and they shall not have hope in altars, nor in the works of their hands, which their fingers wrought.*[363] For most plainly this was said with regard to those who leave idols and believe God our Maker through the Holy One of Israel; and the Holy One of Israel is Christ; and He having been manifested to men — and we have looked well upon Him — we have not hope in altars, nor in the works of our hands.

92. And that He was to be manifested among us, that the Son of God became Son of man, and to be found by us who before were in ignorance, the Word Himself thus says in Isaias: *I have been manifested to those that ask not for me, I have been found by those that sought me not. I said: Lo, here I am, to a nation that did not call upon my name.*[364]

THE GENTILES TO BE A HOLY PEOPLE.

93. And that this nation was to become a holy people was thus announced through Osee in the twelve prophets: *And I will call that which was not my people, my people; and her that was not beloved, beloved. It shall be, in the place where it shall be called not my people, there they shall be called sons of the living God;*[365] that is, what was said also by John the Baptist, *that God is able of stones to raise up children to Abraham.*[366] For our hearts, taken away from stony services through faith see God and become sons of Abraham who was justified by faith.[367] And therefore God says through the prophet Ezechiel: *And I will give them another heart, and put a new spirit into them. And I will take away the stony heart out of their flesh, and will give them another heart of flesh, so that they shall walk in my commandments and keep my judgements, and do them. And they shall be my people, and I will be their God.*[368]

CHURCH MORE FRUITFUL THAN SYNAGOGUE.

94. So through the new calling a change of heart comes about in the Gentiles, through the Word of God, when He became incarnate and tabernacled with men, as also His disciple John says: *and His Word was made flesh and dwelt among us.*[369] For this reason, too, the Church bears fruit in so great a number of saved, for it is no more by an intercessor,

Moses, or by Elias's angel,[370] that we are saved, but by the Lord Himself, who grants more children to the Church than to the Synagogue of the past,[371] as Isaias announced in the words: *Rejoice, O thou barren, that didst not bear* (and "barren" is the Church, which in previous times did not at all bring forth children to God); *shout and call out, thou that wast not in travail; for many are the children of the desolate, more than of her that hath a husband* (and the former Synagogue had a husband, the Law).[372]

THE GENTILES SUPPLANT ISRAEL.

95. But Moses also says in Deuteronomy that the Gentiles are to become *the head*, and an unbelieving people *the tail*,[373] and again says: *Ye have made me jealous with what were no gods, and have angered me with your idols; and I will make you jealous with that which is no people, and will anger you with a foolish nation.*[374] Because they had left the real God and were giving service to unreal gods, and they had slain the prophets of God and were prophesying for Baal, to whom the Chanaanites had an idol; despising also the real Son of God, they rejected Him, but were choosing Barabbas, a robber taken in murder, and they denied the eternal king and were acknowledging the temporal Caesar as their king — God was pleased to grant His inheritance to the foolish Gentiles, and to those who were not God's citizens, and know not who God is.[375] Since, then, life has been given us through this calling, and God has restored again in us Abraham's faith in Him, we should no more turn back, I mean, to the former legislation. For we have received the Lord of the Law, the Son of God; and through faith in Him we learn to love God with our whole heart, and our neighbour as ourselves; but the love of God is without all sin, and love of one's neighbour works no evil to the neighbour.[376]

WE HAVE NO NEED OF THE LAW.

96. Therefore also we have no need of the law as pedagogue.[377] Behold, we speak with the Father and stand face
to face with Him, become infants in malice, and made strong
in all justice and propriety.[378] For no more shall the law say:
Thou shalt not commit adultery,[379] to him who has not *even
conceived the desire of another's wife; [380] or *thou shalt not
kill*,[381] to him who has put away from himself all anger and
enmity; [382] *thou shalt not covet thy neighbour's field, or his
ox, or his ass*,[383] to those who make no account whatever of
earthly things, but heap up profit in heaven.[384] Nor *an eye
for an eye and a tooth for a tooth*,[385] to him who counts no
man his enemy, but all his neighbours, and therefore cannot
even put forth his hand to revenge. Nor will it demand tithes
of him who has vowed to God all his possessions, and who
leaves father and mother and all his kindred, and follows the
Word of God.[386] Nor will he be commanded to leave idle
one day of rest, who is constantly keeping sabbath, that is,
giving homage to God in the temple of God, which is man's
body, and at all times doing the works of justice.[387] For *I
desire mercy*, He says, *and not sacrifice, and the knowledge
of God more than holocausts*.[388] But *the unjust man that
killeth a calf in sacrifice, as if he should immolate a dog; and
he that offereth fine flour, like swine's blood*.[389] But *every
one that shall call upon the name of the Lord shall be
saved;* [390] and *no other name* of the Lord *has been given
under heaven, whereby men are saved*,[391] but that of God
who is Jesus Christ the Son of God, whom even the devils
obey, and the evil spirits, and all rebel powers.[392]

NEARNESS OF ALMIGHTY AID.

97. Through the invocation of the name of Jesus Christ, crucified under Pontius Pilate, *Satan is cast out from men,[393] and wherever anyone shall call upon Him, invoking Him, of those who believe in Him and do His will,[394] He comes and stands close by, accomplishing the petitions of those who invoke Him with a pure heart. Having thereby received salvation, we are constant in rendering thanks to God, our Saviour through His great inscrutable and unsearchable wisdom, and the Preacher of redemption from heaven — the visible coming of our Lord, that is, His human career — which of ourselves we were not able to receive; for *the things that are impossible with men are possible with God.*[395] Therefore also Jeremias says concerning this: *Who hath gone up into heaven and taken her, and brought her down from the clouds? Who hath passed over the sea, found her, and will bring her, of choice gold? There is none, that hath found her way, nor that understandeth her paths. But He that knoweth all things knoweth her with His wisdom, He that prepareth the earth for ever more, and filleth it with fat cattle, He that sendeth forth light, and it goeth, and hath called it, and it obeyed Him with fear; and the stars will shine in their watches and are glad. He called them, and they said: Here we are; with cheerfulness they have shined forth to Him that made them. This is our God, and no other shall be taken into account with Him. He found out all the way by understanding, and gave it to Jacob His servant, and to Israel His beloved. Afterwards He was seen on earth and conversed with men. This is the book of the commandments of God, and of the law, which is for ever. All they that keep it, unto life; but they that have forsaken it shall die.*[396] But " Jacob " and " Israel " he calls the Son of God,

who received from the Father dominion over our life, and having received it, brought it down to us, to those who are far from Him, when *He was seen on earth and conversed with men*, joining and uniting the Spirit of God the Father with what God had fashioned, so that man became according to the image and likeness of God.[397]

CONCLUSION.

98. This, beloved, is the preaching of the truth,[398] and this is the manner of our salvation, and this is the way of life, announced by the prophets and ratified by Christ and handed over by the apostles and handed down by the Church in the whole world to her children. This must be kept in all security, with good will, and by being well-pleasing to God through good works and sound moral character.[399]

ERROR AGAINST THE PERSONS OF THE TRINITY.

99. And now let none think that there is any other God the Father than our Maker, as the heretics think; they despise the real God and make an idol of some unreal one, and create for themselves a father superior to our Creator, and think they have found on their own account something greater than the truth.[400] For they are all wicked men and blasphemers against their Creator and Father, as we have shown in the "Exposure and overthrowal of knowledge falsely so called." [401] And others again despise the coming of the Son of God and the dispensation of His incarnation, which the apostles have transmitted to us, and which the prophets foretold would be the summing-up of humanity, as we have shown you in brief.[402] And such people too should be counted among the unbelievers. And others do not admit the gifts of the Holy Spirit, and reject from themselves the

charism of prophecy, being watered whereby, man bears fruit of life to God.[403] And those are the ones spoken of by Isaias; *for they shall be,* he says, *as a leafless terebinth, and as a garden without water.*[404] And such men are of no use to God, in that they can bear no fruit.

BEWARE OF HERETICS!

100. So error with respect to the three articles of our seal has brought about much wandering away from the truth.[405] For either they despise the Father, or they do not accept the Son, they speak against the dispensation of His incarnation, or they do not accept the Spirit, that is, they reject prophecy. And we must beware of all such men, and flee their ways, if we really desire to be well-pleasing to God and receive from Him salvation.

IRENAEUS'S " PROOF OF THE APOSTOLIC PREACHING "

⚊   ⚊   ⚊

Glory to the all-holy Trinity, one God, Father and Son and all-provident Holy Spirit, for ever, amen.

⚊   ⚊   ⚊

Remember in the Lord the godlike and thrice-blessed Lord Archbishop John,[406] the owner of this book, brother of the holy king; and the humble scribe.

NOTES

ABBREVIATIONS AND TRANSCRIPTION USED.

A.H. = Irenaeus, *Adversus haereses* (cited according to the division in Massuet's edition, which is that printed in Migne's *Patrologia Graeca*; the numbering is the same in Stieren's also).

AR* = J. Armitage Robinson's English *Proof* (cf. n.12 to Introd.)

BK* = Weber's German *Proof* (in the Bibliothek der Kirchenväter; cf. n. 10 to Introd.)

c. = chapter (of *Proof*).

EP* = *editio princeps* of *Proof* (cf. n. 7 to Introd.)

F* = Faldati's Italian *Proof* (cf. n. 12 to Introd.)

HAm. = *Handes Amsorya* (monthly journal of the Mechitarists of Vienna: in Armenian).

L* = Weber's Latin *Proof* (cf. n. 10 to Introd.)

LXX = the Septuagint version of the Old Testament (references to Rahlfs' edition).

n. = note, the reference being to the notes to the text, unless otherwise indicated.

PO* = edition of *Proof* in Patrologia Orientalis 12. 5; unless the context refers to Barthoulot or Tixeront, the reference is to the main body of the edition (Ter Mekerttschian) (cf. n. 8 to Introd.)

S* = Sagarda's Russian *Proof* (cf. n. 9 to Introd.)

TU = Texte und Untersuchungen (Leipzig).

Apart from current use of proper names and the established forms *Handes Amsorya, Huschardzan*, Armenian is transliterated according to the system represented by the following classical-Armenian alphabet:

a	b	g	d	e	z	ē	ĕ	t'	ž	i	l	x	c	k	h
j	ł	č	m	y	n	š	o (ow > u)	č'	p	ǰ	r̄	s	v		
t	r	c'	w (ow > u)	p'	k'										

113

INTRODUCTION

[1] For Irenaeus's friendship with Polycarp, and the latter's with the first disciples, cf. Irenaeus's letter to Florinus, in Eusebius, *Hist. eccles.* 5. 20. 6-8. Regarding Polycarp's appointment as bishop of Smyrna, cf. Irenaeus, A.H. 3. 3. 4 ("ab apostolis . . . constitutus episcopus"), and Tertullian, *De praescr. haer.* 32 (made bishop by St. John).

"He may be said" to have belonged to the third generation of Christian teachers; but as he himself says (letter to Florinus as above), he was only a boy when he knew the aged Polycarp; there is about half a century between their deaths (156?-202?).

[2] Presbyter in Lyons (sent thence on embassy to Rome, to urge leniency towards Montanists), Eusebius, *Hist. eccles.* 5. 3. 4-4. 2. Succession to Pothinus, *ibid.* 5. 5. 8.

[3] Irenaeus is venerated as a martyr by both Greeks (feast August 23) and Latins (feast June 28); but Eusebius does not say he was martyred. The first extant reference to him as a martyr seems to be in the fifth century (no. 115 of the *Responsa ad quaestiones ad orthodoxos* attributed to Justin; there is also a passing reference in our text of Jerome's Commentary on Isaias 64. 4, but the word "martyr" is here probably an interpolation; Jerome makes no mention of martyrdom in his life of Irenaeus, *De vir. ill.* 35). The statement — second half of sixth century — of Gregory of Tours (*Hist. Franc.* 1. 27; *In glor. mart.* [= *Mir.* 1] 50) that Irenaeus was martyred is rendered suspect by his placing the martyrdom under Marcus Aurelius (in former of *loc. cit.* above).

[4] Eusebius, *Hist. eccles.* 4. 25 (treatise against Marcion); 5. 20 (letters to Blastus *On Schism*, to Florinus *On the Sole Sovereignty*, or *That God is not the Author of Evil*; book *On the Ogdoad*, also for Florinus); 5. 24 (letter to Victor of Rome, dissuading him from violence against the Asiatic Churches, who wished to keep to their own tradition in dating Easter, instead of conforming to the Roman custom); 5. 26 (treatises *On Knowledge*, the *Proof*, and a collection of what were probably sermons); 5. 7 and frequent references (*Adversus haereses*).

[5] Zahn argued that the Greek text of Irenaeus was probably extant

in the sixteenth or seventeenth century; cf. *Zeitschrift für Kirchengeschichte* 1878, p. 288-291 (Zahn); 1890, p. 155-158 (Ph. Meyer); *Theologisches Literaturblatt* 1893, p. 495-497 (Zahn).

⁶ The following description of the manuscript is abridged from the full one given in PO* 657 f.: Bound codex, on paper, 245 x 165 mm., in the writing called *boloragir* ("roundhand"), some titles in red ink. 383 sheets remain, but others are missing between nos. 7 and 8. Under the title "Proofs of the Apostolic Preaching" we have: 33ʳ-146ʳ the fourth book of *Adversus haereses*, 146ʳ-222ʳ the fifth book, and 222ʳ-262ʳ the *Proof*.

⁷ TU 31. 1 (1907): *Des heiligen Irenaeus Schrift zum Erweise der apostolischen Verkündigung . . . in armenischer Version entdeckt, herausgegeben und ins Deutsche übersetzt von D. Karapet Ter Mekerttschian und Lic. D. Erwand Ter Minasseantz, mit einem Nachwort und Bemerkungen von Ad. Harnack.*

Though this was the *editio princeps*, there was no description of the manuscript (this was supplied when the text was republished, cf. preceding note), and no *apparatus criticus*, though it is clear from the translation that several emendations were adopted (emendations were referred to in the margin of the republished translation, cf. next note but one). The German translation was in the circumstances a highly meritorious achievement, and not all the criticisms later directed against it (e.g. by Weber, cf. n. 10 to Introd. below) were justified; but inevitably it left much to be desired, and this fact hampered Harnack in his annotations.

The Armenian text (without version) of A.H. 4-5 was published by Ter Minasseantz in TU 35. 2 (1910).

⁸ Patrologia Orientalis 12. 5 (ed. R. Graffin — F. Nau, Paris 1919) 655-731: *S. Irenaeus . . ., The Proof of the Apostolic Preaching . . ., Armenian version edited and translated by His Lordship the Bishop Karapet Ter Měkěrttschian and the Rev. Dr. S. G. Wilson, with the co-operation of H.R.H. Prince Maxe of Saxony, D.D. and D.C.L.* For all that, the version is not infrequently at fault — though it presents several improvements on the original German one — and is further marred by strange misprints.

Tixeront-Barthoulot (cf. n. 11 to Introd. below) is reprinted (747-803) as an appendix to this edition.

⁹ The revised German version was published in Leipzig, 1908; I have not, however, seen it.

The Russian version of Professor N. I. Sagarda (the "Sagrada" of PO* 655 is an error): *Novo-otkrytoe proizvedenie sv. Irineä Lionskago: Dokazateljstvo apostoljskoj propovēdi*, published in *Hris-*

tianskoe čtenie 87 (1907): 476-491 = foreword, 664-691 = c. 1-50, 853-881 = c. 51-100 and closing remarks. This version was made not from the Armenian, but from the German translation of EP*. Hence its independent value lies only in the competent introduction and notes.

[10] German version: Bibliothek der Kirchenväter 4 (Kempten — Munich 1912): *Des hl. Irenaeus Schrift zum Erweis der apostolischen Verkündigung, aus dem Armenischen übersetzt von Dr. Simon Weber, o. Prof. an der Universität Freiburg i. Br.*

The German of this version is superior to that of the first German version, and the text had in the meantime been subjected to discussion; not all the changes so introduced, however, are correct (several were later abandoned by Weber himself).

Controversy: *Zeitschrift für neutestamentliche Wissenschaft* 14 (1913) 258-262 (Ter Minasseantz); *Der Katholik* 94. 1 (1914) 9-44 (Weber); *Zeitschrift für Kirchengeschichte* 35 (1914) 255-260, and 442 as note after the following (W. Lüdtke); *ibid.* 438-441 (Weber).

Latin version: *Sancti Irenaei Demonstratio Apostolicae Praedicationis.* . . . *Ex armeno vertit, prolegomenis illustravit, notis locupletavit Simon Weber* . . . (Freiburg i. Br. 1917). The version is, apart from one or two slips, accurate, but in the nature of things often obscure, ambiguous, or even positively misleading. Though this version is the best means available whereby one who does not know Armenian can form an idea of how the text expressed itself, Latin is not a suitable medium for such a verbal transposition. A Greek version on the same lines would have been more useful. (Lüdtke, *loc. cit.* above, 256, did in fact reconstruct in Greek the second half of c. 34, as a means of judging the merits of the rival German versions).

[11] *Recherches de science religieuse* 6 (1916) 361-432; version and annotations by Barthoulot, introduction and additional notes by Tixeront. Reprinted as appendix to PO*, from which it is cited in these notes. The version is very free, and in some places rather a paraphrase than a translation, and the translator has in several places been misled by lack of acquaintance with the peculiar Armenian style of the text.

A new French version is now being prepared, for the series " Sources chrétiennes."

[12] English version: J. Armitage Robinson: *St. Irenaeus: The Demonstration of the Apostolic Preaching* (Society for Promoting Christian Knowledge: London and New York, 1920). A good version.

Dutch version: H. U. Meyboom (Leyden 1920). I have not seen this version, and take the reference from J. Quasten, *Patrology* 1 (Utrecht-Brussels 1950) 293.

Italian version: Ubaldo Faldati: *S. Ireneo, Esposizione della Predicazione Apostolica* (Roma 1923). A very accurate version, on the whole.

[13] *Hist. eccles.* 5. 26 (cf. § 13 f. of Introd.).

[14] This point is developed by Weber, BK* p.v.

[15] Cf. n. 314.

[16] Cf. § 28 of Introd., and n. 51 thereto.

[17] A.H. 3. 3. 3.

[18] Though O. Bardenhewer (*Geschichte der altkirchlichen Literatur* 1 [2nd ed. Freiburg i. Br. 1913] 409) and others admit the hypothesis that the *Proof* may have been written contemporaneously with the last two books of *Adversus haereses*, there are several points which have seemed to others to suggest that some time elapsed between the two works. Thus Faldati (F* 44) sees in the difference between the exegesis of Isa. 11. 6 f. in c. 60 of the *Proof* and that in A.H. 5. 32 f. a profound change in the author's views, which must have been the work of a considerable lapse of time; but I do not find this conclusion to be inevitable; cf. n. 270.

F. R. M. Hitchcock (*Journal of Theological Studies* 9 [1908] 286) sees in the statement of c. 48, that kings are Christ's enemies and persecutors of His name, a reference to the persecution under Septimius Severus, and so would put the composition of the *Proof* at the end of Irenaeus's life. But the bishop of Lyons did not have to wait for the persecution under Severus in order to make such a statement.

The reference to *Adversus haereses* in c. 99 of the *Proof* comes after the mention of the first of the three classes of heretics there mentioned. Now the other two classes also are dealt with in *Adversus haereses*, but whereas the first class is treated of in books 1 and 2 (though the principal refutation is in book 4), the other two are mentioned in books 3 and 4. Hence the reference to the earlier work does not necessarily imply that the whole work had been finished, indeed the restriction of the reference to the first class might be taken as a suggestion that only the first two books had been completed. It seems, however, on the whole more probable that *Adversus haereses* was completed some time before the *Proof*; but nothing can be affirmed with certainty in this respect.

[19] The fragments are in H. Jordan: *Armenische Irenaeusfragmente*, TU 36. 3 (1913) Fr. 6, 13, 20, 25 (all from the same passage, the

beginning of c. 31 — cf. n. 156), and Fr. 7e (from c. 40 — cf. n. 195).
Cf. next paragraph of Introd., and the notes thereto.

[20] " Stephen the Philosopher": Fr. 20-22 of Jordan, *op. cit.* in preceding note (20 is from the *Proof*, c. 31 — cf. n. 156; 21 is from *Adversus haereses*, and 22 from some other work of Irenaeus).

" Catholicos Sahak ": *ibid.*, Fr. 18 (= 22), 19 (= 21).

[21] For this dating, cf. EP* p. iv-v. Ter Minasseantz, however, in the preface to the Armenian text of A.H. 4-5, in TU 35. 2 (1910) p. v, puts the period of translation at 650-750.

[22] N. Akinean, *HAm.* 24 (1910) 205, puts 604 as the latest date, because of a quotation in a letter of Varthan Kherdogh, and even suggested that the latter was the translator, between 590 and 604.

In 1911 Ter Mekerttschian found yet another manuscript, bearing the title " Seal of the Faith," with a quotation from the *Proof*, distorted however into a Monophysite sense (Fr. 6 of Jordan, *op. cit.* in n. 19 above; from c. 31 — cf. n. 156). This manuscript can be dated to the Catholicate of Comitas, which seems to have been about 611-628 (dating of Ter Minasseantz, TU, Neue Folge 11 [1904] 60-62).

Weber (L* 9-10) suggested that Eznik (early fifth century) knew both the *Proof* and *Adversus haereses*; but this would prove nothing, since Eznik used Greek sources directly.

[23] Jordan, *op. cit.* 203; similarly Ter Mekerttschian in PO* 656.

In addition to the quotations from the *Proof* and from the last two books of *Adversus haereses*, of which we have the Armenian version, there are also Armenian quotations in the same distinctive style from the earlier books of *Adversus haereses*, so that it is clear that the whole work was translated at the same time. Cf. Jordan, *op. cit.* 204 f.

[24] C. F. Conybeare, *American Journal of Theology* 16 (1911) 631 f.; more fully in *Huschardzan* (Vienna 1911) 193-203 (in English).

[25] The classification of the periods of the " Hellenising " school of Armenian, the *Proof* etc. being assigned to the first period, was established by Manandean in his work *Yunaban dproc'ĕ ew nra zargac'man šrǰannerĕ* = " The Hellenising school and the phases of its development" in Armenian (Vienna 1928), which had appeared by instalments in *HAm.* 39 (1925) 225-232, 347-354, 539-548, 40 (1926) 15-23, 121-129, 209-216, 305-313, 437-445, 525-533, 41 (1927) 16-23, 109-116, 289-301, 417-425, 559-569, 42 (1928) 25-30, 109-120, 205-213, 303-310, 401-407.

When Manandean wrote, it was still thought that the school must be dated in the fifth century; since that time, however, this view has been generally abandoned (cf. rest of this paragraph of Introd.). There is a concise account of the development of the Hellenising school, embodying the conclusions of the discussion on the dating, by Akinean, in *HAm*. 42 (1932) 271-292 (in Armenian; German résumé 376-380); and a brief account in English, concerned especially with the first group (to which the *Proof* belongs) in H. Lewy, *The Pseudo-Philonic De Jona* (Studies and Documents 7, London 1936) 9-16.

[26] In the early period of the controversy over the dating of Moses of Khoren the principal opponent of the traditional date was A. Carrière, *Nouvelles sources de Moïse de Khoren: études critiques* (Vienne 1893); *Nouvelles sources de Moïse de Khoren: supplément* (Vienne 1894); or *HAm*. 6 (1892) 250; 7 (1893) 134, 178, 309; 8 1894) 53, 210. C. F. Conybeare: "The date of Moses of Khoren," *Byzantinische Zeitschrift* 10 (1901) 489-504, maintained the traditional dating; so also in *HAm*. 16 (1902) 1, 85, 129, 193, 236; 17 (1903) 30, 33, 152, 215, 317, 325.

For an account of the question in English, cf. H. Lewy, *op. cit.* and two articles in *Byzantion* 11 (1936) 81-96 and 593-596; in the former of these two articles are further references to earlier literature on the subject.

Other modern opponents of the traditional dating: Akinean, *Łewond Erec' ew Movses Xorenac'i* = " Leontius the Priest and Moses of Khoren " (Vienna 1930): suggests identification of " Moses " with eighth-century Leontius; and Manandean, *Xorenac'u ařełcvaci lucumě* = " The solution of the problem of Khorenatzi " (Erevan 1934): puts Moses at beginning of second half of ninth century.

Against the two works mentioned in the preceding paragraph: S. Malkhasean: *Xorenac'u ařełcvaci šurjě* = " Concerning the Problem of Khorenatzi " (Erevan 1940).

For the traditional dating, against Lewy's articles in *Byzantion*, cf. Adontz, after each of those articles (that is, *Byzantion* 11 [1936] 97-100, 597-599), and *Sur la date de l'Histoire de l'Arménie de Moïse de Chorène* (from *Byzantion*, Brussels 1936). Cf. also Abeghian (following note).

[27] Akinean, *Ełišē Vardapet ew iwr Patmut'iwnn hayoc' paterazmin* = " Elisaeus Vardapet and his History of the Armenian War," which appeared in instalments in *HAm*. 45 (1931) 21-49, 129-201, 321-340, 393-414, 449-473, 585-617, 677-690; 46 (1932) 293-298, 385-401, 545-576; 47 (1933) 33-56, 641-679; 48 (1934) 353-414.

A recent, highly authoritative, history of Armenian literature is that of Manuk Abeghian. I have not seen the Armenian original, but only the abridged Russian version, *Istoria drevnearmänskoj literatury* (Erevan 1948 [vol. 1]). He here maintains the traditional dating (mid-fifth century) for both Moses of Khoren (203-209) and Elisaeus (244 f.).

[28] Akinean, *HAm.* 46 (1932) 271-292, referred to in n. 25 above; cf. also Lewy, *op. cit.* at end of same note.

[29] EP* vi-vii; PO* 656.

Latin intermediary: Y. Awger, *Bazmavep* 67 (1909) 59-66, 145-160; and cf. Akinean, *HAm.* 24 (1910) 202 f.; 25 (1911) 305-310; also W. Lüdtke, *Theologische Literaturzeitung* 36 (1911) 541.

[30] The indications of a Syriac intermediary were: (a) the occurrence in *Adversus haereses* of the name "Elisabeth" in the form *Elišabet'*, with the Syriac sound *š* instead of the Greek *s*; (b) the quotation of Zach. 9. 9, in c. 65 of the *Proof*, not according to the Septuagint but in a form agreeing rather with the Syriac version; (c) the rendering of the name of the prophet Malachy, on the two occasions in which it occurs in the *Adversus haereses* (4. 17. 5 and 4. 20. 2, corresponding to 4. 29. 5 and 4. 34. 2 respectively in the Armenian text as in TU 35. 2, which uses Harvey's numbering), as "angel," as if it were the Syriac common noun *mala'kâ*, "angel, messenger."

The first and second of these may be neglected, since (a) such forms as *Elišabet'* are common in Armenian, and are to be found even in works certainly translated directly from the Greek (cf. Akinean, *HAm.* 24 [1910] 201); and (b) the quotation is not taken from the Old Testament directly, but from Matt. 21. 5 or from a collection of texts (cf. § 38 of Introd. and n. 280).

The third point is more difficult to account for. It is true that "Malachy" is not a normal proper name, but a sort of pen name (cf. Mal. 3. 1: *Behold I send* my angel . . . etc.) and so might be rendered "Angel" or "Messenger" in much the same way as "Qoheleth" is rendered "Preacher" (Ecclesiastes); and that the prophet's name is in fact rendered ἄγγελος in the Septuagint (Mal. 1. 1); so that Irenaeus might well have used that word. The difficulty is, that he does not in fact seem to have done so, since the Latin version of *Adversus haereses* has in both places "Malachias." Hence the rendering "angel" of the Armenian version presents a problem; but it does not force the conclusion that the version was made through a Syriac intermediary.

The principal indication of translation directly from the Greek is the style of the version. This is a point which cannot conveniently be documented here; let it suffice to say that the version clearly belongs to a class of servile renderings of Greek texts, so closely modelled on the Greek as to justify the conjecture that they were intended rather as "keys" to the original text than as "translations" in the normal sense. One peculiarity which tells especially against the possibility of a Syriac intermediary is the imitation of the Greek "genitive absolute," of which there are many examples in the version of the *Proof*. This construction is foreign to Armenian, but can be accounted for as a mechanical reproduction of the Greek in a "key"; it is however quite incredible that it can have been transmitted through the Syriac, in which such a construction is incapable of exact reproduction.

Against the use of the form *Elišabet'*, mentioned above, may be set the fact that proper names in general appear in a form which corresponds not to Syriac but to Greek—for example, Sem, Messias, Bethlehem. More telling still is the manner in which the corrupt text of Gen. 1. 1 is transcribed in c. 43: *baresit'*, *sament'ares*, not *barešit'*, *šament'ares*. A Syriac version would have transcribed back into *š* a Greek *s* standing for *š*, and an Armenian version from that Syriac would have reproduced this *š*; transcription in Armenian as *s* argues that the transcription is directly from the Greek transcription. (The corruption of the text in question has also been alleged as an argument against transmission through the Syriac; but corruption may have arisen in the transmission of the version as originally made to the manuscript in which we have it.)

Finally, in c. 25, we read, concerning the Passover, which is put forward as a type of the Passion, "the name of this mystery is *kirk'*." *Kirk'* is a hapax legomenon which seems, as Vardanian pointed out, *HAm.* 24 (1910) 303, to be an attempt to render Greek Πάσχα in the sense "Passion," as if it were related to πάσχειν "suffer" (Armenian *krel*). Now, any Armenian translator must surely have known that the word was a proper name "Pasch," Armenian *Pasek'*; but one can understand how a translator from the Greek, meeting the word here, might have rendered it for the nonce *kirk'*, either thinking that it was in origin a Greek word connected with πάσχειν, or at least thinking that Irenaeus was playing on the similarity of the two words (as indeed he almost certainly was: cf. A.H. 4. 10. 1: cuius et diem *passionis* non ignoravit [sc. Moyses] sed figuratim praenuntiavit eum, *Pascha* nominans; et in eadem ipsa, quae ante tantum temporis a

Moyse praedicata est, *passus est* Dominus adimplens *Pascha*). A Syriac translator from the Greek would surely not have attempted any such rendering, even if he saw that there was a play on the similarity of the words in Greek, for *Pascha* is itself a Syriac word (the Greek having taken this word, like many others, not in the Hebrew form — *pesach* — but in the Aramaic = Syriac form); while an Armenian translating from the Syriac would surely not even have reflected that there had been such a play on words in the Greek original.

[31] For a fuller, but brief, discussion in English of the style of the " Hellenising " school, cf. Lewy, *op. cit.* 16-24.

[32] For examples, cf. Conybeare's articles, references in n. 24 above; this was the peculiarity on which he based his identification of the style of the Armenian Irenaeus with that of the Armenian Philo. Many such "doublets" are mentioned in the notes to the present version: cf. the following paragraph of the Introd., and the Index under "doublets."

[33] It is often exceedingly difficult to determine the correct division and grouping of phrases. As an example of a particular difficulty may be mentioned the use of expressions imitating in various manners the Greek "genitive absolute." Such a construction is foreign to Armenian (cf. above, n. 30), and in several places, where normal Armenian usage would demand a certain interpretation of an expression, it is in fact probable, or at least possible, that the expression should be understood as an "absolute" construction, with a sense sometimes quite different from that which would be demanded by normal usage — a difficulty which is sometimes increased by the fact that in Armenian the genitive and dative of substantives are identical in form. For examples of such ambiguities, cf. n. 43, 195, 200, 201, 222, 249, 341; in the first three of these cases the difference of interpretation is considerable.

[34] There is a list of textual defects in Weber, L* 11.

The *editio princeps* has no *apparatus criticus* (an omission for which the editors were taken to task by Weber, *Der Katholik* 94 [1914] 10), and there are few emendations mentioned in the republication in PO*. The revised edition of the German version of EP* referred to emendations proposed by Nestle and Conybeare; others are to be found in Akinean's article, " St. Irenaeus in Armenian Literature," *HAm.* (1910) 200-208, in Vardanian's articles on the new words in the Armenian Irenaeus, *ibid.* 281-284, 301-306, and on emendations to the *Proof, ibid.* 326-328, in Weber's articles in *Theologische Quartalschrift* 91 (1909) 560-573 and 93 (1911) 162 f., and his " Randglossen," *Der Katholik* 94 (1914) 9-44, and in Lüdtke's reply thereto, *Zeitschrift für Kirchengeschichte* 35 (1914) 255-260, and elsewhere. Weber's Latin version (L*) mentions most emendations made up to its publication. I think I have mentioned in the notes to this version all the important emendations proposed; and I have suggested one or two new ones.

[35] Eusebius, *Hist. eccles.* 5. 26.

[36] So too Faldati has for title " Esposizione . . . ," though he remarks (F* 21 n. 1) that " dimostrazione " would be more accurate as a rendering of the word ἐπίδειξις. The Armenian title is *C'uyc' aṙak'elakan k'arozut'eann.*

[37] Eusebius, *Hist. eccles.* 5. 26.

The name *Marcianus* ought doubtless to have been englished " Marcian," but that the latter form agrees in sound with " Marcion."

[38] *Mart. Polycarpi* 20.

Identification of author of *Martyrium Polycarpi* with addressee of *Proof* was suggested by J. B. Lightfoot, *Apostolic Fathers* 2. 3 (London 1889) 398 f.; he was followed by, for example, T. Zahn (*Realenzyklopädie für protestantische Theologie und Kirche, s. v.* " Irenaeus"). Harnack remarks (EP* 54) that identification is unlikely, the reading " Marcion " being more probable for the name of the author of the *Martyrium.* F. X. Funk–K. Bihlmeyer, *Die Apostolischen Väter* (Tübingen 1924), also read " Marcion."

[39] Insistence on abolition of Old Law: c. 35, 87, 89, 90, 94, 96. For a probable explanation, cf. § 37 of Introd. The suggestion that Marcianus was a recent convert from Judaism was made, to account for this insistence, by F. Diekamp in his review of EP*, *Theologische Revue* 6 (1907) 245, and is regarded as probable by O. Bardenhewer, *Geschichte der altkirchlichen Literatur* 1 (2nd ed. 1913) 411.

[40] " care of souls ": c. 1 (cf. n. 6).

J. Kunze, on the other hand, says it is clear from the whole tenor of the *Proof* that Marcianus was a layman (*Theologisches Literaturblatt* 28 [1907] 26). Similarly Sagarda, who adds however that there is insufficient ground for any certainty in the matter (S* 486).

[41] The confusion and repetitiveness of Irenaeus's exposition is very noticeable in *Adversus haereses.*

[42] Cf. § 45 of Introd. for résumé of probable solution to these " problems."

[43] So Harnack in EP* 55, G. Rauschen in *Literarische Rundschau* 34 (1908) 468, and especially P. Drews in *Zeitschrift für neutestamentliche Wissenschaft* 8 (1907) 226-233, who compares the *Proof*

with Augustine's *De catechizandis rudibus* and with the *Constitutiones apostolicae*. Similarly Sagarda says, " Irenaeus speaks not as a polemist, not even as a scholar, but as pastor and catechete " (S* 487).

[44] c. 1.

[45] c. 1 f. and 99 f.

[46] The word rendered "in its integrity" in c. 1, and similarly rendered elsewhere, is *aῑoἰj*, meaning " entire " in the sense " sound, healthy, lively "; cf. n. 4 and the parallel Tit. 2. 8 there quoted.

[47] So Bardenhewer, *op. cit.* 1. 409, 411. So too Tixeront (PO* 752) and others.

[48] BK* p. xiv.

[49] G. Rauschen, *Literarische Rundschau* 34 (1908) 468.

[50] For Irenaeus's poor opinion of fanciful exegesis and of " mystic numbers," cf. respectively A.H. 1. 8. 1 and 2. 24 f.

[51] *Adversus haereses* (or *Contra haereses*), is given by Eusebius, *Hist. eccles.* 5. 7. 1 etc., its full title, which we find also in c. 99 of the *Proof*: Ἔλεγχος καὶ ἀνατροπὴ τῆς ψευδονύμου γνώσεως, a title which may be variously rendered in English: for example, also " Critique and refutation. . . ." The expression " knowledge falsely so called " is taken from 1 Tim. 6. 20. " Knowledge " (in this sense) is in Greek γνῶσις, and from the related adjective γνωστικός are derived the words "Gnostic," " Gnosticism."

[52] Marcion's system, though it agrees in many general points with those of Gnostics properly so called, is in detail and in spirit as different from them as is orthodox Christianity. Most Gnostic systems, so far as can be judged, were on the intellectual level of the various bogus -osophies which are their modern counterparts; Marcion's, on the other hand, was the work of a misguided genius. He founded a hierarchy, and his sect is said to have persisted into modern times, while other Gnostic systems have been artificially revived in modern times; cf. F. R. M. Hitchcock, *Irenaeus of Lugdunum* (Cambridge 1914) 332 f.; E. C. Blackman, *Marcion and his Influence* (London 1948).

[53] On the word *aeon*, cf. n. 23 to the text.

[54] δημιουργός in Greek means " craftsman, artisan " and was a normal term in Greek philosophy to denote the " creator " or rather " fashioner " of the ordered world. The word seems to have been used in the *Proof* (and in *Adversus haereses*) of the " creative " Word (c. 38, cf. n. 185); it is used of God in A. H. 4. 1. 2 and 4. 20. 4.

[55] So in the *Proof*, c. 4-7, 45.

[56] Identity of God the Father and Creator: c. 3-5, 11, 99; He is universal Lord, Judge and Father: c. 8.

[57] So in the *Proof*, c. 5, 34, 39; for an echo of Plato on the world-soul, cf. n. 171.

[58] So in the *Proof*, c. 7, 45.

[59] " the Son," cf. c. 5 (and n. 32 f. thereto); " inscrutable generation," cf. c. 70 and n. 301 thereto; " always with the Father," cf. " His Son for ever" (c. 10), and His pre-existence, c. 51 f.; and for the question of the Word's eternity and of the Λόγος ἐνδιάθετος and Λόγος προφορικός, cf. c. 43 and n. 205 thereto.

[60] *Proof*, c. 12 (in Paradise), 44 (Abraham), 45 (Jacob, and explicit statement that theophanies are of the Son), 46 (Moses).

[61] Cf. § 33 of Introd. (and n. 70 thereto).

[62] Cf. § 36 of Introd.

[63] This belief in a " seeming " body is called " docetism," and its holders are called " docetes " (from Greek δοκεῖν, " seem ").

[64] Frequent reference to Christ's birth of the Virgin, of the seed of Abraham and of David; and cf. especially c. 33, 38 f.

[65] So in the *Proof* c. 5-8, 49; for the identification Spirit = Wisdom, cf. n. 33 to c. 5; Scripture is the work of the Spirit: c. 49: " it is not a man who utters the prophecy; but the Spirit of God . . . spoke in the prophets"; c. 2: " the Holy Spirit says through the mouth of David"; c. 24: (God testified to Abraham) " saying through the Holy Spirit in the Scriptures"; c. 73: " the Spirit of Christ, who spoke in the other prophets about Him, now also through David says." If Irenaeus sometimes attributes the words of Scripture to the Word, this is not because " the Word articulates the Spirit, and . . . gives their message to the prophets " (c. 5), but because in the particular passages so attributed to the Word the Spirit is speaking " on the part of Christ " (c. 49), and using the first person in uttering words to be attributed to the Son (so c. 34 " the Word says through Isaias: *I refuse not . . .*"; similarly e. g. c. 50, 68); or because the Scripture is reporting the words of the Son in a theophany (so e. g. in c. 9).

[66] Cf. c. 11, 14.

[67] The Spirit in creation and in man, cf. § 33, 34 of Introd. He leads to the Son, cf. § 35 of Introd.

[68] Divinity of the Son: *Proof* c. 47; cf. n. 223 thereto.

[69] c. 99.

[70] " hands ": cf. account of creation in c. 11. In the parallel passage A.H. 4. *Praef.* 4 we have " with His own hands, that is, with the Son and the Spirit"; so too in A.H. 4. 20. 1, 5. 1. 3, 5. 6. 1, 5. 28. 4 the Son and the Holy Spirit are called the two hands of the

Father. Similarly Theophilus of Antioch, *Ad Autol.* 2. 18. Cf. also *Proof* c. 26 (and n. 140 thereto) for a possible reference to the Spirit as the "finger" of God.

"Image" and "likeness" were commonly distinguished by the Greek fathers; the statement that the "image" is ineffaceable, but the "likeness" lost by the Fall was supported by the allegation that the latter word was never used of man in the Scripture after the account of the Fall; but this is a mere chance in the Septuagint version; the Hebrew word *dᵉmût*, to which it corresponds in Gen. 1. 26, occurs also in Gen. 5, 1, where however the Septuagint renders by εἰκών ("image") instead of ὁμοίωσις ("likeness") as in Gen. 1. 26.

For this distinction in Irenaeus, cf. especially A.H. 5. 6. 1, where it is said that the "image" is in the frame (*plasma*) of man and the "likeness" in the spirit; with which cf. *Proof*, c. 11 (n. 65) for the original creation, and c. 97 (n. 397) for the restoration; for the "image" as that of the Son, c. 22: "the 'image' is the Son of God, in whose image man was made"; for the "likeness" as given by the Spirit, c. 5: "the Spirit, who . . . formed man to the likeness of God." (And for free will as especial point of resemblance of man to God, c. 11, n. 66.)

⁷¹ Man created free and lord of world and its angels: c. 11, 12; immortality, c. 15; "self-mastery" as especial resemblance to God, c. 11 (n. 66); man intended to develop, etc., c. 12 (n. 70); the Fall and its effects, c. 16 f.; loss of immortality, c. 15, 37 f.; "image and likeness," cf. n. 70 above; Incarnation as restoration, cf. § 36 of Introd.

⁷² A.H. 5. 9. 1 f.; Plato, *Phaedrus* 246a; 253c; cf. following note.

⁷³ All three elements necessary, cf. A.H. 5. 9. 1 f.; 5. 6. 1, etc. Body and soul, cf. *Proof* c. 2 (n. 8); necessity of Spirit, c. 7, 14, 41 f., 89; Spirit a special "godlikeness," cf. n. 70 above, and A.H. 5. 9. 1-3, 5. 10. 1; 4. 6. 1; 4. 8. 1; cf. also c. 42 and n. 201.

⁷⁴ Body also part of man, c. 2 (n. 8); and A.H. 5. 6. 1: "the soul and the spirit can be part of man, but by no means 'a man'"; cf. also insistence on "incorruption" (cf. § 36 of Introd.). All things created by the one God, c. 3 f., 10.

⁷⁵ "Material": Greek ὑλικός < ὕλη, "matter"; ("earthly": χοικός, "carnal": σαρκικός); "sensual": ψυχικός < ψυχή, "soul"; Latin *homo animalis*; "spiritual": πνευματικός < πνεῦμα, "spirit."

Cf. 1 Cor. 2. 14 f.: *But the sensual man perceiveth not these things that are of the Spirit of God. . . . But the spiritual man judgeth all things*; and 3. 1: *And I, brethren, could not speak to you as unto spiritual, but as unto carnal*; and Jude 19: *sensual men, having not the spirit.*

[76] Not that the Gnostics were necessarily licentious; some of them were, if we are to believe Irenaeus; but others were ascetical. The Marcionites in particular affected an extreme asceticism.

[77] 1 Cor. 15. 50, on which text in A.H. 5. 9. 1 f. Irenaeus explains the necessity of spirit *as well as* soul and body. For the Gnostics, "flesh and blood" did not participate in salvation.

[78] 1 Tim. 1. 9, quoted in the *Proof*, c. 35.

[79] *Proof*, c. 14 (spirit knows no evil), 89 f. (newness of spirit supersedes the law); 61, 95 f.

[80] *Proof*, c. 8.

[81] Cf. n. 70 above.

[82] *Proof*, c. 5 (n. 34).

[83] *Proof*, c. 5-7.

[84] *Proof*, c. 7.

[85] "Recapitulation" or "summing-up," Greek ἀνακεφαλαίωσις. The corresponding verb is rendered "re-establish" in Douay in Eph. 1. 10: *in the dispensation of the fulness of times, to re-establish all things in Christ.* In Irenaeus (cf. rest of this paragraph) the sense is rather "re-establish." Principal references in the *Proof*: c. 30 (end), 31-34, 37 f. (and cf. parallels cited in notes thereto).

[86] "Communion": Armenian *hasarakut'iwn miabanut'ean*, literally "community of agreement," or more freely rendered, "terms of good fellowship," "friendly relations." In A. H. 4. 20. 4, however, (4. 34. 4 in Harvey's numbering, used in the edition of the Armenian text, TU 35. 2), the same expression corresponds to the Latin version's *communio*. Elsewhere (A.H. 4. 14. 2, Harvey's 4. 25. 2) twice the word *communio* has as its Armenian correspondence *hasarakut'iwn* alone (cf. n. 195, and variants in fragments of c. 31: n. 156). In the *Proof*, c. 6; and, with explicit reference to "incorruptibility," c. 31, 40.

[87] Cf. *Proof*, c. 7, 31, 39, 40, 55; and the continuation of 1 Cor. 15. 50, cited above (n. 77); after stating that *flesh and blood cannot possess the kingdom of heaven*, the apostle goes on: *neither shall corruption possess incorruption.*

Not merely the spiritual principle, but the whole man to be saved, cf. A.H. 5. 6. 1, cited in n. 74 above.

[88] F. Loofs, in his posthumously published work on the sources of Irenaeus, *Theophilus von Antiochien Adversus Marcionem und die anderen theologischen Quellen bei Irenaeus*, TU 46. 2 (1930), regards Irenaeus's reputation for original thought as exaggerated, and suggests that he reproduces incompatible views from his various

sources. There is however much that is controvertible in the views expressed in that work (including, for example, the suggestion of "binitarianism" alluded to in § 32 of this Introd.

[89] J. Rendel Harris, *Expositor* 7. 3 (1907) 246-358 (on the *Proof*) and 7. 2 (1906) 385-409 (on "Testimonies"); these articles are repeated, along with other matter, in the same author's book, *Testimonies*, 2 vols. (Cambridge 1916, 1920).

[90] Harnack, EP* 58; Tixeront, PO* 771 n. 3.

[91] Description of Leviticus, c. 26; of Deuteronomy, c. 28. Note the inaccuracy of the Deuteronomy quotations in c. 29 (n. 152, 153).

[92] For composite quotations cf., in the *Proof*, c. 24 (n. 127), 29 (n. 152), 43 (n. 206), 79 (n. 324), 88 (n. 352).

[93] For false attribution: c. 43 (n. 206), 65 (n. 280: here note parallel in Justin gives different false attribution), 72 (n. 307), 97 (n. 396).

Apocryphal quotations from rubrics or glosses: cf. c. 43 (n. 207), 68 (n. 289).

[94] Cf. c. 5 (n. 31), 77 (n. 318); but the fact that the former is a commonplace and the latter inaccurately quoted lends support to the suggestion that Irenaeus may here be quoting from memory; c. 86 (n. 346), but here the fact that the quotation echoes two different prophets might have accounted for the expression "the prophets"; cf. also c. 38 and 62 (Amos, cited also in Acts), 72 (Ps. 20), 86 (Isaias, cited also in Romans).

[95] C. 54 (n. 247), 56 (n. 251); cf. also Isa. 53. 4 quoted c. 67 as in Matt. 8. 17, and (in longer citation) c. 68 as in LXX (n. 283, 288).

[96] Cf. c. 35 (n. 176), 63 (n. 277), 65 (n. 280: note that the different false attribution in the Justin parallel suggests common source, not the gospel), 67 (n. 283), 93 (n. 365). In Rendel Harris's theory this agreement with the New Testament is due to the use by the latter also of the book of "Testimonies against the Jews."

[97] C. 81 (n. 328).

[98] C. 8 (n. 55). In A.H. 4. 5. 2 correct attribution to Christ of the gospel's addition.

[99] A.H. 3. 21. 1-4. In the *Proof*, c. 69, there is a notable omission which is to be accounted for by use of the Septuagint (n. 295).

[100] In c. 3 (n. 18) I have even ventured to emend a quotation into agreement with the Massoretic text.

The immediate source not the New Testament: cf. n. 96 above.

The style of the translation of the *Proof* — a key to the Greek original — makes it reasonable to suppose that the translator has simply translated Irenaeus's quotations as they stood in the Greek original, instead of substituting — as translators not uncommonly did — the (Armenian) version of the Scriptural passage quoted. In one or two places, it is clear that the translator has retained peculiarities of the original (cf. e. g. n. 324 to c. 79 of text).

It is interesting to note in the *Proof* a couple of striking agreements with the so-called "Western text" of the New Testament in the quotations of Mich. 5. 2 (= Matt. 2. 6; c. 63, n. 277) and Isa. 52. 7 (= Rom. 10. 15; c. 86, n. 346); and cf. n. 264, 329 (Codex Bezae).

[101] Jeremias: c. 78 (n. 320); David: c. 68 (n. 289).

[102] Cf. c. 9 (n. 60), 20 (n. 105), 43 (n. 207), 57 (n. 257).

[103] C. 4 (n. 28); A.H. 4. 20. 2.

[104] C. 18 (n. 100).

[105] C. 9 (n. 57); other "echoes" of *Ascensio Isaiae* are c. 10 (n. 62) and 84 (n. 338).

[106] Abraham: c. 24 (n. 124); star: c. 58 (n. 264).

[107] The "elders": or "ancients" or "presbyters" (οἱ πρεσβύτεροι, *presbyteri, seniores*), a word commonly so used, and regularly added by Irenaeus when he refers to the preceding generation of tradition, the "disciples of the apostles"; so in the *Proof*, c. 3 and (without the expression "disciples of the apostles") c. 61. In A. H., 2. 22. 5, 3. 2. 2, 5. 5. 1, 5. 33. 3, 5. 36. 1 and 2. For the word "elders," cf. *Ancient Christian Writers* 6 (*The Didache* etc.) 107 ff.

Chiliasm: c. 61; for an account of this doctrine, see n. 270. It has recently been called in doubt whether Irenaeus did in fact hold millenarian views; cf. the article of V. Cremers, "Het millenarisme van Irenaeus," *Bijdragen* 1 (1938) 28-80. Even on the millenarianism of Papias doubts have been expressed, by L. Gry, "Le Papias des belles promesses messianiques," *Vivre et Penser* 3 (1943-4) 112-124.

[108] C. 74 (n. 314); A.H. 2. 22.5.

[109] Chiliasm (in *Proof*, c. 61, n. 270) in Justin, cf. esp. *Dial.* 80 f.; Papias, cf. (Eusebius, *Hist. eccles.* 3. 39. 12 and) A.H. 5. 33. 4; but cf. end of n. 107 above.

[110] Papias and chiliasm, cf. preceding paragraph of Introd.

Polycarp quoted by name: A.H. 3. 3. 4; echo in *Proof*, c. 95 (n. 376). In the last postscript to the *Martyrium Polycarpi* in the Moscow manuscript we are told that Irenaeus "wrote a solid refutation of every heresy, and, besides, handed down the ecclesiastical and Catholic rule of faith, just as he had received it from the saint," that is, from Polycarp. The "solid refutation of every heresy" refers obviously to *Adversus haereses*; it is possible that the "ecclesiastical and Catholic rule of faith" handed down by Irenaeus as he received it from Polycarp refers to the *Proof*.

[111] Cf. Index.

[112] Cf. Index. In his introduction to the *Proof* (AR* 6-23) Robinson gives a detailed comparison between certain parts of the *Proof* and parallel passages in Justin (c. 57 and *Apol.* 1. 32; c. 44 f. and *Dial.* 56, etc.; and c. 53 as "cleared up" by *Apol.* 2. 6). So also F. R. M. Hitchcock, *Journal of Theological Studies* 9 (1908) 284-289, lists several parallels between the *Proof* and Justin.

It must be noted that there are many differences of Scriptural reading between Justin and Irenaeus; in the *Proof*, cf. n. 277, 302, 317, 318, 320, 322; cf. different attribution, n. 280.

[113] Cf. § 38 above, and Harris (references in n. 89 above). Loofs, *op. cit.* (n. 88 above) 5 n. 1, thinks the parallels between Justin and Irenaeus may be attributed to what was already traditional.

A notable difference between the two lies in Irenaeus's frequent use of St. Paul, whom Justin never mentions or quotes.

[114] Two particular examples, taken from the *Proof*, given by Harris, *Expositor* 7. 3 (1907) 255-257, and *Testimonies* 1. 68 f.: in c. 57, after quoting Gen. 49. 10 f., Irenaeus continues, "He is also *the expectation of the nations*, of those who hope in Him . . ."; in *Apol.* 1. 32, after quoting Gen. 49. 10 f., Justin passes on to a composite quotation (Num. 34. 17, Isa. 11. 1, Isa. 11. 10; the whole attributed to "Isaias") ending *and in His arm shall the nations hope*. In c. 72, Irenaeus applies Isa. 57. 1 to the death of Christ and also of "those who believe in Him and like Him are persecuted and slain"; in *Apol.* 1. 48, Justin refers the same passage to Christ and "those who hope in Him." In both these cases it is more likely that the "echo" in Irenaeus is due to an adjacent text in the common source, than to a reminiscence of Justin.

[115] Reference to treatise against Marcion, A.H. 4. 6. 2; Loofs, *op. cit.* (n. 88 above) 5.

[116] *Proof*, c. 12, 14; Theophilus, *Ad Autol.* 2. 25.

[117] Account of Aristo, Origen, *C. Cels.* 4. 52.

For references to echoes of apologists, cf. Index.

[118] A.H. 3. 3. 3.

[119] Holy Spirit and Scripture, cf. n. 65 above; fourth gospel, c. 43, 94; trinitarian formula, c. 3.

Interesting also is what seems to be an allusion to the formula of exorcism "in the name of Jesus Christ, crucified under Pontius Pilate" (c. 97 n. 393).

[120] E. g. H. Jordan, *Theologischer Literaturbericht* 30 (1907) 78. (Weber, L* 13, refers to Krüger in the same sense, but as his reference, which is false, is to the same volume of the same periodical, it may well be a mistake for Jordan as above.)

[121] Good works: c. 2, 98; dogmatic faith: c. 1-3, 100; redeemed man: c. 61, 93, 94, 96.

[122] C. 43 (n. 205).

[123] Seven heavens, c. 9; Pontius Pilate, c. 74 (n. 314).

[124] C. 61 (n. 270).

[125] Adam and Eve, c. 12, 14; man lord of world and its angels, c. 11, 12; theophanies, c. 12, 44-46 (Sodom and Gomorrha, c. 44); decalogue, c. 96.

[126] Sem and Japheth, c. 21, 24, 42; Adam and Christ, c. 32; Spirit and Wisdom, c. 5; distinction between Persons, c. 47.

[127] There is an "Irenaean" Creed, drawn up from his works, at the end of F. R. M. Hitchcock, *Irenaeus of Lugdunum* (Cambridge 1914). See also J. N. D. Kelly, *Early Christian Creeds* (London 1950) 76-82.

NOTES TO TEXT

[1] Marcianus: cf. § 14 of Introduction.

"I . . . congratulate you": *xndakic' em i k'ez*, more literally "I am partaker in thy joy" (cf. etymology of "congratulate"); but used simply as equivalent of our "congratulate," corresponding to συγχαροῦμαί σοι.

[2] "set forth . . . the preaching of the truth," cf. the title of the work.

[3] "in the form of notes on the main points": *ibru t'ē glxaworagoyn yišatakaran* = ὡσεὶ κεφαλαιῶδες ὑπόμνημα, "as it were a summary memoir."

"all the members of the body of truth": an Irenaean metaphor, cf. A.H. 1. 9. 4 (and n. 40 below).

[4] "those who hold false views": AR* ". . . inculcate falsehood," and PO* "the false boasters"; but *zsut karcec'ołsn* = τοὺς ψευδοδόξους, the contrary of "orthodox."

". . . what we have to say in its integrity and purity": more literally "our word (λόγος) sound and blameless," as in Titus 2. 8: *the sound word that cannot be blamed*; but Irenaeus uses the adjectives predicatively. "Sound" is *ařolj*; the "integrity" referred to is that of correctness rather than of completeness.

With the opening section of the *Proof* compare the prefaces to the books of *Adversus haereses*, especially to book 1, with which there are a couple of verbal parallels ("so far as may be," "you will draw much profit from what we have expressed in brief").

[5] Cf. the opening words of the *Didache*: "There are two ways, one of life and one of death," and Barnabas, *Ep.* 18: "There are two ways of doctrine and power, that of light and that of darkness"; and Prov. 4. 18 f. (*But the path of the just, as a shining light, goeth forwards and increaseth even to perfect day. The way of the wicked is darksome*) and 12. 28 (*In the path of justice is life; but the byway leadeth to death*).

[6] "who look after the salvation of souls": if this rendering is correct, Marcianus may have been a bishop, or at least a cleric. The text has however *ork' hogan anjanc' p'rkut'ean*, and in Armenian the word *anjn*, "soul," is frequently used as a reflexive pronoun; such a use would give here the sense "who have a care for their (own) salvation"; so EP* ("das eigene Heil") and Weber in BK* ("ihr Heil"). Weber L* however has "animarum," and Faldati "delle anime," and Weber L* 15 refers to Marcianus as one who had care of souls. The renderings of PO* ("of their souls," and Barthoulot "de leur âme") keep the word "soul," but supply the possessive; if however *anjanc'* be understood as the substantive, then "of souls" is the only possible rendering; "of their souls" would demand the expression of the possessive *iwreanc'* in Armenian (as in Greek, or English). Moreover, *anjanc' iwreanc'* would be a normal rendering even if the Greek were simply ἑαυτῶν, "their own." It seems to me that *anjanc'* must be understood as the substantive, "of souls." The sense so given agrees with the reference to Marcianus as confounding heretics and preaching the truth. The translator of the *Proof* does not, so far as I have observed, use *anjn* as a pronoun; he follows the Greek and uses *anjn* for "soul," while had the Greek here been ἑαυτῶν he would surely have rendered, as he does elsewhere, *iwreanc'*; if he had used *anjanc'* for ἑαυτῶν, he would most likely have added *iwreanc'*, in view of the ambiguity of the context; but it must be admitted that he did not habitually concern himself greatly with the avoidance of ambiguity in his version.

[7] "remain at a standstill": *anc'c'en mnasc'en*, literally "pass-remain," an apposition giving more or less the sense "come to stop" or, with the sense of the perfect, "be at a standstill"; cf. in the *Proof* the use of *anc'anel kal*, "come-to-stand," or, with the sense of the perfect, simply "be standing" (e. g. c. 44, where *anc'eal kayin* corre-

sponds to εἱστήκεισαν in the LXX; cf. n. 211), and the frequently used compound *kal mnal*, "stand-remain," in the sense "remain (constantly)," and also *barjeal krel*, "to carry" (cf. n. 45). Such appositions are common in Armenian, and especially in the Armenian of the school to which the version of the *Proof* belongs. Hence there is no need to render *anc'c'en* independently "transgress."

⁸ Composition of man, cf. Introd. § 33.

"that must come about through the instrumentality of both of these": *i jeṙn erkuc'unc' aysoc'ik linel nma part ew aržan ē*; "it is necessary (*linel nma*) through both of these" (*part ew aržan ē* is simply an expanded version of χρή or δεῖ). In *linel nma*, the dative pronoun *nma* has previously been taken to refer to "man," and the infinitive *linel* to mean "be (exist)," giving a curious expression with the not very satisfactory sense "it is necessary *for him to exist* through both of these." Barthoulot paraphrases freely: "il est juste et nécessaire *de tenir compte* de ces deux éléments" (italics mine). But *linel* should correspond to γίνεσθαι "come to be" rather than to εἶναι "be," and *nma* may be understood as a neuter (Armenian does not distinguish gender) referring to the following — or not following — of the way of life, so giving the relevant sense "it is necessary *for that to happen* through both of these."

"both of these," that is, not soul alone (against the Gnostics, cf. n. 10, and n. 74 to Introd.). The sense "*he* must *have his being* through both of these" would be equivalent to the statement that soul alone is not "man," cf. A.H. 5. 6. 1, quoted in n. 74 to Introd.

⁹ "mind": here the word *ogi* ("spirit," etc.) is used; in the following, "if truth be not in the soul," the word is the normal *anjn*. (*oč' eteloy čšmartut'eann yanjin*, "genitive absolute").

¹⁰ This chapter is directed against the Gnostic view that the body was outside the scheme of salvation, and good works necessary for the "sensual" man only, not for the "spiritual"; cf. § 34 of Introd.

¹¹ "to set man in the presence of God": *zi zmardn yandimanakac' arasc'en Astucoy*. Barthoulot (PO* 757 n. 3) attributes to *yandimanakac'* (which he presumably regards as corresponding to ἐναντίον) what he calls the pejorative sense "in opposition to" instead of "in presence of." Here "these two" would be the vicious and the impious; otherwise, he asks, how explain the struggle ("fight side by side": more literally "become comrades-in-arms"; one might render "ally themselves"), and the following Scriptural quotations. But "these two" are obviously the just-mentioned holiness of body and truth in the soul, and the struggle not against but for man; and *yandi-*

manakac' does not correspond to ἐναντίον ("against" would be *hakaṙak*), but generally to παρών ("present") or the like, while here it goes with the following word, *yandimanakac' aṙnel* (*Astucoy*) being simply παριστάναι (Θεῷ).

[12] Ps. 1.1, continued in the following.

[13] An etymological explanation; the Greek would be ἀσεβεῖς . . . οὐ σέβονται, a correspondence which is reproduced by the Armenian *amparištk'* . . . *oč' pašten*, and may be imitated in English by rendering: "those are *impious* who have *not piety* towards . . . God."

[14] Exod. 3. 14.

[15] "sinners" = "scornful, disdainful folk" ("scornful, disdainful" surely a doublet for a single Greek word): an etymological explanation, like the preceding one? If so, where is the association (with ἁμαρτωλοί, "sinners")? Or a reference to the arrogance of the Gnostic view that good works were unnecessary for the initiate? Cf. also *Didache* 12, where it is said that "meekness and patience are far from" sinners. Most likely the allusion is simply to the fact that, knowing God, they neglect Him.

[16] "sit and are brought to corruption": or "they sit, and those are brought to corruption (who take the poison of their doctrine)"; but not "they sit and corrupt," unless the verb is to be emended from passive to active (an easy emendation, however).

So Hermas, *Mand.* 11 (beginning), describes a vision of the "spirit of the world" seated on a chair and expounding error to the faithful seated on benches before him.

[17] "rule of faith": κανὼν τῆς πίστεως, *regula fidei*, a common expression; cf. the "rule of truth" received in baptism, A. H. 1.9.4. Κανών = "Rule" in the sense of a stick serving as a standard of judgement, the meaning being, that the test of any view proposed for our acceptance is, does it *square with* the formula called the "rule."

Harnack remarks (EP* 56) that the conjunction belief — love (Lord — Father) is common in Irenaeus.

[18] *unless . . . *continue*: Isa. 7. 9: the manuscript here has *unless you believe*, says Isaias, *you shall not understand*; this reading agrees with the Septuagint, but it makes the argument inconsequential: "Action is preserved (or acquired) by faith, BECAUSE unless you believe you shall not understand, AND faith is given by truth, since faith rests on reality" (the "because" is not part of the quotation from Isaias, but belongs to Irenaeus). It seems to me therefore that the reading of the manuscript is due to scribal "correction" (deliberate or not) into conformity with the "received text" — a not

uncommon phenomenon — and that Irenaeus must have quoted from a version agreeing with the Massoretic text, whose reading is rendered by Douay's *you shall not continue* (= " persevere "). The argument then makes good sense, especially with the rendering " is preserved," and agrees with what is said later in the chapter: " Since, then, it is faith that maintains our salvation, one must take great care of this sustenance, to have a true perception of reality."

" for we shall believe . . . keep ": or " that we may believe . . . keep," or " for let us believe . . . keep " (*zi . . . hawatasc'uk' . . . pahesc'uk'*).

" believing what really is ": the text has the unintelligible reading *hawatagol zēsn*. Akinean (*HAm.* 24 [1910] 207 n. 2) emends to *hawata gol zēsn*, but this does not give very good sense ("believe that what is exists," " believe " being imperative).

[19] " this sustenance ": AR* has " the maintenance thereof " (that is, " its sustenance "), which may possibly correspond to the sense of the original Greek. The Armenian however has *bazum xnam darmanoy* nma *part ew aržan ē ařnel*. The word rendered " sustenance " (*darman*) means " medicine," but also " food " in general.

[20] " the elders, the disciples of the apostles ": cf. § 40 of Introd. (and n. 107 thereto).

[21] The text does not say " in *the name of* the Holy Spirit," but the reference to the trinitarian formula is clearer than that in Justin, *Apol.* 1. 61.

[22] " seal ": σφραγίς, commonly used in this connection (cf. *Epistola* 2 attributed to Clement of Rome, 7. 6 and 8. 6), and of the Sign of the Cross, and of circumcision (so in c. 24, echoing Rom. 4. 11). In c. 100 baptism is referred to simply as " our seal." Cf. the theory of sacramental " characters " elaborated by later theologians.

[23] " that the eternal and everlasting One *is* God ": *zmištn ew zyar ēn astuacanal* (*zyar ēn* Vardanian's emendation of manuscript's *zyarēn*, *HAm.* 24 [1910] 207 n. 2). PO* has " that our abiding and continuing portion may partake of the divine nature ": but there is no " our," and the use of the third-person article *-n* instead of the first-personal *-s* excludes the sense " our " even if the expression " *mišt ew yar ē* could be understood as " abiding and continual portion "; moreover the syntax requires accusative-and-infinitive of statement rather than infinitive of purpose (the preceding final clause was conjunction-and-subjunctive). AR* has " that what is everlasting and continuing is made God," and says (AR* 72 n. 2) that the Armenian translator has misunderstood Greek θεοποιεῖσθαι, used in Hippolytus,

Philos. 10. 34, of our "deification"; cf. also reference in Irenaeus to this deification, e. g. A.H. 4. 38. 4, and 3. 6. 1. But the continuation of the sentence as it stands requires the subject to be the "eternal and everlasting" God just referred to. The use of the verbal form "be-divine," "act-as-God," suggests the emphatic rendering "*is* God," and the expression may be directed against the Gnostic view that the Absolute is aloof from "acting-as-God," or may mean that the (unique true) "Aeon" is God (cf. Introd. § 29).

"Aeon" (αἰών = "age, perpetuity") was earlier used as a personal name for the cosmic god (Latin Janus) transcending the change of subcelestial time; for Irenaeus this one Aeon was obscured by the multiplicity of Gnostic Aeons, but cf. A.H. 1. 1. 1 for the unique transcendent Aeon, and this may be the sense of "the eternal and everlasting One" here ("eternal and everlasting" being a doublet probably due to the translator), though αἰών is normally rendered literally, *yawitean*, in Armenian, even when used in the Gnostic sense. In *Verbum Domini* 27 (1949) 287-290 I have suggested a similar interpretation of Wisd. 13. 9.

"all things whatsoever are subject to Him": or "He subjects (*or* has subjected) everything to Him(self)," *zamenayn inč' ĕnd novaw dnel* so being the "put all things under him" of 1 Cor. 15. 27 f. (cf. Ps. 8. 8. — The manuscript's expressly passive *dnil* is of course a late form, due doubtless to the scribe); in 1 Cor. however the reference is to the subjection of all things to *Christ*, whereas here the passive is more in accordance with the argument, whose point is not that God "subjects" things to Himself but on the contrary; they are of their nature subject to Him (cf. following notes).

[24] "and that what is subject to Him was all made by Him": *ew zedealsn ĕnd novaw zamenesin nma ařnel.* The sense "that He subjects all things to Himself" (cf. F*) is repetitive, inconvenient (cf. end of preceding note) and syntactically impossible, as the definite *zedealsn* must be subject or object, not predicate-complement, of the infinitive, which must then be independent "make," not merely an element of "make-subject." Better is the rendering of the German versions (and AR*): "all that is subject to Him is made His own," or the like; but it is difficult to see how this can be the sense, and the whole point of the argument should be that all things *are*, of their nature, God's own. Weber L* has "et subiectos sub se omnes *eum* facere" (my italics) taking the dative *nma* as agent of the verb. This is surely correct: καὶ τὰ ὑποτεταγμένα αὐτῷ πάντα αὐτῷ πεποιῆσθαι. (Note the position of "all"; hardly "all that is subject . . . ," but

"... was all made. ....") The statement is made against the Gnostic view that God the Father was not the creator, but had "taken over" the creatures of the demiurge (cf. Introd. § 29 f.; also following note).

[25] "so that God is not ruler and Lord of what is another's, but of His own": or "for God ...," but "so that ..." is better: *zi oč' ayloy uruk' išxel ew tēr linel Astucoy, ayl iwroc'n*. Not simply "God is ruler and Lord of none other than His own": *uruk'* is personal ("any*body*"), which seems pointless with such a sense (though indeed this distinction is only in the Armenian; but it points to a Greek τῶν ἄλλου τινός), and genitive, which suggests possessive rather than complement (dative: though genitive just possible as *tēr linel* is used instead of *tirel*); and *ayl* surely corresponds to ἀλλά, not ἤ. Moreover the sense is that required against the Gnostic view of the "other God" interfering in the creation of the demiurge; cf. preceding note, and A. H. 4. 20. 2: non enim aliena, sed sua tradidit ei (sc. Father to Son), and "He came into His own" of John 1. 11 (because He was the maker of all).

Here, as in the preceding phrase, the dative (*Astucoy*) is taken as agent of the verb. It is just possible to take *astucoy* as genitive along with *ayloy uruk'*, and render "for He is not ruler and Lord of what is another god's, but of His own," an (inverted) allusion to the distinction between the demiurge and the "other God."

[26] "Almighty": *amenakal* = παντοκράτωρ, that is, universal, absolute ruler; a constant epithet of God (cf. n. 49).

[27] Not mere repetition, but a confirmatory argument; in "the Origin of all is God" "Origin" is the subject, "God" being predicate, and it is the subject that is taken up by the pronouns in the following clauses, hence I render "It" instead of "He"; Irenaeus is not so much concerned to say that the world was created, as to insist that the Creator is fully divine: "Everything must have *one supreme cause*; since *this cause* is cause of all, itself uncaused, it must be God." He is still concerned with the Gnostic distinction (Introd. § 29) between creator and Absolute.

[28] The whole of this sentence agrees, with slight verbal differences (Irenaeus adds "the Father" after "God"; and cf. next paragraph of this note), with Hermas, *Mand.* 1; the same passage is quoted (without the differences just mentioned) in A.H. 4. 20. 2, as "Scripture."

"brought being out of nothing": *arar zoč' ēsn i gol* = ἐποίησε τὰ μὴ ὄντα εἰς (τὸ) εἶναι, "(made =) brought what-was-not into being"; but Hermas and A.H. (cf. above) have (ποιήσας) ἐκ τοῦ μὴ ὄντος εἰς τὸ εἶναι τὰ πάντα, "who (made =) brought everything into being out of what-was-not." Cf. 2. Mac. 7. 28, quoted at end of next note.

"while holding all things, is alone beyond grasp": zamenayn inč' tanelov miayn ē antaneli: the meaning of antaneli ("not [to be] held") has been disputed (cf. L* 19 note h), and Barthoulot takes "hold" to mean "uphold," so that antaneli means in effect "independent" ("qui soutient tout sans avoir besoin de soutien"), which is indeed suggested by Irenaeus's context; but the sense of "hold" must be "contain, grasp," since Hermas has πάντα χωρῶν μόνος δὲ ἀχώρητος ὤν (and A.H. 4. 20. 2: omnium capax et qui a nemine capiatur). The reference is doubtless, as Weber suggests (loc. cit.), to the immensity of God rather than to His incomprehensibility. Cf. n. 39 (antar).

[29] This addition, which may seem pointless to a modern reader, is directed against a variety of Gnostic views, distinguishing the origin of matter and spirit etc. (cf. Introd. § 29).

"in 'all things' is included this world of ours, with man in it": more literally: "in everything, this world of ours, and in the world, man." The absence of a verb suggests that the Greek had "holding all things . . . , and in 'all things' this world . . . ," as in the parallel passage A.H. 4. 20. 1; but in the Armenian "this world" and "man" are nominative.

For the addition of "man," cf. also 2. Mac. 7. 28: God made them (= heaven and earth and all that is in them) out of nothing (ἐξ οὐκ ὄντων = "from what-was-not") and mankind also.

[30] Characteristically, Irenaeus here adds "invisible"; the invisibility of the Father has for him an especial moment; cf. Introd. § 30, 31 for this point, and for the rôle of the Son as His visible reproduction.

"above whom . . . , and after whom . . .": God is neither subordinate like the Gnostic demiurge, nor the aloof Absolute, nor the supreme God with the "God" of the Old Testament as His subordinate (cf. Introd. § 29, 30). This passage tells against the view that Irenaeus "subordinated" the Son (Loofs, TU 46. 2. 343 f.); God the Father is of course the unique source of divinity.

[31] "God is rational, and therefore produced creatures by His Word": an etymological argument, like that following ("God is a spirit, and so fashioned everything by His Spirit"), but, unlike the latter, not reproduced in the English. "Rational" = Greek λογικός, Armenian banawor; "Word" = Greek Λόγος, Armenian Ban. The English equivalent would be "God is reasonable and so produced creatures by His Reason."

By the word of the Lord . . . : Ps. 32. 6, but Irenaeus omits the words τοῦ στόματος from τῷ πνεύματι τοῦ στόματος αὐτοῦ (LXX), thus producing a reading which fits the argument (the true reading means " and by the breath of his mouth all their army," that is, the stars; " power " here, as once in English — cf. " force " even in modern English — meaning " army "; " breath of his mouth " so parallels " word " and " army " parallels " the heavens "). The same quotation, with the same omission and similar exegesis, is found in Theophilus of Antioch, *Ad Autol.* 1. 7; it is also found in A.H. 1. 22. 1, 3. 8. 3, but quoted correctly.

[32] " works bodily and consolidates being ": a version which aims at reproducing so far as possible the ambiguity of the manuscript's *marmnoy gorcē ew goyac'ut'iwnn eloy šnorhē.*

Marmnoy gorcē as it stands seems to mean either " works for body " or perhaps " does the work of body." Weber (L* 30 note f) suggests emendation to *marmnov gorcē* " works with (the) body," and Vardanian (*HAm.* 24 [1910] 326 f.) to *marmnagorcē* for σωματοποιεῖ (" corporealises, gives ' body,' gives substance "; used in A.H. 1. 5. 2).

In the second member we must surely emend *goyac'ut'iwnn* to an accusative (*goyac'ut'iwn*, supposing dittography, or *zgoyac'ut'iwnn*, supposing confusion of similar letters z, g, and haplography). *Eloy* may be genitive or dative of participle or infinitive of " be "; if genitive, it should rather have the article itself, instead of *zgoyac'ut'iwnn*, but that rule is not very strict, and is certainly neglected in the style of the version of the *Proof.* Hence possible senses are " and confers substance on what exists " (so Weber, Faldati), or " and confers solidity of existence " (PO* " power of existence ") or the like.

The fact that the whole expression is an exegesis of " establishes " might suggest Vardanian's emendation and the rendering " gives-substance and confers solidity-of-existence." On the other hand, the conclusion drawn from the exegesis is that the Word is fitly called " Son "; and this suggests reference to His rôle as the Father's reproduction on the level of contact with bodily things. Cf. following note; also n. 171.

[33] " powers ": in the Psalm, the word means, " army " (cf. n. 31), and refers to the stars. Irenaeus commonly understands the word of the spiritual " powers " of the heavens (and it is the " power " of the heavens, formed by the Spirit, which is here in question), and there is contrast with the " bodily " work of the Son; it might therefore seem that here " powers " was understood of the spiritual creation, and that the sense of the preceding phrase had to be " works in the

body" or the like. But in fact the Son's work is all-pervading (cf. the "world-soul," n. 171), and comparison with other passages in which Irenaeus associates Word and Wisdom in regard to creation, shows that he rather means that the Word "gives substance *or* subsistence," and Wisdom develops the "powers = potentialities," or "orders" creation (cf. A.H. 3. 34. 2: Verbo suo confirmans et Sapientia compingens omnia; 4. 20. 2: qui omnia Verbo et Sapientia adornavit; 4. 20. 4: qui Verbo et Sapientia fecit et adaptavit omnia). This agrees also with what is said of Wisdom in the Sapiential books (cf. Prov. 8. 27-30; Wisd. 7. 17-21; Ecclus. 16. 25-27; 24. 5 on), and is the sense required by the argument whereby the Spirit is here identified with Wisdom (cf. last paragraph of this note).

"the Word is fitly and properly called the Son ": that is, because He "establishes," with the exegesis "works bodily and consolidates being." This is an obscure statement; Weber (L* 31 note a) suggests that Irenaeus means that the Psalmist attributes to the Word what is elsewhere attributed to the Son, referring to John 1. 1 f., Col. 1. 15 f.; this is very tenuous and in any case would merely serve to identify the Psalmist's "Word" with the Son, whereas Irenaeus is arguing to the propriety of the term "Son" as applied to the Word. The sense seems to be, that the Word is a "Son" of the Father because He is the expression or reproduction of the Father on the plane of possible contact with created things (cf. § 31 of Introd.). This is the explanation of the term "Son" given by Athenagoras, *Suppl.* 10 (and cf. Tatian, *Or. ad Graecos* 5), and corresponds to the theory of the Λόγος προφορικός, for which cf. n. 205.

"but the Spirit (is fitly called) the Wisdom of God": that is, because He orders and develops the "powers" of created things. So too Theophilus of Antioch (*Ad Autol.* 1. 7, citing Ps. 32. 6, as here) speaks of creation through the Word and *Wisdom*; but for the latter he cites Prov. 3. 19 f. Again, for creation through Wisdom (= Spirit), cf. Ps.-Clement of Rome, *Hom.* 16. 12. On the other hand, Wisdom is identified (not with the Spirit but) with the Word by Justin, *Dial.* 61 and 100, and by Athenagoras, *Suppl.* 24, and by Clement of Alexandria, *Strom.* 4. 25 and by other Fathers (cf. Prov. 8. 22 f., where Wisdom is spoken of as being "conceived" and "brought forth" by God).

[34] Eph. 4. 6, which however has "one God *and* the Father *of all*, who . . ." (italics for words lacking in Irenaeus); the word "and," however, is lacking also in the Syriac (Peshitta) version. Quoted also A.H. 2. 2. 6, 4. 20. 2, 4. 32. 1, 5. 18. 2, always with Irenaeus's

peculiar omission of the words " of all." The exegesis here given —
with reference to creation — is new, though the context in A.H.
4. 20. 2 is similar; in A.H. 5. 18. 2 the exegesis refers to Christ and
the Holy Spirit in the Church.

[35] Gal. 4. 6.

[36] " likeness of God " (given by the Spirit): cf. Introd. § 33.

[37] " the Word articulates the Spirit ": " articulates " is *yawadac'-uc'anē* = (δι)αρθροῖ; Weber has BK* " wehen macht," L* " fingit ";
PO* " gives expression to "; Faldati " esprime "; AR* " utters "; but
Barthoulot " sert de lien à " is surely right in taking " articulate " not
in the secondary sense " utter " but in the primary sense " link up."
" Utter " might pass with the following " therefore it is Himself who
gives their message to the prophets " (where the text has literally
" Himself is announcer of *or* to the prophets "), but it fails to account
for the rest of the sentence: " and takes up man and brings him to
the Father." For this " linking-up," cf. Introd. § 35, and St. Basil,
De Spir. Sancto 18: " The Holy Spirit is linked to the sole Father
by the sole Son." For the message to the prophets, cf. A.H. 4. 20. 4:
et propterea prophetae ab eodem Verbo propheticum accipientes
charisma praedicaverunt eius secundum carnem adventum.

[38] " drawing-up ": *das kargi*, a doublet; either word alone would
correspond to Greek τάξις, the word normally used by later Fathers
(the Cappadocians, etc.) for the " order " of the divine activity,
having its source in the Father, realised by the Son, perfected by the
Spirit (cf. account of creation in preceding chapter and notes
thereto). Here, however, Irenaeus seems to be using the word simply
in the sense " drawing-up in order " of the faith (cf. following meta-phors). AR* has " the order of the rule of our faith," a rendering of
the doublet which is misleading in that it suggests reference to the
" rule (κανών) of the faith " (cf. n. 17).

" way of life ": the word used is *gnac'k'* = " way " or " way of life,"
" course of life," " behaviour," Latin *conversatio*.

[39] " beyond grasp ": *antar*, which I take, like *antaneli* (c. 4, n. 28)
to stand for ἀχώρητος in the passive sense, though the Armenian
Lexicon (Venice 1836-7) has for the equivalence ἀχώρητος the sense
" unreceptive," and the primary sense of *antar* is ἀφόρητος " unbear-able." If we suppose haplography and emend to *antarr* (" not-com-posite, immaterial ") we have a statement, reinforcing " invisible "
and the contrast with the visible Son and His Incarnation, of the
simplicity and immateriality of the divine nature; hence AR* has
" not material." PO* has " incomprehensible," as for *antaneli*, and

Barthoulot "inengendré," explained as "sans support" (PO* 756 n. 8); cf. his view of *antaneli*, Weber's Latin "independens (seu immensus)" also as for *antaneli*.

"article" here and for all other occurrences in the *Proof* is my rendering of *glux* (κεφαλή, κεφάλαιον, "head[ing]") in this sense.

[40] "according to the design of their prophecy": cf. A.H. 4. 33. 10 on, where we are told the prophets are "members of Christ," each giving his own part of prophecy according to what member he is, all together giving the "whole body" of the work of the Son of God.

"and through Him . . .": literally "(. . . of the Father), through whom . . ."; the relative surely refers back to the Word.

[41] *in the end of times*: Dan. 11. 13.

Such expressions are common both in the Scripture and in the Fathers, referring to the time of the (first) coming of Christ. So in the *Proof*, in addition to *in the end of times* (c. 6 twice; c. 8), we have also *in the last times* (c. 22, where it is taken from 1 Peter 1. 20; also in 1 Tim. 4. 1; and cf. 1 Peter 1. 5: *in the last time*), "in the end of this age" (c. 21, 30), "in the end of days" (c. 89; cf. 2 Tim. 3. 1: *in the last days*). Cf., with respect as here to "recapitulation," *in the fulness of times*, Eph. 1. 10.

[42] "for the recapitulation of all things": in the text, "to recapitulate all things," the verb being rendered by a doublet, *glxaworel ew bovandakel* ("sum up and contain"). In the Armenian New Testament ἀνακεφαλαιοῦσθαι is rendered by *bovandakel* both in the "profane" sense (Rom. 13. 9: *and if there be any other commandment, it is comprised in this word*) and with reference to Christ (Eph. 1. 10: *in the dispensation of the fulness of times, to re-establish all things in Christ*). In the Armenian *Adversus haereses* it is rendered by *glxaworel* alone when the reference is not to Christ (so three times in 5. 29. 2, and cf. *glxaworut'iwn* "recapitulation," same reference and same sense), but the two verbs are used together (as here) of Christ's "summing-up in Himself" (so in 4. 38. 1, 4. 40. 3, 5. 1. 2, corresponding respectively to 4. 62, 4. 66. 2, 5. 1. 2 of the Armenian text of TU 35. 2, which has Harvey's division). In this sense, however, Irenaeus says "recapitulate *in Himself*," and "in Himself" is left untranslated (save in so far as it may be said to be implied by the added *bovandakel*) in 4. 38. 1 = 4. 62; perhaps we should here render "recapitulation in Himself."

Irenaeus's theory of "recapitulation": cf. Introd. § 36.

"to abolish death and bring to light life": cf. 2 Tim. 1. 10: (God's purpose and grace given us in Jesus Christ before the times of the world) *is now made manifest by the illumination of our Saviour Jesus Christ, who hath destroyed death, and brought to light life and incorruption by the Gospel* (so Douay; but *abolished* rather than *destroyed* in the Greek); and Barnabas, *Ep.* 5. 6 (quoted in n. 186).

"communion": cf. Introd. § 36.

[43] Cf. A.H. 4. 33. 15: in novissimis temporibus nove effusus est in nos.

"over all the earth renewing man to God": alternatively "when God renewed man over all the earth"; Barthoulot not only adopts this alternative but cites Marr as saying it is the only possible interpretation (PO* 759 n. 10; "Jacques" for "Nicolas"). On the contrary, it seems to me rather less likely than the one I have adopted. For similar ambiguities (due to similar causes) cf. n. 195, 200 (and cf. next note).

The text has *yamenayn erkir norogelov zmardn Astucoy*, and in normal Armenian usage the version I have adopted imposes itself, *Astucoy* being taken as a dative. The ambiguity arises from the fact that the style of the *Proof* uses such constructions as an equivalent of the Greek "genitive absolute," *Astucoy* so being the genitive subject (examples in n. 201, 239).

Here and in the other examples just referred to the construction is, though abnormal, technically justifiable in that the "gerund" is the instrumental case of the infinitive, and the subject of the infinitive used substantivally is in the genitive (but the construction corresponds formally not to the genitive absolute of Greek, but to [ἐν] τῷ followed by accusative-and-infinitive). One also finds, however, direct transpositions of the genitive absolute (genitive of subject and genitive of participle: cf. n. 9, 106, 133, 201, 222, 341, though the last case is capable of straightforward interpretation), and the use of nominative instead of genitive with the "gerund" (cf. n. 249, 281, but the former is doubtful) or participle (cf. n. 200).

[44] "rebirth (unto God)," cf. A.H. 1. 14. 6, 1. 21. 1.

"comes through (these three articles)": a literal translation; the sense is clear from what follows in the chapter; cf. A.H. 5. 36. 2, where it is said that the guidance of the saved "passes through the following degrees," Spirit—Son—Father; cf. Introd. § 35.

"articles": cf. end of n. 39.

"granting": *šnorhelov*; Faldati points out the connection with *šnorhk'* "grace," and translates equivalently to "giving us the grace (of rebirth)"; but this seems to me inadvisable.

"granting us rebirth unto God the Father . . .": Armitage Robinson has "God the Father bestowing on us regeneration. . . ." Presumably he first rendered "bestowing on us regeneration unto God the Father . . . ," and later changed to "God the Father etc." without consulting the Armenian, supposing that "unto God" was *Astucoy*, and deciding that this was not after all dative but genitive, in a "genitive absolute" construction (cf. preceding note). In fact, however, the manuscript has *zyAstuac Hayrn i verstin cnundn mez šnorhelov*, that is, not παλιγγενεσίαν . . . Θεῷ (Θεοῦ), but unambiguously τὴν εἰς Θεὸν . . . παλιγγενεσίαν.

⁴⁵ "who are bearers of the Spirit of God": *ork' barjealn kren zHogin Astucoy*, literally "who having-taken-up bear the Spirit of God." Barthoulot understands the participle as passive, and meaning "taken-up" from the baptismal water, ("those who have been baptised and bear the Spirit of God"), but in fact *barjeal krel* is simply a doublet; in c. 16 we have "(the serpent) who had been the bearer of the slanderer": *or barjeal kreac' zbansarkun*. Cf. A.H. 4. 20. 6, 4. 14. 2 etc. for the expression "portare Spiritum."

Leading by Spirit to Son and by Son to Father (Introd. § 35), cf. A.H. 5. 36. 2, quoted in preceding note, and 4. 20. 5: Spiritu quidem praeparante hominem in Filium Dei, Filio autem adducente ad Patrem, Patre autem incorruptelam dante in aeternam vitam (here the doctrine is attributed to "the elders, the disciples of the apostles"). Note the leading up to "incorruptibility" as the ultimate fruit of the redemption (Introd. § 36).

⁴⁶ Cf. and contrast A.H. 4. 6. 1-3, where Irenaeus says, as here, that the Son is knowledge of the Father, but that "knowledge of the Son is in the *Father*," and "none may know the Son save according to the *Father's* good-pleasure" (on Matt. 11. 27: *no one knoweth the Son, but the Father*).

⁴⁷ "charismatically": *paštawnabar*, which may be rendered "by way of service"; *paštawn* and the corresponding plural *paštamunk'* mean "service" in a variety of senses (divine service, liturgy, ministry, office) including that of "favour" (χάρις). In c. 9 (n. 58) the gifts of the Holy Spirit are called *paštamanc' jewk'*, "forms of service." The sense required, in both passages, seems to be that of *charisma*, the special gift (of prophecy, of tongues etc.) given to some by the Holy Spirit for the service of the community: cf. 1 Cor. 12. 4-11. Χάρισμα is normally rendered in Armenian by *šnorhk'* (= χάρις, "grace"), both in the New Testament and in

Adversus haereses (not only in quoting, as 4. 20. 6 from 1 Cor. 12. 4, but also 4. 20. 4 contextually; for the Armenian text of TU 35. 2, which has Harvey's numbering, the references are 4. 34. 6 and 4), and cf. *Proof* c. 99; while *paštamanc'* is used in 1 Cor. 12. 15 for διακονῶν, parallelling the χαρισμάτων of the preceding verse (*there are diversities of graces, but the same Spirit; and there are diversities of ministries, but the same Lord*). Hence, though the correspondence *paštawn* = χάρισμα is *a priori* reasonable, in fact the correspondence is probably with διακονία, and it would doubtless have been verbally more accurate to render " ministerially " (and in c. 9 " ministries "); but the sense is surely better rendered by " charismatically " (" charismata ").

[48] " as the Father will, to those to whom He will ": the order of words of the text is represented by " quibus voluerit et sicut voluerit Pater." I have inverted the order of the clauses, and suppressed the conjunction, in order to leave so far as possible in English the same possibility of understanding the " He " of " to whom He will " as the Word (in the text the preceding subject), or even as the Spirit (in the text the nearest noun); but though both of these interpretations might be supported from Scripture, the reference is surely to the Father.

[49] " by the Spirit ": that is, in Scripture, the work of the Holy Spirit (cf. n. 65 to Introd.).

Most High (*barjreli* = ὕψιστος): one of the commonest epithets of God in the Old Testament; it occurs more than a hundred times in the LXX.

Almighty (*amenakal* = παντοκράτωρ, that is, universal, absolute ruler): in the LXX even more frequent than *Most High*.

Lord of Hosts: that is, of Armies (*zawrut'iwn* = δύναμις, " power, force," used — as " power " was formerly and " force " still is in English — to mean " army "); also more than a hundred times in the LXX.

[50] Note that it is the God of the Old Testament who is all this; Irenaeus is insisting here, against Marcion in particular, that the God of the Old Law is not a peculiarly Jewish demiurge, just but harsh, but is the supreme and merciful God of all (cf. § 30 of Introd.). He nevertheless admits — cf. the rest of this chapter — that God does not stand in quite the same relation to the various classes of men (cf. the Gnostic threefold classification, Introd. § 34).

" the whole world ": the Armenian uses the " first-person " article -s, which gives the sense " this (world) of ours," but the Greek original probably had the simple article.

[51] " opened (the testament) ": that is, revealed it (and so, made it operative); a regular word in Irenaeus in this sense, cf. e. g. A.H. 3. 10. 5, 5. 9. 4, 5. 33. 1; and in the *Proof* also c. 91.

[52] " in the mean time ": that is, before the appointed " end of times."

" brought them into subjection ": that is, not mankind in general, but the Jews.

This identification of the kind Father of the faithful and the severe God of the Law is especially directed against Marcion (Introd. § 30).

[53] This statement is directed especially against the Gnostic distinction of three classes of men, and their " Aeons " corresponding to the " angels " (cf. Introd. § 34).

[54] Rom. 2. 4-6.

[55] " in the law," that is e. g. Exod. 3. 6, for the words *the God of Abraham and the God of Isaac and the God of Jacob*; the comment *He is not the God of the dead but of the living* is added in Matt. 22. 32. In A.H. 4. 5. 2 however Irenaeus correctly assigns the latter comment to Christ.

[56] That is, the close relation of creatures to God just described does not detract from God's transcendence and absoluteness — against the Gnostic view (cf. Introd. § 29).

[57] It seems unlikely that Irenaeus took over the " seven heavens " and their angels from the Valentinian Gnostics, whose similar doctrine he records in A.H. 1. 5. 2 simply as a Gnostic view, showing no more respect for it than for the more extravagant cosmologies of other Gnostics, reported in A.H. 1. 17. 1, 1. 24. 3, 2. 35. 1. He probably took it over, directly or indirectly, from the Jewish tradition as found for example in the *Testamentum Levi* (3), or in the *Ascensio Isaiae* (10: here there are six heavens, but the firmament is not included in this enumeration; there are other parallels in the *Proof* to *Ascensio Isaiae*, cf. n. 62, 338). Moreover Maximus (*Scholia in Dionysii* De mystica theologia, 1) attributes this view to Aristo.

For the " seven heavens " doctrine, cf. H. St.-John Thackeray, *The Relation of St. Paul to Contemporary Jewish Thought* (London 1900) 172-179, and (for the doctrine in Christian apocalyptic literature) R. H. Charles in the preface (xliv-xlvii) to his edition of W. R. Morfill's translation of the Slavonic *Book of the Secrets of Enoch.* (The doctrine is found in this *Secrets of Enoch,* 3 f.)

The angels do homage to keep themselves out of mischief; there may be some special reference here; " lest they *too* be . . . accursed "

seems to allude to the rebel angel(s) — cf. the rebuking of the
tempter, c. 16; and Weber L* 34 refers to Matt. 25. 30 (the un-
profitable servant) and 34 f. (last judgement; works of mercy done to
Christ; *Depart ye cursed . . .*) and Luke 13. 9 (parable of the barren
fig tree). With the reason for the angels' homage as here expressed
by Irenaeus, Robinson (AR* 78 n. 1) aptly compares Justin, *Dial.*
22, where it is said that the temple-worship was given to the Jews
by God not because He had need of it, but because worshipping
Him would keep them out of idolatry. This already approaches
more closely to the true reason, which however is here not so clearly
expressed; namely, that God has no need of homage, and draws
no profit from it for Himself, but creatures have need to give Him
homage, and themselves receive the profit therefrom. Cf. A.H.
4. 18. 6: Deus non indiget eorum quae a nobis sunt . . . nos indigemus
offerre aliquid Deo; and the statement that God takes in order to
reward His own gifts, and later, with a closer verbal parallel to this
passage of the *Proof*: sicut igitur non his indigens, vult tamen a
nobis propter nos fieri, ne simus infructuosi.

[58] "charismata": *Yewt'n paštamanc' jews*, "in seven forms of service" (cf. n. 47). I render simply "charismata" instead of "charis-
matic forms," supposing the use of *jewk'* to be accounted for by the
need of showing the plural, *paštamunk'* being a "plurale tantum."
The following participle, "resting," agrees not with *jews* but with
paštamanc'.

[59] Isa. 11. 2 f. In our manuscript the words *the spirit of knowledge* are missing, but I have supplied them, the omission being clearly
a slip of the pen, since Irenaeus refers in what follows to all seven
gifts (and in c. 59, as also A.H. 3. 9. 3, 3. 17. 3, quotes the same
passage without this omission).

[60] Irenaeus counts the heavens downwards, instead of in the more
usual ascending order, in order to keep to the order of the gifts in
Isaias, while giving the highest heaven to Wisdom, and the firmament to the Fear of God.

"firmament . . . full of the fear of this Spirit, who lights up the
heavens": from an apocryphal source? Or simply an application to
the Spirit of a Sun-metaphor, more usually applied to the Word, but
in Ecclus. 24. 6-8 used of Wisdom (= the Spirit, for Irenaeus),
though in c. 34 Irenaeus echoes it of the Word? The reference to
Wisd. 1. 7 (*the Spirit of the Lord hath filled the whole world*) is not
very relevant. For the "lighting up," cf. perhaps Job 26. 13: *His
spirit hath adorned the heavens.*

[61] For both quotation and exegesis, cf. Heb. 8. 5: *who* (= priests) *serve unto the example and shadow of heavenly things, as it was answered to Moses, when he was to finish the tabernacle: See (saith He) that thou make all things according to the pattern that was shown thee on the mount* — the Old Testament reference being Exod. 25. 40.

[62] "their Powers": that is, their angelic forces, armies; the text has the singular, perhaps as Weber suggests (L* 35 note l) by confusion EI-I (ΔΥΝΑΜΙΣ for ΔΥΝΑΜΕΙΣ).

For Cherubim as "Powers of the Word," cf. Melito of Sardis, Fragment 15 from the *Tractatus de fide*, where Christ is called the "charioteer of the Cherubim, leader of the army of the angels" (cf. Ps. 17. 11: *he ascended on the Cherubim, and he flew; he flew upon the wings of the winds*). Cf. also (as pointed out by AR* 39-43) the liturgical association of Cherubim and Seraphim (e. g. in the *Te Deum*) with the glorification of God; and perhaps also *Ascensio Isaiae* 9. But all the angelic hosts are subject to the Word and Wisdom (A. H 4. 7. 4), being made through them (A.H. 3. 8. 3 — corresponding to the statement of c. 5: cf. "powers of the heavens" there).

[63] Angels included in the world created by God, that is, not intermediate between the supreme God and this world, like the Gnostic Aeons, still less creators of the world, like the Gnostic demiurge (or creator-angels, cf. A. H. 1. 23-25): cf. Introd. § 29. Instead they were for Irenaeus administrators of the world: cf. next chapter. He seems however here to be making a distinction between the angels belonging to the "establishment of heaven" and the terrestrial ones. Note the law that each keep to his own place (cf. n. 98).

[64] Creation of man: Gen. 2. 7.

"But man . . .": or "But the man . . . ," as the reference is to *the* Man, Adam. Here I have preferred to omit the article, but I use it in subsequent references to Adam.

"with His own hands": ". . . , that is, the Son and the Spirit," adds the parallel passage A.H. 4. *praef.* 4 (cf. n. 70 to Introd.).

[65] Man was created in the "image" of the Son, which is in his "frame" ($\pi\lambda\acute{a}\sigma\mu a$); and the added gift of the Spirit gave him "likeness" to God: cf. Introd. § 33.

"He gave his frame the outline of His own form, that the visible appearance too should be godlike": *stełcuacin ziwrsn paragreac' jews, zi ew or tesanic'inn Astuacajew ic'ē*, more literally "for the formation He outlined His own form, that also what would be seen

,hould be deiform "; there can be no doubt that Irenaeus is here teaching man's bodily resemblance to God. God is of course invisible, for Irenaeus too, precisely as God; the bodily resemblance is to the Son = Christ. The word rendered "formation" corresponds to πλάσμα, echoing the ἔπλασε "formed" of Gen. 2. 7: *God formed man of the slime of the earth.* For the statement that man is like God in figure Harnack (EP* 58) refers to Melito of Sardis; but Melito says (*Or. ad Anton.* 6) that it is in man's spirit that there is likeness to God, who is invisible and intangible "and has no outward form."

breathed into his face the breath of life: Gen. 2. 7.

" so that the man became like God in inspiration as well as in frame ": *orpēs zi ew ĕst p'č'mann ew ĕst stełcuacin nman linel zmardn Astucoy* = " so that both according to in-breathing and according to formation man became like God," where " in-breathing " stands for ἐμφύσημα and " formation " for πλάσμα, echoing the ἐνεφύσησεν " breathed (into) " and ἔπλασε " formed " of Gen. 2. 7.

In A.H. 5. 12. 2 Irenaeus says God first "formed" man (that is, his body), and gave him his soul, and lastly gave the Spirit. Here however the distinction between soul and spirit is not clear. The " breath of life," breathed into man, as Irenaeus here says " that he might come to life," is surely the soul, but the " likeness to God " here referred to in contrast with the " image " in man's frame seems to show that Irenaeus understands it of the spirit; and the reference in c. 14 to the " breath of life " also seems to identify it with the spirit (I have even translated " spirit of life " in c. 14; cf. n. 82).

[66] " So he was free . . .": for man's freedom as a point of likeness to God, cf. A.H. 4. 37. 4.

" his own᾿ master ": *ink'nišxan* = αὐτεξούσιος. Perhaps this word was used alone in the Greek, " free and " being an expansion of the Armenian translator's.

[67] " domain ": *vayr* = τόπος, meaning the " place " assigned to man in the scheme of things (cf. end of preceding chapter). For man as lord of the earth, cf. Gen. 1. 28: *fill the earth and subdue it and rule over* (the various animals). Irenaeus develops this into understanding man as lord of the angels and of the world as well (cf. next sentence, and next chapter).

[68] For the (arch)angel of the world, cf. Hermas, *Sim.* 8. Hermas's angel is Michael, whereas a tradition represented the angel of the world as having become the devil (cf. the " spirit of the world " of Hermas, *Mand.* 11, referred to in n. 16; and the " prince of this world " in John 12. 31; 14. 30; 16. 11; and the " prince of the power

of this air" of Eph. 2. 2; and the alternative version of 1 John 5. 19: *the whole world is under the wicked one*). In the *Proof* Irenaeus refers to the tempter simply as "the angel" (c. 16). It seems, however, that for him the rebel angels were subcelestial ones.

"the servants were angels, but administrator-in-chief the archangel": the subjects of these two clauses are "servants" and "the archangel"; the predicates "angels" and "administrator-in-chief" (*tnawrēn hazarapet* = οἰκονόμος χιλίαρχος, more or less "Colonel Manager").

⁶⁹ An important point, remarks Harnack, EP* 58.

"in secret" (*zanxlabar*): the "secrecy" is probably to be explained by the fact that man, though lord by right, and destined to rule in fact, was not yet capable of doing so (cf. what follows), so that his lordship was not yet made known to his subjects.

A traditional account of the fall of the angels represents their trial as having consisted in the command to submit to man, whose dignity was not revealed to them; but in the tradition the "man" was Christ. Irenaeus seems to identify the sin whereby the devil "fell" with his tempting of man from motives of jealousy (c. 16; cf. n. 88).

⁷⁰ "full development": the word so rendered is *karelut'iwn*, which would mean "possibility." Though the text as it stands is capable of interpretation in the sense evidently required ("possibility" being understood not as undeveloped potentiality but as meaning that what was possible for them, they had), on other grounds Weber is probably right in suggesting (L* 37 note b) that one should read *katarelut'iwn* (the word rendered "full perfection" at the end of the sentence).

For the representation of Adam (and later, of Eve) as children, cf. A.H. 3. 22. 4, 4. 38. 1-4, 4. 39. 1, and Theophilus of Antioch, *Ad Autol.* 2. 25. Clement of Alexandria, *Protr.* 11. 111. 1, also calls Adam παιδίον τοῦ Θεοῦ before his fall, and adds the interesting statement that in the fall he became a grown man by his disobedience, ὁ παῖς ἀνδριζόμενος ἀπειθείᾳ.

In A.H. 4. 38, Irenaeus explains how man was destined, in God's original plan, to evolve into an ever more and more perfect likeness of the uncreated God.

⁷¹ "in luxury": *xraxut'eamb p'ap'kut'eamb*, a "doublet" meaning roughly "with-festivity," "with-delight (delicacy)."

For the description of Paradise Harnack refers (EP* 58) to *Apocalypsis Petri* 15 (= TU 9. 2. 17); but the resemblance is not very close.

"the Garden": following Weber (L*) I have rendered the word

drast " Garden," reserving " Paradise " for the form *draxt*, used in Gen. 2. 8 for the " Garden " of Eden (both words mean " garden ").

[72] The Word walked in the Garden: cf. Theophilus of Antioch, *Ad Autol.* 2. 22. All " theophanies " are attributed to the Word — cf. Introd. § 31.

" prefiguring ": that is, by His action, which was a " type " of what was to come; not that He spoke with Adam on those topics. PO* has " to impress on his mind beforehand," owing to failure to realise that *yaṙajagoyn tpaworelov*, which is capable of the literal rendering " impressing beforehand," is simply a doublet for προτυπῶν (" on his mind " is added by PO*).

[73] Gen. 2. 19. Our text has *asēr anun nma* " was called its name," but a slight emendation (*sa ēr anun nma*) gives " this was its name." Note the dative *nma* (ἐλέγετο ὄνομα αὐτῷ or, with the emendation, τοῦτ' ἦν ὄνομα αὐτῷ).

[74] Gen. 2. 18.

[75] Cf. Gen. 2. 20.

[76] Gen. 2. 21.

[77] " that one work be accomplished out of another ": *zi gorc i gorcoy kataresc'i*, " that work from work be accomplished." Barthoulot's rendering " pour l'accomplissement de son chef-d'œuvre," explained (PO* 763 n. 2) as literally " une œuvre parmi les œuvres," does not agree with the text, which has *i gorcoy*, singular (though *i gorcoc'* is a very slight emendation; *y* and *c'* are easily confused); and the sense is not very likely (it would have to be understood, of course, of the accomplishment of *man*, as God's *chef d'œuvre*, by the creation of woman).

[78] Gen. 2. 21 f. The words " in this wise " seem to be intended as part of the quotation, but are not in the Old Testament form. Most likely Irenaeus was not deliberately quoting here and in similar cases, but merely using the words of Scripture to tell his story.

[79] Gen. 2. 23.

[80] Gen. 2. 25.

[81] " of the sort that is engendered ": *yaync'anē*, or *inč' miangam . . . cnani*, literally " from whatever is engendered."

" concupiscence ": *hešt c'ankut'iwnk'*, literally " pleasurable desires," commonly a doublet for ἡδοναί, " pleasures."

" lust ": *amawt'ali c'ankut'iwn*, literally " shameful desire."

[82] " for what had been breathed into their frame was the spirit of life ": *vasn zi p'č'ec'ealn i stelcuacn šunč' ēr kenac'*; *-n* of *p'č'ec'ealn* surely not phrase-article, but determining subject, *šunč'* being predi-

cate; hence not simply " for the spirit of life had been breathed . . ."; nor is AR* correct ("since they still had the breath of life which was breathed on their creation "). "into their frame": *i stełcuacn* = "into the *plasma*"; and " spirit ": *šunč'*, which corresponds to πνοή, " breath," (or to πνεῦμα in that sense), and is the word used in Gen. 2. 7 — *breath of life*; here however I render " spirit," since it is hardly possible to use "breath" in what follows ("so long as the spirit remains. . ."). " Frame," " breath," cf. n. 65.

[83] " so long as the spirit still remains in proper order and vigour ": this seems to be the sense of *kalov mnalov šunč'n yorum dasun ew zawrut'ean*, the syntax of which may be rendered by the Latin "manendo spiritŭs in quo ordine et virtute." Weber adds " [datus est] " and suggests supplying *kargec'aw* in the text (L* 39 note k).

[84] Adam and Eve represented as children: cf. n. 70.

[85] " have thoughts of grandeur": *mecamecs xorhesc'i*, a doublet for μεγαλοφρονήσῃ.

" become lifted up ": a doublet, *hambarjeal barjrasc'i*.

" because of the dominion that had been given to him, and the freedom, fall into sin against God his Creator": the syntax is obscure. In the first place, translators have commonly thought it necessary to supply a conjunction; but where? " And " may be supplied in any one of three places: before "as if" earlier in the sentence, before "because," or before " fall into sin." I have preferred to leave the text as it stands. The words " that had been given to him " may of course be applied to " freedom " as well as to " dominion."

More important is the possible variant rendering "because of the dominion that had been given him, and the freedom towards God his Creator, fall into sin " (PO* renders in this sense), " freedom " being understood of " unconstrained terms, unceremoniousness." The word used is in fact *hamarjakut'iwn*, which corresponds to παρρησία, and " towards God his Creator " in the text may be taken either with " freedom " or with " fall into sin " (. . . *hamarjakut'ean ař i yararoǐn iwr Astuac sxalesc'i*).

Note the reason here assigned by Irenaeus for the prohibition of the Tree of Knowledge: a token of subjection to God.

[86] " certain conditions": *sahmans omans*. EP* rendered " Grenzen," to which Weber (L* 40 note l) objected that the corresponding Greek was ὅρους τινάς, and rendered " regulas "; PO* however keeps " limits " but Faldati follows Weber with " regole." Obviously the Greek was ὅρους τινάς, but it might be maintained that " bounds "

was a better rendering of that expression than " rules," even in this context; the correct rendering is " terms, conditions," a normal use of the word ὅροι.

" melting into earth, whence his frame had been taken ": cf. (Gen. 2. 7 and) Gen. 3. 19 (after the fall: *dust thou art and unto dust thou shalt return*).

[87] Gen. 2. 16 f., with slight variants from LXX.

[88] Temptation by angel, and fall: cf. Gen. 3. 1-6 (" serpent " as tempter), Wisd. 2. 24 (" devil ").

" looking on him with envy ": *č'arakneal* = βασκαίνων: more literally " evil-eyeing." Some have remarked on the motive (envy) assigned to the devil, as if it were a theory peculiar to Irenaeus, but cf. Wisd. 2. 24: *by the envy of the devil, death came into the world.*

" both ruined himself ": Irenaeus thus seems to identify the sin whereby the devil himself fell with his tempting of man (cf. also rest of this chapter); as for the other rebel angels, cf. c. 18 for their unlawful unions with man (n. 98). Cf. n. 69.

[89] " having become by falsehood . . .": cf. John 8. 44: (the devil) *was a murderer from the beginning, and he stood not in the truth . . . for he is a liar and the father thereof.*

[90] " rebel ": or " apostate " (*apstamb* = ἀποστάτης). So also in A.H. 5. 21. 2. This meaning for the word " Satan " is doubtless taken from Justin, who derives the word from *satá* " apostate " and *nâs* " serpent " (*Dial.* 103 .5), that is, from Hebrew *sāṭāh* " deviate " and *nāḥaš* " serpent "; in fact, it is derived from *sāṭan* " oppose," and means " adversary." The rendering " Widersacher " given in EP* misled Hitchcock (*Journal of Theological Studies* 9 [1908] 285 f.) into thinking that Irenaeus had found the true meaning of the word since writing A.H. 5. 21. 2.

" Slanderer ": *bansarku* = κατήγορος or διάβολος (whence is derived the English word " devil "), " accuser, informer, talebearer " (and in that sense " adversary "). Cf. Job 2, where " Satan " is represented as intriguing against Job at the court of God.

[91] Curse of the serpent: Gen. 3. 14.

" rebuked ": " cursed " seems not the best word to render the text's *lutac'aw* " abused, scolded "; " cursed " is e. g. *nzakeac'*.

" had been the bearer ": *barjeal kreac'* (cf. n. 45).

" sent away to dwell ": *p'oxeal bnakec'uc'eal*, literally " changing making-to-dwell," a doublet for μετοικίσας.

" by the road into the Garden ": *aṙ i drastn čanaparhi.*

Harnack's remark (EP* 58) that this sentence supposes that man's return to the Garden was envisaged is perhaps due to the ambiguous rendering of EP*: " auf den . . . Weg versetzte " (and cf. e. g. AR* " on the way to Paradise," L* " in horti viam "). Though the return to Paradise (after the Resurrection and the Judgement) was regarded as envisaged by the text of Genesis, cf. e. g. Theophilus of Antioch, *Ad Autol.* 2. 26, the present passage does not especially suggest such a view. Cf. Gen. 3. 24: *And he cast out Adam; and placed before the paradise of pleasure Cherubims, and a flaming sword, turning every way, to keep the way of the tree of life.*

" since the Garden does not admit a sinner ": note the difference from the reason alleged in Gen. 3. 22 (lest man eat of the tree of life and live for ever). In A.H. 3. 23. 6 Irenaeus says (after Theophilus of Antioch, *Ad Autol.* 2. 25 f.) that God cut off man's access to the tree of life not as grudging him the tree, but because immortality, in his fallen state, would have been an immortality of sin.

⁹² " miseries of mind and body ": *alēts tarakusi c'awoc'*, more literally " miseries of doubt *or* despondency, of pain *or* toil."

⁹³ Cf. Gen. 3. 17-19.

⁹⁴ Gen. 4. 1 f.

⁹⁵ Cf. Gen. 4. 8, which however has no reference to the devil, and 1 John 3. 12: *Cain, who was of the wicked one.*

⁹⁶ Descendants of Cain, cf. Gen. 4. 17-24. The statement that they became like their forefather is doubtless to be accounted for by the theory that curses or blessings in general are inherited; or to some peculiar interpretation of Gen. 4. 23 (*Lamech said . . . I have slain a man to the wounding of myself and a stripling to my own bruising*). The depravity leading to the flood was not, seemingly, confined to the descendants of Cain, and there does not seem to have been any definite Jewish tradition of the effect of the curse of Cain on his descendants in general. Lamech's words were accounted for by the legend that in his old age he had slain, accidentally, his great-great-great-grandfather Cain, and his own son, the youth responsible for the mistake whereby he slew Cain (Cain's bloodguilt thus being visited on him in the seventh generation — cf. L. Ginzberg, *Legends of the Jews* 1 [Philadelphia 1909] 115-118).

⁹⁷ Cf. Gen. 4. 25.

⁹⁸ " For (unlawful unions . . .) ": the text has *ew k'anzi*. Weber (L* 43 note b) rejects *k'anzi* " because," and translates only *ew* " and." It seems better on the contrary to translate " for " and leave " and " untranslated; *ew k'anzi* here as elsewhere seems to stand for καὶ γάρ.

" *unlawful (unions)": *tarrawrēn*, a hapax legomenon which has been understood as meaning "heterogeneous" (cf. EP* "Vermischungen zwischen verschiedenen Elementen "), and connected with *tarrawor* or *tarrelēn*, though these words mean rather "material, elemental" or the like, from *tarr* "element." The version "unlawful" supposes emendation to *tarawrēn*, proposed by Vardanian, *HAm.* 24 (1910) 327. The "law" so broken would be that of "each keeping to his own place" (cf. end of c. 10); cf. Justin, *Apol.* 2. 5, who refers to the transgression of this law in the unions between angels and women; and Jude 6: *the angels who kept not their principality, but forsook their own habitation.* . . .

⁹⁹ The Giants: cf. Gen. 6. 2-4; Bar. 3. 26-28; Wisd. 14. 6; Ecclus. 16. 8.

"Giants": in view of the context I have used this word to render the text's *erkracink',* literally "earthborn" (γηγενεῖς), a common appellation of the Giants. Weber (L* 43 note d) suggests that the word *hskayk'* = γίγαντες, "Giants," has fallen out after *erkracink'*; but this is hardly necessary. In c. 27 both words occur in "giants, sons of the Titans," where "Titans" is my attempt at a rendering of *erkracink'.*

The explanation of the origin of the giants from unions between angels and men is due to the natural interpretation of the expression "sons of God" in Gen. 6. 2 as meaning the angels (cf. the "sons of God" with Satan among them before Him in Job 2. 1), and is developed in Jewish apocrypha, cf. Jubilees 5. 1; 1 Enoch 6 (cf. following note).

¹⁰⁰ The whole of this chapter is based on Jewish apocrypha; cf. especially 1 Enoch 6-9, where the "teachings of evil" are set forth in detail. This book and others were commonly accepted as having almost Scriptural authority; there are echoes of them in the New Testament, especially in the epistle of St. Jude, in which 1 Enoch 1. 9 is quoted (Jude 14 f.).

"virtues of roots and herbs": these may not seem to be "teachings of evil," but 1 Enoch 7. 1 and 8. 3 show that the reference is not to their medicinal or other innocent properties, but to their use in magic.

"cosmetics": *zšparans*, Vardanian's emendation, *HAm.* 24 (1910) 304, for the text's *zšaprans.*

"discoveries of precious materials": *zgiwts patuakan niwt'oc'*, an enigmatic phrase. Along with the various aids to beauty, we are told in 1 Enoch 8. 1, Azazel taught men also the use of weapons and armour and metalworking in general (cf. Gen. 4. 22, Tubalcain the metalworker), and also "all manner of precious stones." The "discoveries of precious materials" may refer to alchemy, or to precious stones or other finery, or also to metalworking and like crafts.

"love-philtres": or "beauty-medicaments"? The word is *šnorhadelut'iwn*, which rendered literally into Greek would give *χαριτοφαρμακεία* "grace-medication." Hence L* "medicamentum venustatis," EP* "Mittel zur Beförderung der Anmut," F* "la cosmesi della bellezza." The sense may however be connected rather with that of *χαριτήριον*, hence my rendering (so too AR*). PO* has "magic" and Barthoulot "la magie."

"constraints of love": *br̄najgut'iwns siroy*, of which the meaning is obscure.

"bonds of witchcraft": *kapans kaxardut'ean*: that is, the binding of spells.

All this traditional expansion of the legend of the giants is lacking in the parallel passage A.H. 4. 36. 4, but in the parallel, Justin, *Apol.* 2. 5, it is briefly referred to, and in A.H. 4. 16. 2.

[101] "in the tenth generation": cf. genealogy in Gen. 5: Adam — Seth — Enos — Cainan — Malaleel — Jared — Henoch — Mathusala — Lamech — Noe.

"Noe alone was found just": cf. Gen. 6. 8.

The ark: cf. Gen. 6. 18 ff.; 7. 1 ff.

"with all animals which God ordered Noe to bring into the ark": this phrase is omitted by an oversight in AR*.

[102] Cf. Gen. 9. 18 f.

[103] Cf. Gen. 9. 21-27.

[104] Gen. 9. 25. The Massoretic text is rendered by Douay's: *Cursed be Chanaan: a servant of servants shall he be unto his brethren* (the cursing of Chanaan rather than Cham is explained by a Jewish tradition as due to the boy's having been the first to find Noe, and having told his father). The LXX however renders a variant in which "servant of servants" becomes παῖς οἰκέτης, giving, according to the punctuation, *Cursed be the boy Chanaan: a servant shall he be to his brethren* (Χαναὰν παῖς· οἰκέτης), or, with the more usual punctuation, *Cursed be Chanaan: a servant boy shall he be to his brethren* (Χαναάν· παῖς οἰκέτης). Moreover several cursives have the variant reading Χάμ instead of Χαναάν. Our text not only has the less usual punctuation, but reads "Cham" instead of "Chanaan" not only here, but also in verses 26 and 27, quoted in the next chapter; in these verses the variant in the LXX is very rare (one cursive in Holmes and Parsons). The reading and punctuation Χὰμ παῖς·

οἰκέτης has been explained by taking Χάμ as a genitive ("the son of Cham; a servant"); but in the first place, the Armenian translator, at least, did not so understand it, since he here leaves the name, which is normally declined, in the form of the nominative; and in the second place, this explanation does not account for the reading "Cham" in verses 26 and 27.

[105] "fourteen generations": from an apocryphal source? Gen. 10. 6-20 (progeny of Cham) does not help, and the genealogy which is ostensibly complete, that of Sem (Gen. 11. 10-26) gives ten generations to Abraham (cf. n. 108), after which we have Isaac, Jacob, and the four generations from Levi to Moses (cf. n. 128), giving sixteen generations to the "mowing down" of the Egyptians, and so seventeen to that of the Chanaanites.

"his race was . . . mown down": that is, in the plagues of the Egyptians (for Irenaeus is speaking of the Hamites, not only of the Chanaanites) and in the delivery of the land of the Chanaanites to the Jews. How Irenaeus explained the "mowing down" of other (non-Palestinian) "Hamites" is not clear. Cf. next note.

[106] The nations "mown down" by the Jewish inroad are named as six, namely Chanaanite, Hittite, Pherezite, Hevite, Amorrhite, Jebusite, in Exod. 3. 8, 3. 17, 33. 2, 34. 11; Deut. 20. 17; Jos. 9. 1, 11. 3; the seventh (Gergesite) is added to the same list in Deut. 7. 1 and Jos. 24. 11 (cf. the "seven nations descended from Cham" of c. 24). Gen. 15. 19-21 gives six of the seven, omitting the Hevites, but including Cineans, Cenezites, Cedmonites, and Raphaim, which are not on Irenaeus's list. Of the "seven," all but the Pherezites are mentioned in the list of Cham's offspring, Gen. 10. 6-20. As for the other peoples listed by Irenaeus:

Sodomites: cf. Gen. 10. 19, the limits of Chanaan are *until you enter Sodom*. In fact the Sodomites were not reckoned as Hamites. EP* has "Zidoniter" instead of Sodomites, but in Gen. 10. 15 "Sidon" is a Hittite, and the "dwellers in Phoenicia" are mentioned later by Irenaeus; PO* returns to "Sodomites." It seems most likely that the Sodomites were included because they lived in the neighbourhood of the Chanaanites and were "mown down" by a punishment from heaven.

Arabs: the Arabs are traditionally not Hamitic but Semitic, descended from Abraham's son Ishmael. Nestle may be right in saying that "Aradians" (Gen. 10. 18) should be read; or it may be "Aracites" (Gen. 10. 17); much more likely, however, "Arabs" is correct, and has been thrown in because they too lived in that part of the world.

Dwellers in Phoenicia: probably added for the same reason; but cf. Sidon, Gen. 10. 15, though he is there a Hittite, and Gen. 10. 19, Sidon as limit of Chanaan; also Jos. 9. 1: *in the places near the sea, and on the coasts of the great sea, they also that dwell by Libanus.*

Egyptians: cf. Gen. 10. 6 and 13 (Mesram, Mesraim).

Lydians: EP* emends to "Libyans," an easy emendation and one suggested by the proximity of Egyptians; so too AR*, and adds (87 n. 2) that "Irenaeus seems to have drawn on Acts 2. 9-11 to amplify his list," a suggestion that can scarcely be taken seriously. Most likely "Lydians" is correct. Gen. 10. 13 has "Ludim" as sons of Mesraim (that is, Egypt) and for "Lydians" as an African (and so, Hamitic) people cf. Isa. 66. 19: *Africa and Lydia*, Ezech. 30. 5: *Ethiopia and Libya and Lydia*, 27. 10: *Lydians and Libyans* (note therefore that this "Lydia" is not simply a variant name for Libya).

Other progeny attributed to Cham in Gen. 10. 6-20 is not mentioned, e. g. the Babylonians and Assyrians; important as those peoples were, the boot was on the other foot in the matter of being conquered by the Jews.

"for long was the curse spread over the ungodly": *yerkar jktec'eloc' ndovic'n i veray ambarštac'n*, a "genitive absolute"!

[107] Gen. 9. 26 ("Cham" for "Chanaan," cf. n. 104).

[108] "a peculiar possession of worship": *stac'uac ašogi astuacpaštut'eann.* The word *ašogi* is obscure, but the meaning is fairly certainly "special, peculiar, own, apart," cf. *aṙošogi* "apart"; Vardanian, *HAm.* 24 (1910) 283, suggests reading *ušogi*, though that seems strange.

"burgeoned when it reached Abraham": *busaw . . . yAbraham haseal*; an excellent metaphor, not conveyed in the rendering of *busanel* ("grow" etc., but primarily of plants) as "increase" (PO*) or "extend" (AR*). Cf. "blossomed forth" in the parallel reference to the blessing of Japheth, below.

Genealogy of Abraham (Gen. 11. 10-26): Sem — Arphaxad — Sale — Heber — Phaleg — Reu — Sarug — Nachor — Thare — Abram.

[109] Exod. 3. 6 etc.

[110] 'was carried over": or "was meant for," "was aimed at" or the like: *karkaṙeal yaṙec'aw*; more literally "being-extended attained"; but both verbs of the doublet occur as equivalents of παρακύπτω ("regard obliquely" etc.).

[111] Gen. 9. 27. "Cham" for "Chanaan," cf. n. 104; "let him *dwell": the text has *awrhnesc'ē* "may he bless," but later in this chapter Irenaeus gives the exegesis of "dwells in the house of Sem,"

and in c. 42 the fruit of the blessing of Japheth is described as " dwelling in the house of Sem." Hence I render " let him dwell," which may stand for the normal LXX " make him dwell " (κατοικισάτω) or for a variant (κατοικησάτω) corresponding to the Massoretic "may he dwell."

In the Hebrew the word " enlarge " is a play on the name Japheth," " may . . . enlarge " being in Hebrew *yaft*.

¹¹² ' and *this blossomed forth in the end of this age,* in the manifestation of the Lord to the Gentiles of the calling ": the manuscript's *ews ē: i vaxčan yawitenis calkeac' erewec'eloc' Teařn i koč'-manēn het'anosac'* is best reproduced in Latin: " adhuc est: in fine saeculi (huius) floruit manifestatis Domino ex vocatione gentium " or ". . . gentibus " (" manifestatis . . . gentibus " either dative or ablative absolute). For " manifestatis " Weber has " visis," which he says seems to mean " beneplacitis " (L* 46 note h), but it seems preferable to emend the text. Vardanian, *HAm.* 24 (1910) 327, emends *ews ē* " adhuc est " to *ew Sēm* " et Sem," and *erewec'eloc' (Teařn)* " manifestatis (Domino) " to *erewec'eloy (Teařn)* " manifestato (Domino)," taken as a rendering of a Greek genitive absolute.

The latter of these emendations is almost inevitable; the sense so given, " in the manifestation of the Lord," is called for both by the context and by the choice of verb (*erewim* = ἐπιφαίνομαι, cf. the very word " Epiphany "); *c'* and *y* are easily confused, and to an Armenian scribe the syntax might seem to demand *erewec'eloc'*. The other emendation is not so good; surely it was not Sem (rather Japheth than Sem), but the blessing which " blossomed forth " (cf. " the blessing burgeoned " above). Hence I render " and this " (*ew sa*; the text's *ews ē* would emend more easily into *ew sē* or *ews ew*; but the form *sē* is uncalled-for and unlikely, while *ews ew* would leave the verb without an expressed subject, and would still be best rendered " and *this* too ").

" in the end of this age " (*i vaxčan yawitenis*): cf. n. 41.

" to the Gentiles of the calling " (*i koč'manēn het'anosac'*): more literally ". . . out of the calling "; a curious expression, but the rendering " out of the calling of the Gentiles " does not fit the context, so *het'anosac'* must be taken as dative instead of genitive, and *i koč'-manēn* as qualifying it. Emendation to *i koč'mann*, however, would give " in the calling of the Gentiles."

¹¹³ Ps. 18. 5, quoted in Rom. 10. 18.

¹¹⁴ Cf. c. 26 (tabernacle figure of the Church), c. 41, 42 (the calling of the Gentiles, realised in the Church, is the fruit of the blessing of Japheth); and cf. Justin, *Dial.* 139.

"the calling from the Gentiles, that is to say, the Church": in A.H. 4. 20. 12 the Armenian version has the same expression "calling from the Gentiles" where the Greek text has ἡ ἐξ ἐθνῶν ἐκκλησία. The use of the expression here along with the explanatory "that is to say, the Church" tends to show that in A.H. the Armenian version was accurate, and — as was already suspected — the ἐκκλησία of our Greek text an error for κλῆσις.

[115] "and for all living beasts": the insertion "other" ("all other living beasts") is due to misunderstanding *ayl* in *aylews* (= *ayl-ews*) as the adjective "other"; in fact *ayl ews* = ἀλλὰ καί.

God's pact with Noe, Gen. 9. 9 on.

When the sky . . .: the quotation does not correspond with either of the two versions in Gen. 9. 14-17.

"covenant" (both in the quotation and earlier in the sentence) is rendered by a doublet: *uxt ktakarani* ("a pact of covenant"), *zuxt ktakaranin imoy* (*the pact of my covenant*).

[116] Gen. 9. 1-6 (with some omissions and some departures from LXX readings).

"flesh of the blood of life": the word rendered "life" is *šunč'*, ("breath" etc., cf. n. 65; here = ψυχή).

[117] Man made in image of Christ, and Christ "image" of God, cf. Introd. § 33 and 31.

[118] 1 Peter 1. 20.

"in the last times" (*i verjin žamanaks*): cf. n. 41.

[119] Gen. 11. 1 (LXX).

[120] Cf. Gen. 11. 2-4.

[121] Cf. Gen. 11. 5-9.

[122] Cf. Gen. 11. 28 (Aran's birthplace "the land of the Chaldees": so LXX for "Ur of the Chaldees") and 11. 31 (Abram departs from Ur: same readings as in verse 28).

[123] "tenth generation": genealogy of Abraham, n. 108.

"rightful due . . .": cf. c. 21 (blessing of Sem).

[124] "going all about": the manuscript has *šurj goyr*, "was (existing) around"; read *šurj gayr* (= περιεπάτει).

"was growing faint and beginning to desist from the discovery": *tkaranayr ew kasēr i giwtēn*; probably *tkaranayr ew kasēr* "was-weakening and was-desisting" is a doublet for a single Greek word, and "was failing" might serve as an English rendering provided it was understood in the sense "falling off"; but AR* "and failed to find out" does not render the text correctly.

This representation of Abraham as going about seeking God and like to fail is founded on Jewish tradition; cf. e. g. N. Bonwetsch's commentary on his edition of *Apocalypsis Abrahami* (*Studien zur Geschichte der Theologie und Kirche* 1. 1, Leipzig 1897) 42-48.

" through the Word ": all theophanies being of the Son, cf. Introd. § 31.

[125] Gen. 12. 1. The following " and dwell there " seems to be presented as part of the quotation, but is not in the text quoted.

[126] " *while he was seventy years old, and had a wife, *and while she herself was of a ripe age ": the Armenian text of EP*, and all the translations, have the order of clauses: " while he himself was of a ripe old age, and while he was seventy years old, and had a wife." In making my translation I emended the order to that here given, " he himself " now becoming " she herself " (Armenian does not distinguish the genders), and the use of the emphatic " herself " being so accounted for. On collating with the Armenian text of PO*, I find that it gives this emended order. As there is no note indicating editorial emendation, it is to be concluded that this change represents a correction of the text printed in EP*, and that the manuscript had the order given by PO*. The translation, however, which accompanies the text in PO*, follows the old order.

Abram's age at the time is given as seventy-*five* years in Gen. 12. 4; Sarai was ten years younger than her husband (cf. Gen. 17. 17) and still, seemingly, young enough to be coveted by Pharaoh (Gen. 12. 15 on) and — when she was ninety — by Abimelech (Gen. 20. 2).

Abraham's departure: Gen. 12. 4 f.

[127] " seven nations, descended from Cham ": cf. n. 106.

to thee . . . : a composite quotation, formed apparently out of Gen. 12. 7 (*to thy seed will I give this land*), 13. 15 (*all the land which thou seest, I will give to thee, and to thy seed for ever*), 17. 8 (*I will give to thee, and to thy seed after thee* [so LXX], *the land of thy sojournment, all the land of Chanaan for a perpetual possession*).

[128] Cf. Gen. 15. 13-16; Acts 7. 6 f.

Sagarda says (S* 678 n. 23) that Harnack thought this passage might be an interpolation. I do not know where Harnack expressed this opinion; not in his commentary in EP*. In any case, there seems to be no reason for such a view. As Sagarda points out, the passage is accounted for by Gen. 15. 13.

" fourth generation ": *sic* (so Gen. 15. 16, and cf. the genealogy Levi — Caath — Amram — Moses and Aaron, in Exod. 6. 16-20).

[129] " splendour ": not simply " glory " or the like, because the reference is to the brightness of the stars; cf. c. 35 (n. 174).

Look up . . . : Gen. 15. 5. Cf. Rom. 4. 18.

[130] Gen. 15. 6, quoted in Rom. 4. 3.

[131] Rom. 4. 11 (*a seal of the justice of the faith which he had, being uncircumcised*); cf. Gen. 17. 10 f.

*a seal of the *justice*: the manuscript has "a seal of uncircumcision," but emendation to agreement with Rom. 4. 11 seems called for, though EP* attempts to render the text as it stands, and so too PO*: "as a seal of his faith of uncircumcision which he had in uncircumcision." If we retain "uncircumcision" it seems to me that we should render simply "a seal of his faith of uncircumcision," and reject the then repetitive "which he had in uncircumcision" as a gloss, based on Rom. 4. 11, added to explain the curious expression "faith of uncircumcision," and later mistakenly integrated into the text.

"seal": cf. n. 22.

[132] Cf. Acts 7. 8; and Gen. 21. 1-4 (Isaac), 25. 25 (Jacob).

[133] "the Spirit assigning to them the inheritance": *Hogwoyn žaṙanduṭ'iwn bažanec'eloy i nosa*, a "genitive absolute"; not simply e. g. "as the inheritance of the Spirit divided among them" (PO*): the inheritance did not simply come to them, but was definitely "assigned" to Isaac (not Ishmael) and Jacob (not Esau), cf. Rom. 9. 7-13, and Gen. 21. 12 (Isaac), 25. 23, Mal. 1. 2 (Jacob) there quoted. "The Spirit" assigned the inheritance, that is, in the Scripture, the work of the Spirit (n. 65 to Introd.), cf. "saying through the Holy Spirit in the Scriptures" of the testimony to Abraham, above, and the quotation which here immediately follows.

the God of Abraham . . . : Exod. 3. 6 etc.

[134] Cf. Acts 7. 8; Gen. 35. 23-26.

[135] Cf. Acts 7. 11-15; Gen. 41. 54, 45. 5 f.

[136] "seventy-five souls": cf. Acts 7. 14; Gen. 46. 27; Exod. 1. 1-5 (the "seventy" of Douay for Gen. 46. 27 follows the reading peculiar to the Massoretic text for that one place).

"as the oracle had said": that is, in Gen. 15. 13 (Acts 7. 6), referred to in the preceding chapter.

"four hundred years": cf. Gen. 15. 13; in Exod. 12. 40 the length of stay is given as having been four hundred and thirty years.

"six hundred and sixty thousand": the number is given as 603,550 in Exod. 38. 25 (LXX reference varies according to edition; Rahlfs 39. 3) and Num. 1. 45 f.; and this represents only "men able to bear arms."

[137] Cf. Exod. 7-10 (first nine plagues), 11-12 (tenth plague).

[138] Institution of Passover, Exod. 12.

"the Passover": the manuscript has *kirk'*, apparently an attempt to render Πάσχα in the sense "Passion," as if connected with πάσχειν "suffer" (Armenian *krel*); cf. last paragraph of n. 30 to Introd. The word (Hebrew *pesaḥ*) means "passing-over" in the sense "sparing" = not "visiting" with the plague; can the following expression, "source of freedom," be intended by Irenaeus as an explanation of the meaning of the name? With this interpretation of the word "Pasch" cf. the Georgian gloss on the same word: after Luke 2. 41 (... *at the feast of the Pasch*) the Djrutch and Parkhal MSS add: *which is the Passion*.

[139] Cf. Exod. 14.

[140] Cf. Exod. 20. 1-17, 24. 12, 31. 18.

tablets . . . : Exod. 31. 18.

"'finger of God' is that which is put forth by the Father in the Holy Spirit"; or ". . . from the Father . . ."; or ". . . He who is put forth . . ."; or ". . . (in)to the Holy Spirit"; or, with a slight emendation: ". . . He who is put forth by the Father, the Holy Spirit": *matn Astucoy ē ayn or jgeal ē i Hawrēn i Surb Hogin*; the form *jgeal ē* should correspond to a perfect (ἐκτέταται), so expressing the permanent relation of origin. Omission of *i* before *Surb Hogin* gives the sense ". . . is . . . the Holy Spirit."

Vardanian, *HAm.* 24 (1910) 327, takes this last sense; so too PO*, "is the one who proceeds from the Father, the Holy Ghost," which is a modernisation, the verb used not being the later-canonised "proceed." This would make good sense; not only have later Fathers called the Holy Spirit the finger of God (e. g. Ambrose, *De Spir. Sancto* 3. 3, with reference as here to the writing of the Law; Gregory the Great, *Hom. in Ezech.* 1. 10. 20, of Christ's fingers used in healing, referring to the gifts of the Holy Spirit), but in the parallels Luke 11. 20, Matt. 12. 28 "finger" (*if I by the finger of God cast out devils*, Luke) and "spirit" (Matt.) correspond; moreover Barnabas, *Epist.* 14. 2, has "written by the finger of the hand of the Lord in the Spirit," and Ps.-Clement of Rome, *Hom.* 11. 22 and 16. 12, has close parallels with the expression here used by Irenaeus, but with "hand" instead of "finger"; and Irenaeus himself calls the Holy Spirit the hand of God (cf. n. 70 to Introd.).

EP* took the sense ". . . into the Holy Spirit . . ." ("das, was vom Vater zu dem heiligen Geist ausgestreckt ist"), and Bonwetsch (*Theologische Literaturzeitung* 32 [1907] 176), Kunze (*Theologisches Literaturblatt* 28 [1907] 29) and Sagarda (S* 679 n. 24) take this to mean the Word.

Note the juxtaposition "and the commandments . . . ," which suggests that the reference is simply to revelation, through the Holy Spirit, of the Law. The rendering I have adopted for the exegesis of "finger of God" aims at reproducing so far as possible the obscurity of the original and allowing the same interpretations.

[141] Tabernacle: cf. Exod. 25 f.

Likeness of heavenly things: cf. end of c. 9 (n. 61) and Heb. 8. 5 (quoted in n. 61).

Prophecy: cf. Heb. 10. 1 (*the law having a shadow of the good things to come*) and in similar sense Col. 2. 17, etc.

Furniture: cf. Exod. 25 and 27; tablets in the ark, cf. Heb. 9. 4 (and 3 Kings 8. 9 = 2 Paral. 5. 10).

[142] Priesthood to Aaronites: cf. Exod. 28. 1; Num. 3. 10. Of the tribe of Levi, cf. genealogy, n. 128.

Levites: cf. Num. 1. 48-53, 3. 5-12.

"for the character and behaviour of those . . .": literally "how and in what wise they should be. . . ." This closing passage may be intended as a description of the book of Leviticus: cf. Introd. § 38.

[143] Cf. Num. 13. 2-21.

[144] Change of name: cf. Num. 13. 17 ("Jesus" represents the form used in the LXX: "Jesus" and "Josue" represent two Greek forms of the same Hebrew name); and Exod. 23. 21 *My name is in him* (= in Josue), quoted in the parallel passage, Justin, *Dial.* 75 (cf. also *ibid.* 113, and Barnabas, *Epist.* 12. 8 f.).

"and so it came to pass": or *eiewn* = ὅπερ ἐγένετο (-περ > -n), which some have taken as qualifying "the name," and so been forced to render abusively "which was given."

[145] Cf. Num. 13. 22-14. 4.

"They did return . . . but (some of the envoys)": The manuscript has *isk k'anzi . . . ew*, literally "But since . . . and."

"Titans": *erkracink'* = γηγενεῖς, literally "earthborn," a common appellation of the giants (cf. n. 99).

"so that they could hold the land," so the manuscript; "they" refers of course to the inhabitants. Others insert a negative, and understand "so that they could not take the land," "they" being the Israelites. The verb is *unel* = ἔχειν, "have, hold."

[146] Cf. Num. 13. 33.

[147] Cf. Num. 14. 6-9.

[148] "punishing": *ožbilov*, a hapax legomenon (postclassical form, passive, of gerund of verb *ožbel*) whose meaning can only be conjectured from the context.

[149] Cf. Num. 14. 26-38.

"not knowing their right hand from their left" = commonly, "not able to distinguish good and evil," not morally responsible.

[150] Cf. Num. 26. 3, 26. 63, 36. 13.

[151] Account of Deuteronomy, cf. Introd. § 38. The name is derived from the Greek δεύτερος "second" and νόμος "law." The various points mentioned by Irenaeus can be referred, more or less, to Deuteronomy, *passim* (Weber L* gives references, of sorts), though it would be difficult to find the alleged "many prophecies."

[152] From Deut. 32. 49, with considerable omission. The following words, "for thou shalt not bring my people into the land," also seem to be intended as part of the quotation, but are not in the Old Testament (v. 52 however has *thou shalt not enter into it* = into the land).

[153] *died* . . . : from Deut. 34. 5, with omission.

Succession of Josue: Deut. 34. 5-9. (Form "Jesus," cf. c. 27, n. 144.)

[154] "dividing the Jordan" (*hatanelov zYordanan*): or simply "crossing the Jordan" (so Faldati); cf. Jos. 3.14-17.

"seven nations": cf. n. 106.

Josue's occupation of Chanaan: cf. Jos. 2-11.

"distributed it among the people; here is Jerusalem": (for Josue's distribution of the land, cf. Jos. 12); I have supplied "it" and "is." Some have taken *asti Erusalēmn* as τὴν ἐνταῦθα Ἱερουσαλήμ ("distributed among the people the earthly *or* the temporal Jerusalem," literally ". . . the Jerusalem here"), but this would be *zasti Erusalēm(n)*; the text's *asti Erusalēmn* can only stand for ἐνταῦθα ἡ Ἱερουσαλήμ. Besides, Jerusalem can hardly be said to have been "distributed."

Tabernacle on the pattern of heavenly things: cf. end of c. 9 n. 61) and Heb. 8. 5 (quoted in n. 61).

[155] Pre-existence and birth of Son: cf. n. 205.

"in the end of this age" (*i vaxčan yawitenis*): cf. n. 41.

resuming anew . . . : Eph. 1. 10; cf. Introd. § 36.

[156] Cf. A.H. 3. 18. 7, 3. 19. 1, 3. 20. 2.

This sentence corresponds to Fr. 25 of the *Armenische Irenaeusfragmente* published by Jordan in TU 36. 3. Fr. 6, 13, and 20 contain in addition the following sentence. For our texts's *Ard zmardn miaworec'uyc' ěnd Astuac ew hasarakut'iwn miabanut'ean Astucoy ew mardoy gorceac'* ("So He united man with God and brought about a communion of God and man"), Fr. 20 ("Stephen the Philosopher") has simply *or ekn ew miaworut'iwn gorceac' Astucoy ew*

mardoyn ("who came and brought about unity of God and man "),
while Fr. 6 (from the Monophysite "Seal of Faith") has *uremn ew
mi bnut'iwn Astucoy ew mardoy gorceac'* ("then also He brought
about one nature of God and man," but *uremn* "then, so" should
perhaps be emended into *or ekn* "who came," as Fr. 20). Note the
ease of the corruption *miabanut'iwn* ("concord") > *mi bnut'iwn*
"one nature." Other variants are unimportant.

"communion" (*hasarakut'iwn miabanut'ean,* "community of concord"): cf. Introd. § 36.

"in any other wise": the text has *ayl awrinakabar inč'.* As was
pointed out by Akinean, *HAm.* 24 (1910) 207 n. 2, *aylawrinakabar*
is to be read, a single compound word; hence there is no point in
Barthoulot's objection (PO* 771 n. 4) that since *ayl* ("other")
cannot qualify an adverb, *ayl* must here be "but," and the sense
"we could receive only figuratively." Nor is the English version of
PO* justified, "we could not receive legally . . . in any other way";
the connection with *awrēnk'* ("law") is purely etymological.

[157] Cf. Introd. § 36.
"that we might be taken into full communication with incorruptibility": *zi ēst amenayn masin kc'ordut'iwn ĕndunelut'ean ařc'uk'
zanapakanut'eann,* literally "that we might according to every part
take communication of acceptance with respect to incorruptibility."

[158] Cf. Rom. 5. 12 and 19.
"being all implicated in the first *formation of Adam, we were
bound to death through [the]disobedience" (sc. of Adam): a doubtful rendering of *i naxastelcec'elumn Adamay amenek'in šalealk'
kapec'ak' ĕnd mahu i jeřn taralsut'eann.* Here *naxastelcec'elumn* as
it stands can only be an unusually-formed locative, giving the sense,
word for word: "in the first-formed (πρωτόπλαστος) Adam all implicated we were bound . . ." (so BK*, L*, and both versions of PO*).
The same unusual form *naxastelcec'elumn* occurs again below in
this chapter in a context where, as it stands, it can be understood only
as a dative, an irregular use of *-um* in such a word (n. 161). Hence
it seems not unlikely that the text is in both places corrupt. The later
passage is set right by understanding a noun of action in the accusative (a misreading of *-umn?*), and the same sense fits the present
passage. The word was so interpreted in the version of EP*, and
AR* and F* return to this interpretation. In either case the participle "implicated" (*šalealk'* — note that it is declined) should be
taken, as F* takes it, with what precedes ("implicated in the first-
formation"), not along with the following word to give a "doublet"

šatealk' kapec'ak' ("we were [implicated and] bound"). With the emended interpretation this grouping is called for also by the sense.

"implicated in the first formation": that is, integrated into the human race, as descendants of Adam, not "another formation"; cf. later in this chapter (n. 161) and the following two chapters (n. 163, 166).

"the bonds of death . . . to be loosed": more literally simply "death . . . to be undone" (*lucanil mahun*, with late form *-il*).

159 "it was necessarily through the body that it (= death) should be done away with and let man go free from its oppression": *i jeřn marmnoy part ew aržan ēr xap'anumn ařeal i bac' t'olul zmardn i harstaharut'enēn iwrmē*. A rendering "it was necessary that by suffering destruction in the flesh it let man go free . . ." or the like, though it would suit Rom. 6. 6 *that the body of sin may be destroyed*, does not do justice to the syntax of the opening words of the text, or to the sense of the verb which I render "do away with" (*xap'anumn ařeal* may be rendered "being put a stop to," and probably corresponds to ἀναιρεθέντα in the original). Still less can one admit the rendering which changes the subject to Christ: "it was necessary that by suffering destruction in His flesh He liberate man from its oppression"; apart from the syntactical difficulties and the sense attributed to the verb, the possessive in "its oppression" is *iwr*, reflexive, so that the subject ought to be "death." Cf. also the following sentence, "sin, destroyed by means of that same flesh. . . ."

160 John 1. 14.

161 Cf. Rom. 6. 6 (*our old man is crucified with Him, that the body of sin may be destroyed, to the end that we may serve sin no longer*). Tixeront remarks (PO* 772 n. 1) that this chapter contains a résumé of Irenaeus's Christology and Soteriology as exposed in *Adversus haereses*.

"took up the same first formation for an Incarnation": *znoyn naxastelcec'elumn zmarmnut'iwn ěnkalaw* (which calls for emendation—cf. n. 158): that is, became man by reproducing the creation of Adam and integrating Himself into the race of Adam; cf. n. 158 above, and n. 163, 166 below, and what follows.

"join battle on behalf of His forefathers": because He was a member of the human race, His battle was that of "His forefathers," of the race descended from Adam. Cf. A.H. 3. 18. 6: erat enim homo pro patribus certans; similarly A.H. 5. 21. 1, of the war with Satan. With the end of this chapter and the whole of the next there is a close parallel in A.H. 3. 21. 10.

[162] Gen. 2. 5.

[163] Cf. n. 158, 161 above, and 166 below; and A.H. 5. 1. 2. Christ could not have redeemed us unless He had summed up afresh in Himself the original formation of Adam (εἰ μὴ τὴν ἀρχαίαν πλάσιν τοῦ 'Αδὰμ εἰς ἑαυτὸν ἀνεκεφαλαιώσατο).

"summing up afresh": cf. Introd. § 36 ("recapitulation").

"reproduced the scheme of his incarnation . . . copy the incarnation of Adam": more literally "took up the same dispensation (οἰκονομία) of incarnation with him . . . show the likeness of incarnation with respect to Adam."

"man might be made, as was written in the beginning . . .": elic'i grec'ealn i skzbann mardn; note that grec'eal and mard both bear the article; hence not "that He might become the man written in the beginning," but "what was written (grec'ealn = τὸ γεγραμμένον) in the beginning might be realised, man . . ." (or "he who was written [ὁ γεγραμμένος] in the beginning might come into being, man . . ."?)

according to the image and likeness of God: Gen. 1. 26 etc., with Θεοῦ for ἡμῶν.

Cf. Col. 3. 10 (the new man, *who is renewed unto knowledge, according to the image of Him that created him*) etc.

[164] "man resuscitated by life received life": i verstin arcarceal mardn kenawk' ĕnkalaw zkeansn. I take i verstin together as "again," so that mardn becomes the subject; others have taken i as governing mardn, "again" being verstin alone, so giving the sense "in the man resuscitated by life he received life" (not "he received the life [that is] in the man . . ."; that would be zi verstin. . .). This interpretation seems to me less likely, in spite of John 1. 4 (*in Him was life*) and 1 John 5. 11 f. (*God hath given us eternal life. And this life is in His Son. He that hath the Son, hath life*).

(i) verstin arcarceal means "rekindled"; kenawk' "by life" is difficult to interpret. Perhaps it should be taken with the following verb ("by life received life"), but more probably it should be taken with the preceding participle (although it is separated from it by mardn), so giving "resuscitated by life," an expression in which, in English, "by life" might be omitted as superfluous.

"Again" is i verstin, not verstin alone, e. g. in the preceding chapter's "summing up afresh" (i verstin glxaworelov) and twice later in this chapter, "seek back" (i verstin xndrel) and "to be restored" (i verstin glxaworeln) and elsewhere in the Proof; but verstin alone is also found.

The difficulty, however, in the interpretation of this sentence is to determine the identity of "(the) man resuscitated": the human race, or Christ? The statement is applicable to either, but it seems to me that the reference is to the human race, although to be sure represented in the concrete by Christ (cf. n. 166 below). In this chapter it is *Eve* who is "restored" in the Mother of God, and Adam in Christ; the comparison is no longer, as in the previous chapter, with the earth whence Adam's frame was taken, and in any case he did not receive life from the earth, but it was breathed by God into the frame taken from the earth; and Eve is *the mother* not of Adam, but *of all the living* (Gen. 3. 20). Nevertheless, the chapter is directed against the view of Marcion and others that Christ was not in the proper sense of the word born of the Virgin, but "became incarnate" by a special act (cf. Introd. § 31). In general the "incarnation" of those views was only a seeming one, but the argument here presented by Irenaeus would hold against a genuine incarnation by a special act, not birth of the human race.

[165] Christ came to seek the lost sheep: cf. parables of lost sheep and of Good Shepherd, and Matt. 15. 24, Luke 19. 10.

"it was man who was lost": *koruseal mardn ēr*; Weber is probably right in suggesting (L* 59 note i) that *oč'xar* has dropped out after *koruseal*, and that the text should be "and man was the lost sheep" (cf. PO*: "the lost sheep was man"). Cf. 1 Peter 2. 25; Isa. 53. 6. Irenaeus often refers to the *plasma* of humanity as the lost sheep; so A.H. 3. 19. 3, 3. 23. 1, 3. 23. 8, 5. 12. 3, 5. 15. 2; and cf. 5. 14. 2 quoted at the end of the following note.

[166] "He did not become some other formation": *ayl stełcuac inč' oč' ełeal*. Alternatively "there was not made some other formation" (AR*), which agrees with the close parallel A.H. 3. 21. 10 (quoted below); but the construction of the sentence is there different, and here the version I have given is defensible both in syntax, keeping the same subject, and in sense, though the expression may seem curious. "Formation" means not only "process of formation" but also "product of formation" (*plasma*, used constantly by Irenaeus in this sense); the sense would thus be, that Christ, by reproducing the (process of) formation, integrated Himself into the same (product of) formation, that is, into the human race, which He so saved; otherwise He would, as it were, have constituted in Himself *another* "formation" or human race; cf. A.H. quoted below.

"He likewise, of her that was descended from Adam, preserved the likeness of formation": a doubtful version of *i nmanē yaynmanē, or yAdamay zazgn unēr, znmanut'iwn stełcuacin paheac'*. The difficulty here is in the expression *i nmanē yaynmanē*. It seems to me possible, if not very probable, that *nmanē* is not, as has always been supposed, the pronoun (*na*) but the adjective *nman*, and that *i nmanē* renders literally ἐξ ἴσου, "on the same footing," a suitable enough expression in the context. Hence I render "likewise," which may also stand as a free paraphrase if *nmanē* is the pronoun. The following "of her" supposes that *yaynmanē* refers to the Mother of God; which is far from certain.

In A.H. 3. 21. 10 Irenaeus explains why God, in reconstituting in Christ the formation of Adam, did not, as for Adam, take clay, but formed Him from the Virgin; this was ἵνα μὴ ἄλλη πλάσις γένηται, μηδὲ ἄλλο τὸ σωζόμενον ᾖ, ἀλλ᾽ αὐτὸς ἐκεῖνος ἀνακεφαλαιωθῇ, τηρουμένης τῆς ὁμοιότητος ("so that there should not be made a new formation, and what was saved should not be something else, but that same one should be recapitulated, the likeness being preserved"). Here "that same one" seems to be Adam, since the masculine is used; but in our text we can hardly understand "He who was descended from Adam preserved from that same one (= Adam) . . . ," because in the original the pronouns precede the mention of Adam. AR* has "in that same which had its descent from Adam He preserved the likeness of the (first) formation," here, as in the preceding clause, perhaps being influenced by the parallel just quoted.

If *nmanē* be taken as the pronoun we have for *i nmanē yaynmane* literally ἐξ αὐτ- ἐξ ἐκείν- (gender uncertain), and it might seem that the meaning was "of (from) that same one," the pronouns being taken together as in the αὐτὸς ἐκεῖνος of the passage just quoted. Not only, however, does this interpretation disregard the repetition of the preposition (which may easily enough be disregarded) and suppose *nmanē* to be a misrendering of emphatic αὐτός (for *nmin*); but it is not easy to determine the identity of "the same one that was descended from Adam," "out of" whom or which Christ is said to have "preserved the likeness of formation." If the reference is to the Mother of God, then why "same," which seems to be opposed to "other" and refer to the identity of formation? If on the other hand the reference is to the human race, the syntax is strange ("*out of* that same one . . . He preserved the likeness of formation"; AR* seeks to smooth the expression by rendering "in the same one" instead of "out of the same one"). Moreover the context suggests strongly that there is a reference to the Mother of God (cf. end of n. 164).

This difficulty is removed by taking into account the repetition of the preposition, and placing a comma between the two expressions, though if *nmanē* be taken as the pronoun the sense still demands that it be regarded as a misrendering due to neglect of the article with αὐτός in the original. The emendation gives: *i nmin, yaynmanē,* "out of the same one, of the one that was descended from Adam ...," where, if the second pronoun be taken as an original feminine, "of *her* that was descended from Adam," the second expression uses the preposition in a natural sense, and the first preposition is explained by the apposition of the two expressions. This is perhaps the most likely explanation of the text, but I leave "likewise" in the version, partly to allow for the possibility that *i nmanē* = ἐξ ἴσου, and partly because even if the text be emended to *i nmin* = ἐκ τοῦ αὐτοῦ [sc. πλάσματος — or ἐκ τῆς αὐτῆς sc. πλάσεως), "likewise" still serves well enough, by conveying the general sense of an expression hardly translatable straightforwardly into English.

With the doctrine cf. A.H. 5. 14. 1, where it is said that Christ would not have become flesh and blood, but that flesh and blood needed to be saved, and that had He not become flesh and blood according to the "original formation," He would not have "summed up all things in Himself"; and A.H. 5. 14. 2: Si autem ob aliam quandam dispositionem Dominus incarnatus est, ex altera substantia carnem attulit, non ergo in semetipsum recapitulatus est (se) hominem. . . . Nunc autem quod fuit qui perierat homo, hoc salutare factum est Verbum . . . non alteram quandam, sed illam principalem Patris plasmationem in se recapitulans, exquirens id quod perierat.

[167] " to be restored " (= " recapitulated "): cf. Introd. § 36.

Parallel Adam-Christ: cf. 1 Cor. 15. 53, 2 Cor. 5. 4; A.H. 3. 22. 3. Eve-Mary: cf. A.H. 3. 22. 4, 5. 19. 1; Justin, *Dial.* 100.

[168] In PO* the chapter-division departs here from that of Harnack, this first sentence of c. 34 being printed as the end of c. 33. This change is doubtless due to the translation: " and the transgression, which was by means of a tree, should be put away ... ," continuing the purpose-construction of the end of c. 33. This is however a mistranslation, for the verb is indicative ("was undone" *lucaw*, not continuing the subjunctive of "should undo" *lucc'ē*).

" by the obedience of the tree, obedience to God whereby ... ": literally " by the obedience of the tree, obeying which to God ... " ("internal accusative"). Others have rendered " by the tree of obedience,"but the version I have given suits better both the parallel "sin which was wrought through the tree" and the taking-up of "obedience" by the relative. In the strictest Armenian *i jeřn p'aytin hlut'ean* is indeed as I have translated "by the obedience of the tree," and not "by the tree of obedience," since it is the qualifying genitive that should have the article; but this rule, never strict, is commonly ignored in our version.

"evil is disobedience to God, as obedience to God is good": cf. A.H. 4. 39. 1.

[169] "the Word says": cf. n. 65 to Introd.

"it was because they told the future that they were 'prophets'": not "they were 'prophets' in order to foretell the future"; the verb is indicative (*zi . . . patmein*). Cf. A.H. 4. 20. 5: prophetia est praedicatio futurorum. Greek προφήτης "prophet," derived from πρό-φημι understood as "fore-tell," that is, tell beforehand. In fact "prophet" originally meant the "mouthpiece" of an oracle, the verbal sense being not praedicere but praedicare; in Hebrew also the word "prophet" (*nābī'*) meant not necessarily one who foretold the future, but one commissioned by God to speak to men.

I refuse not . . . : Isa. 50. 5 f.

[170] "obedience, whereby He obeyed unto death . . .": cf. Phil. 2. 8 ("whereby": again an "internal accusative").

[171] "in His invisible form": the text has not "His" but simply the ("third-person") article; not simply "in *an* invisible form, but with contrast of the invisible and visible forms; cf. A.H. 5. 18. 3.

Cf. Eph. 3. 18: *the breadth and length and height and depth.*

"in these": that is, in these "dimensions"; not "in it" (that is, the world), as AR* renders. "World" in Armenian is singular, and the plural can hardly be explained as an error due to the use of a plural expression for "world" in Greek.

"imprinted in the form of a cross on the universe" (PO*: "putting the sign of the cross on all things"): cf. Plato, *Tim.* 36 b-c, paraphrased by Justin, *Apol.* 60. 1, as ἐχίασεν αὐτὸν (= the world-soul) ἐν τῷ παντί (Justin says Plato must have taken this from Moses — cf. Num. 21. 8 f., the brazen serpent on the cross); cf. also A.H. 5. 17. 4 (and 2. 24. 4, on the "five summits" of the cross), and Justin, *Apol.* 55.

[172] "to bring to light the universality of His cross": more literally "to bring to light His cross-sharing with the universe": *yerewelis acel zamenaynis zxač'akc'ut'iwnn iwr*, rendered by Lüdtke, *Zeitschrift für Kirchengeschichte* 35 (1914) 256, εἰς τὸ φανερὸν ἄγειν τὴν τῷ παντὶ σταυροκοινωνίαν αὐτοῦ. Failure to realise that *yerewelis acel* is simply

εἰς τὸ φανερὸν ἄγειν has led to such renderings as "to set upon all things visible the sharing of His cross" (AR*), where *zamenaynis* is referred, in defiance to syntax, to *yerewelis*.

"in order to show openly through His visible form that activity of His": *zi znergorcutʻiwnn iwr zayn i yerewelwoǰn cʻucʻcʻē i jeřn ereweli jewoyn.* "His visible form": the text has simply "the visible form"; cf. "His (for the) invisible form" above (preceding note). Again, *i yerewelwoǰn* is simply ἐν τῷ φανερῷ "openly," not "on visible things" (AR*).

For "activity" W. Bousset, *Zeitschrift für neutestamentliche Wissenschaft* 14 (1913) 274 n. 1, suggested "brightness" (because of the following "makes bright the height"), supposing a misreading in the Greek whereby ἐνάργειαν became ἐνέργειαν.

[173] Cf. Ecclus. 24. 6-9: *I (= Wisdom) made that in the heavens there should rise light that never faileth. . . . I dwelt in the highest places. . . . I alone have compassed the circuit of heaven, and have penetrated into the bottom of the deep . . . and have stood in all the earth and in every people*; and *ibid.* 44 f.: *I make doctrine to shine forth to all as the morning light. . . . I will penetrate to all the lower parts of the earth.*

"holds the deep": the verb is *šarunakel* "contain, conserve."

"navigating": the verb is *nawastel* = κυβερνᾶν "pilot, steer." PO* renders "sails through," and AR* "steers across," but surely the sense is "guiding." In c. 39 the same verb is used in a context where "guiding" seems to be the only possible sense, but PO* retains "sail through" with bizarre effect (cf. n. 192).

"calling in all the dispersed . . .": cf. John 12. 32: *And I, if I be lifted up from the earth, will draw all things to myself*; 11. 51 f.: *that Jesus should die for the nation, and not only for the nation, but to gather together in one the children of God, that were dispersed.*

[174] Promise to Abraham: cf. Gen. 15. 5.

"lights in the world": referring to the brightness of the stars, cf. c. 24 (n. 129); cf. Matt. 5. 14 (*you are the light of the world*) and Phil. 2. 15 (*among whom you shine as lights in the world*). Cf. A.H. 4. 5. 3, where Phil. 2. 15 is quoted in exegesis of Gen. 15. 5.

[175] Gen. 15. 6, quoted in the same argument in Rom. 4. 3, Gal. 3. 6; cf. James 2. 23.

[176] Hab. 2. 4, as quoted in Rom. 1. 17; Gal. 3. 11 (and cf. Heb. 10. 38).

[177] Rom. 4. 13, but not accurately.

[178] 1 Tim. 1. 9.

[179] Cf. Rom. 3. 21 f.: *but now without the law the justice of God is made manifest, being witnessed to by the law and the prophets, even the justice of God, by faith of Jesus Christ. . . .*

"through the faith of Him to whom witness was borne": *i jer̄n hawatoc'n, vkayec'eloyn.* AR*: "by faith, which is witnessed to"; similarly PO* and BK*, but L*: per fidem testificati. The version of AR* PO* BK* supposes emendation of *vkayec'eloyn* to *vkayec'eloc'(n).* L* however is surely right in dropping the comma and keeping *vkayec'eloyn* (cf. "by faith of Jesus Christ," Rom. 3. 22 quoted above; and that our faith is faith in "Him to whom witness was borne by the law and the prophets" is the main thesis of the *Proof*).

[180] Promise made to David: cf. 2 Sam. 7. 12 f.: *I will raise up thy seed after thee, which shall proceed out of thy bowels, and I will establish his kingdom; he shall build a house to my name, and I will establish his kingdom for ever.*

"from the fruit of his bowels": the text has *i ptłoy orovaynē nora*, and as this can hardly be an instance of the idiom whereby a genitive is sometimes replaced by an apposition, the literal sense should be "from his belly of fruit" (but cf. n. 343 for a similar case, there taken as a scribal error). In c. 64 the same inversion is found (*i ptłoy orovaynē k'ummē*, "from thy belly of fruit"). In the parallel expressions later in this chapter it is uncertain whether this inversion is intended, since the genitive and ablative of each of the three nouns involved are formally indistinguishable (*i ptłoy mijoy, i ptłoy erikamanc'*). I have given all these expressions their normal form, and so here (and in c. 64) "from the fruit of his (" the," below, and "thy," c. 64) bowels," as if the reading were *orovayni* (and in c. 64 *orovayni k'oyoy*), since in the parallel passage A.H. 3. 21. 5 we have ἐκ καρποῦ τῆς κοιλίας αὐτοῦ, "de fructu ventris" (similarly 3. 10. 4, 3. 16. 2; but 3. 21. 9 "de ventre David"), "de fructu lumborum eius," "de fructu renum eius"; and in any case the reading here and in c. 64 can only be a corruption, since had the Greek employed such an inversion the order of words would have been different, as the possessive should then go with "fruit," not with "bowels"; this objection does not apply to the expression later in this chapter — cf. the following note — whence the suggestion there made of a possible origin of the corruption.

"bowels": the word so rendered (by Douay in the passage quoted above; I have kept Douay's word) is *orovayn* = κοιλία "belly," a word which may be used in the present connection — as here — of a man, but which is in such uses normally understood as "womb"; hence the argument developed in the following sentence.

¹⁸¹ "from the fruit of the bowels," "... loins," "... reins": the text has "from the fruit's bowels" (cf. preceding note); here however the omission of the possessive makes the phrase readily intelligible, the most natural sense being "from the womb of the fruit," which fits the argument; doubtless the corruption began in this place and was extended to the other places in order to bring them into conformity. As was remarked in the last note, the other two expressions are capable, in their Armenian form, of being understood as "from the loins (reins) of the fruit."

"separately and specially": that is, "precisely," but I render literally because the same expression is repeated later in the sentence in a context where "precise" is impossible.

"of a woman," "*of a man": clearly the opposition called for by the argument; hence with Weber, *Theologische Quartalschrift* 91 (1909) 560, read *aṙn cenund* ("birth of a man") in place of the text's *aṙ i cenund* ("with regard to birth"). In the parallel A.H. 3. 21. 5 the corresponding expressions are: quod est proprium virginis praegnantis, quod est proprium viri generantis et mulieris conceptionem facientis. In the *Proof*, however, Irenaeus does not go so far as to say that "from the fruit of thy bowels" is of itself proper to *virgin* birth, but only that the choice of that phrase rather than one of the others points to virgin birth, the phrase itself being proper to birth of a woman.

¹⁸² Cf. Luke 1. 32 f. (Gabriel to Mary): *the Lord God shall give unto Him the throne of David His father ... and of His kingdom there shall be no end.*

¹⁸³ "In such wise ... was His triumph of our redemption": *ayspēs šk'akoxēr zp'rkut'iwnn mer*, more literally "thus was He gloriously marching-over our salvation."

¹⁸⁴ "summing up": cf. Introd. § 36.

"to be born *through* sinfulness": so the text (*i jeṙn melanut'eann cnic'eloc'*), not "in," as AR* renders.

¹⁸⁵ "the creative Word": "creative" = *aruestagēt*, "craftsman" (*aruest* "craft," *-gēt* "versed in") = δημιουργός("demiurge," cf. Gnostic word for the creator, Introd. § 29, and n. 54 thereto). So too EP* "schöpferische"; in PO* "the Master" must mean "the master (-craftsman)." The suggestion that in the present context *aruestagēt* = θαυματουργός "wonder-worker" (*aruest* also = "wonder, miracle"), which accounts for the versions of BK*, L*, F*, and perhaps also

Barthoulot ("fécond en ressources"), seems to me unlikely. In the Armenian of *Adversus haereses*, δημιουργός used substantivally, "Demiurge, Creator," is rendered *ararič'* "maker"; but in 5. 15. 2 and 5. 24. 4 we have *aruestagēt* corresponding to "artifex" of the Latin version's "artifex Verbum."

"put Himself in our position, and in the same situation in which we lost life": an attempt to interpret *i noyn vayrs mez ew i noyn telis elew, yors mek'n linelov korusak' zkeans*, more literally "became in the same place (space) with us and in the same place (situation), in which when we were, we lost life."

[186] "abolished death . . . showed forth the resurrection": cf. Barnabas, *Epist.* 5. 6: "to abolish death and show forth the resurrection from the dead"; and 2 Tim. 1. 10 (quoted at end of n. 42).

first-born from the dead: Col. 1. 18; or *first-begotten of the dead*, Apoc. 1. 5.

[187] Amos 9. 11 (Acts 15. 16); again in *Proof*, with exegesis, c. 62.

[188] "in the triumph": *šk'akoxelov*, cf. n. 183.

"setting us free": *aprec'uc'eal* = σώζων (σώσας etc.), "saving (life)" rather than "making to live" of EP*.

[189] This passage (with the following sentence) is directed against the denials of the genuineness of Christ's birth referred to in the last paragraph of n. 164 above, to c. 33, and opposed by the intervening chapters.

[190] For the argument, cf. 1 Cor. 15. 12-17.

"from the beginning": the text has *i skzbanēk's*; read *iskzbanēk's* = (ἡμεῖς) οἱ ἀπ' ἀρχῆς. . . .

[191] "those who exclude redemption . . . despise also our Lord's birth": the converse of the preceding thesis that rejection of genuine birth excludes redemption. The reference is here to the view that matter was incapable of redemption, the body unable to receive "incorruption" (cf. Introd. § 29, 33, 34, 36). The two views, as Irenaeus here points out, imply each other.

"take the lead of all in heaven": not simply "precede all"; the reference is to Christ's primacy, cf. what follows here and at the beginning of c. 40 (*yamenesean yaṙajasc'i*, cf. "hold the primacy" of Col. 1. 18, quoted c. 40; n. 193).

[192] "as the . . . as the . . . as the . . .": the various rôles in which Christ "takes the lead of all," as first-born (a) of God: the eternal Word, (b) of the Virgin: in His life on earth, (c) from the dead: after His resurrection. Cf. opening sentence of c. 40: true man (= b), God the Mighty (= a), giving incorruptibility (= c).

" Himself in the world making all things perfect by His guidance and legislation": the reference is not to Christ's ministry, which comes under the following heading, but to the Word immanent in creation, cf. end of c. 34. PO* has the bizarre rendering "fulfilled all things, sailed through all and gave a law on the earth"; "sail through" is accounted for by the metaphor used, the verb being *nawastel* = κυβερνᾶν "navigate," cf. n. 173.

" as the first-born of the Virgin": the text has " as He was the first-born of the Virgin," but the sense is clearer without the verb. The rendering " only-begotten " instead of " first-born " not only fails to correspond to the text, but obscures the argument, which is based on the triple " primogeniture " of Christ.

" first-born of the dead": cf. Col. 1. 18, Apoc. 1. 5.

[193] Col. 1. 18.

" hold the primacy": *yamenayni yaṙajac'eal*, cf. " take the lead of all " in the previous chapter (n. 191).

[194] Isa. 9. 6 (LXX 9. 5, but obelised by Origen, hence not in e. g. Rahlfs), quoted again, with exegesis, c. 54 (-55); in c. 56 the passage of Isaias in which the words occur is quoted in a different form, omitting these words.

[195] This section ("calling man back . . . have part in incorruptibility") corresponds to Fr. 7e of the *Armenische Irenaeusfragmente* published by Jordan in TU 36. 3.

" communion," " incorruption": cf. Introd. § 36. Here the first " communion " renders *hasarakut'iwn miabanut'ean*, and the second *hasarakut'iwn* alone.

" calling man back again into communion with God": *i hasarakut'iwn miabanut'ean zmardn andrēn verstin koč'ec'eal Astucoy*. In normal Armenian, though the subject of a participle used as a finite verb or in apposition to a finite verb may be in the genitive, *Astucoy* here can hardly be so taken, since the clause would then seem to be used "absolutely." In the style of the *Proof*, however, it is not impossible that the clause is a rendering of a Greek genitive absolute. But this is unlikely in the present case, as the resulting sentence would be clumsy (" Thus then does the Word . . . hold the primacy, for He is true man . . . and God the Mighty, God having called man back into communion, that by communion with Him . . .").

[196] This sentence summarises the main thesis of the *Proof*.

" He who was preached": cf. section C of the *Proof* (c. 42-85).

" Most High," " Almighty": cf. n. 49.

" Source of all things": in apposition to " Son," not to " Father."

"He who spoke with Moses": cf. c. 44 (n. 211).

"came into Judaea ... of the seed of David and of Abraham": cf. especially c. 63 f.

"God's anointed": ("anointed" = Greek Χριστός) — cf. c. 49 etc.

"showing Himself to be the one who had been preached in advance through the prophets": cf. c. 86: Christ took up and fulfilled the prophecies, so our faith is well-grounded — the chief "proof of the apostolic preaching."

[197] Cf. John 1. 32 f.; Isa. 11. 2 (*the spirit of the Lord shall rest upon Him*).

[198] "Taught by Him and witnesses ... were the apostles": *sora ašakertk' ew vkayk' ... ařak'ealk'n*, literally "His disciples, and witnesses ..." (but this is predicate, "apostles" being the subject, hence I render "taught by Him"), and there is no verb expressed.

"after the descent of the power of the Holy Spirit": the text has simply "after the power of the Holy Spirit," and the word rendered "after" may mean "according to"; but in the context the temporal sense seems called for.

"turning them back from idols and from fornication and from selfish pride": Harnack remarks (EP* 60) that the three vices mentioned were for the early Christians the special characteristics of paganism. "Selfish pride" is my attempt at rendering *awelastac'ut'iwn* = πλεονεξία.

"baptism of water and of the Holy Spirit": cf. John 3. 5.

[199] I am not sure whether this sentence refers to what precedes or to what follows. In either case it is suitably used as a link after the subheading.

[200] "For so (they said) do the faithful keep, when there abides constantly in them the Holy Spirit, who is given by Him in baptism": *k'anzi ayspēs unel zhawatac'ealsn kac'eal mnac'eal i nosa Hogin Surb, or tueal lini i mkrtut'eann i nmanē*. The version given takes *unel* as ἔχειν "keep" used intransitively (a normal use of that word) and infinitive of virtual indirect speech, continued from the end of the preceding chapter, hence I add "(they said)." There is no need to render "so the faithful *ought* to keep *themselves*." In A.H. 4. 6. 2 the Latin equivalent "se habere" corresponds to *unel* of the Armenian version (4. 11. 2 in Harvey's division, used in the text as published in TU 35. 2). As the style of our version uses "absolute" constructions I have taken *kac'eal ... Surb* as a "nominative absolute." The alternative, emendation to *zHogin* and rendering "... keep constantly abiding in them the Holy Spirit," is rendered

less likely by the following " and is kept . . ." and by the outline of the argument (the faithful keep fit for resurrection and incorruptibility when the Spirit abides in them, for it is resurrection of this spirit that comes to them). The " by Him " is very strange, but one can hardly render ". . . keep . . . *what* is given by Him " (that is, by the Spirit).

[201] " for it is resurrection of this spirit that comes to the faithful "; sic! (*k'anzi aysr ogwoy yarut'iwn lini hawatac'eloc'n*), not " for it is of (= from, through) this spirit that resurrection comes . . ." or the like. The Armenian translator has here used for " spirit " the word *ogi* (" spirit " in general), not *Hogi* (" Spirit," of the divine Spirit); this formal distinction did not, of course, exist in the Greek.

" when the body receives once more the soul and . . . is raised . . . and brought into . . .": *marmnoy andrēn ĕndunelov zanjnn ew . . . yaruc'eloy ew i nerk's muceloy*, a " genitive absolute " in which the genitive subject is followed first by a gerund (active voice) and then by two genitive participles (passive voice).

[202] Cf. c. 21; " God's promise " seems to mean Noe's blessing of Japheth, Gen. 9. 27.

" in constant obedience ": *kac'eal ansac'eal*, an enigmatic expression. AR* has " standing in readiness," PO* " which was expecting," understanding the participles as referring to " the Church "; this, however, is awkward both syntactically (*i jeřn ekełec'woy ereweal, kac'eal ansac'eal*) and in sense. More likely the reference is to the Gentiles " hearing " (obeying) the call; the " fruit of the calling " is " by obedience to receive." The form of the participles can here be accounted for by supposing the Greek to have had an indefinite singular accusative; but *kac'eal* is still strange.

[203] This introduction, and the conclusion, in c. 86, that the apostolic preaching, and our faith, is true because Christ fulfilled the prophecies, " bracket " the main thesis of the *Proof* (section C), the main " proof of the apostolic preaching," that is, the Old Testament witness to Christ. To this introductory passage there is a very close parallel in Justin, *Apol.* 1. 33.

[204] Perhaps this sentence should be assigned to the end of the preceding chapter; in the text, however, it is run on to what follows (cf. following note).

[205] The text's punctuation would give: " For God is in all things truthful; also that there was born . . . before the world was made. Moses. . . ."

" was born ": *ełew* strictly = ἐγένετο: cf. *ełanel* in c. 48 (n. 238).

For the sense of the expression in the context, cf. later in the present note (under " A Son in the beginning . . .").

" Moses, who was the first to prophesy ": " *qui* primus prophetavit Moyses " (*or*, not *zor*), not " quem . . ." (" whom [= and Him] Moses was the first to prophesy ") as in L*. For Moses as the first prophet, cf. Justin, *Apol*. 1. 32.

" BARESITh . . .": that is, *baresit' bara elovim basan benuam sament'ares*. The first three words correspond to those of Gen. 1. 1, " in the beginning God created " (Massoretic $b^e r\bar{e}$'$s\hat{i}\theta$ bārā' 'ĕlōhîm, or pointed bārēš$\hat{i}\theta$), and the last word seems to correspond to the rest of the verse, " heaven and earth " ('ēθ haššāmayim w^e'ēθ hā'āreṣ). This leaves *basan benuam* to be accounted for. From the translation given, the Hebrew bārā' " created " seems to have been taken as the Aramaic bārā' " son," so *basan* may correspond to " established " and *benuam* to " then," but I am unable to suggest an origin for the words. E. Nestle suggested (*Berliner philologische Wochenschrift* 57 [1907] 134) that Irenaeus may have taken the first word, *baresith*, to mean " a Son in the beginning," and this would account for the order of the opening words of the translation, but the suggestion made above seems more likely. This corrupt reading of Gen. 1. 1, with the corresponding version, is not found outside the *Proof*, although other Fathers have seen in the verse a reference to the Word. So, before Irenaeus, Justin, *Apol*. 1. 59, quotes ἐν ἀρχῇ, and later on says ὥστε λόγῳ Θεοῦ, but this may simply allude to " and God said " of Gen. 1. 3. More clearly Theophilus of Antioch, *Ad Autol*. 2. 10, quotes ἐν ἀρχῇ and a little later takes this as creation ἐν Λόγῳ, and *ibid*. 13, he explains ἐν ἀρχῇ as meaning διὰ τῆς ἀρχῆς. In both Fathers, however, the interpretation is a question of the exegesis of the expression " in the beginning," not of a different reading of the text. Jerome (*Quaest. hebr. in Gen.* on 1. 1) attributes to Aristo, however, the statement that the Hebrew had " in the Son God made."

" of which the translation is ": the Armenian has: " and this, translated into Armenian, means." As the Greek must also have translated the alleged Hebrew, probably only " into Armenian " is not original in this expression. PO* (692 n. 1) has however the curious reflection " the Armenian translator has interpreted ' Bereshit bara'. . . ."

A Son in the beginning God established then heaven and earth: deliberately left unpunctuated, but the only reasonable way to punctuate is to put a comma after " established." In the Armenian " Son " might be nominative or accusative, but the sense is surely " God established a Son." Perhaps Irenaeus might not have approved of such an expression, but doubtless his source understood "God established a Son in the beginning" of the "uttering" of the Word as the first act of creation (not itself a "creation" but the first "moment" of the creation of heaven and earth). The Stoic distinction between the λόγος ἐνδιάθετος and the λόγος προφορικός, taken up by Philo, was adopted also by Christian theologians as a distinction between the Word as eternally with the Father (Λόγος ἐνδιάθετος) and the Word as "uttered" in the beginning (Λόγος προφορικός). So, before Irenaeus, Justin, *Apol.* 2. 6; Tatian, *Orat.* 5; Athenagoras, *Suppl.* 10; Theophilus of Antioch, *Ad Autol.* 2. 10. The doctrine was supported not only by such passages as Prov. 8. 22 f. (Wisdom "brought forth before the hills ") or Ecclus. 24. 5 (*I came out of the mouth of the Most High, the first-born before all creatures*), but also, and especially, on Ps. 44. 1: *My heart hath uttered a good word.* The same doctrine accords with other expressions used by Irenaeus ("ἐγένετο a Son of God . . . before the world was made," above, and " the Son ἐγένετο as a beginning for God before the world was made " below; and γενέσθαι in c. 48 " He came into being long before ") and with his explanation that the " Son " is fitly so called because He " establishes " (c. 5, cf. n. 33), and was general in Irenaeus's time, and held by his chief sources; so it is strange that in A.H. 2. 13. 8 he expresses comparative disapproval of expressions whereby " generationem prolativi hominum verbi transferunt in Dei aeternum Verbum "; and he nowhere clearly propounds the theory. It may be, however, that he held the theory in fact, while objecting to the terminology and to the suggestion that this " utterance " of the Word was the " undeclarable " divine generation, for that of course was not " in the beginning " but eternal. The difference of outlook between the *Proof* and the passage of *Adversus haereses* just referred to would be no greater, on the supposition that Irenaeus is here consciously expounding the substance of the Λόγος προφορικός doctrine, than that between his attitude to Chiliasm in *Adversus haereses* and in the *Proof* (cf. n. 270). In sum, the doctrine is implied in the *Proof*, and we may agree with Loofs (*Theophilus von Antiochien* Adversus Marcionem *und die anderen theologischen Quellen bei Irenaeus*, TU 46. 2. 351) that Irenaeus may well have held it himself, unless one is to agree with Loofs' view that he reproduced what was in his sources in spite of resultant self-contradiction.

[206] Not Jeremias, but a composite quotation from Ps. 109. 3 (*from the womb before the daystar I begot Thee*) and Ps. 71. 17 (*His name*

continueth before the sun). The same two texts are so associated by Justin, *Dial.* 76, and by later Fathers. Cf. J. R. Harris's suggestion that the source was a catena against the Jews (cf. Introd. § 37-38). The composite text and the attribution to Jeremias could then be accounted for by supposing the source to have had, for instance: "Jeremias: *Before I formed Thee in the womb, I knew thee*; also: *from the womb before the daystar I begot Thee; His name continueth before the sun.*" The text attributed correctly to Jeremias (Jer. 1. 5) has been omitted as less suitable for the present purpose, but the two Psalm-texts have been mistakenly supposed to be a single quotation from the same source as the preceding one. The source would not necessarily indicate, or the reader might easily overlook, the source of each text or the division between texts taken from different places. Note that the quotation fits the Λόγος προφορικός doctrine mentioned in the preceding note; and cf. the following note.

²⁰⁷ "again he says": the Armenian has "again He Himself says" (my capitals; *darjeal ink'n asē*), but the "again" and the attribution of the same apocryphal quotation to Jeremias in Lactantius, *Inst. div.* 4. 8, and the ease with which the error arises (it is in fact not infrequent) make it more probable that *ink'n* "Himself" (= αὐτός) is an error for (ὁ αὐτός =) *noyn* "the same" (that is, Jeremias).

Harris (*Testimonies*, vol. 1. 73) suggests that the quotation in Lactantius (ref. above) may have its origin in an apocopation of a variant of Ps. 71. 17 (quoted in preceding note): "beatus qui erat antequam nasceretur (sol)," the reference to Jeremias being accounted for in the manner described in the preceding note. The juxtaposition in the *Proof* of the Psalm-quotation and this alleged corruption of it makes this suggestion less likely to be correct.

Note that the sense is "before He was made man," not "before man was made" (the text has *yaṙaj k'an zelaneln mard nma*).

²⁰⁸ "was as a beginning for God": more literally "became *or* was made a beginning ..." (*elew skizbn* = ἐγένετο ἀρχή); cf. n. 205 (under *A Son* ...).

"in that we knew Him not": literally "who knew Him not"; or "who for our part did not know Him," in the Armenian interpretation (*ork' oč's gitēak' zna*, with the "first-person-article" appended to the negative).

²⁰⁹ John 1. 1-3. For Irenaeus's introductory words, cf. the following note.

²¹⁰ Both the passage introducing the quotation, and the one following it, are syntactically very obscure. The rendering I have given

fits the text (but so would others) and seems to me to be that called for by the argument; obviously the "Word" of the gospel is the Son; the argument is, that since all things were made by Him, He pre-existed. (The text: . . . *patmelov mez ov ē Ordin Astucoy, or ērn ar̄ Hawr yar̄aj k'an zašxarhs elanel, ew zi i jer̄n nora elealk's amenayn elen asē ayspēs:* . . . *zi or i skzbanē Bann ēr ĕnd Hawr, i jer̄n nora amenaynk' elen, say ē Ordin nora.* I have rendered it as it stands, but emendation has been proposed of *i jer̄n nora* [second occurrence] to *ew i jer̄n oroy.* The note whereby Weber [L* 71 note b] refers to this emendation is misleading for those who do not know Armenian: the "eius" of the note does not refer to the "eius" of the text, but to that of a literal rendering "in manu eius" of *i jer̄n nora,* which appears in the text as "per id"; hence the change mentioned in the note — of "eius" to "cuius" — when applied to the text becomes a change of "per id" to "per quod.")

[211] "that the Son of God drew near": Moses does not, of course, say so explicitly; but for Irenaeus all material manifestations of God are to be attributed to the Son (cf. next chapter, and Introd. § 31).

and God appeared . . . : Gen. 18. 1-3 (with omissions).

were standing: Armenian *anc'eal kayin,* literally "passing-stood," whence misrendering as if *anc'eal* had independent force "passing by." The expression is a doublet (cf. n. 7) corresponding to LXX εἰστήκεισαν.

[212] Cf. Gen. 18. 22-32.

[213] Angels go to Lot in Sodom: Gen. 19. 1 on.

and the Lord . . . : Gen. 19. 24.

[214] That is, the double "Lord" of the text is explained by taking it as referring on its first occurrence to the Son, and on the second to the Father.

For this chapter's interpretation of Abraham's visitors and of the destruction of Sodom and Gomorrha (and that of Jacob's dream, in the following chapter) cf. Justin, *Dial.* 127 f.

[215] "So Abraham was a prophet": cf. A.H. 4. 5. 5.

"saw . . . the Son of God in human form, that He was to speak": or simply "saw . . . that the Son of God was to speak," according to the common Greek idiom; but as Abraham did in fact, according to Irenaeus, "see the Son of God," I have preferred to reproduce the text's expression. (The Armenian cannot mean "saw the Son of God to be born in the future in human form" or the like.)

[216] Jacob's dream: cf. Gen. 28. 12-15.

"the tree": that is, the Cross.

"from *earth even to heaven": the text has "from heaven" instead of "from earth," an easy slip of the pen (*yerknē* instead of *yerkrē*). Parallel in Justin: cf. n. 214.

[217] Isa. 66. 1 f., quoted in Acts 7. 49, where however "saith the Lord" is inserted after "build for me."

[218] Cf. Isa. 40. 12.

[219] "would stand": *anc'eal kac'eal*, literally "passing-standing," the same doublet as for the "were standing" of Gen. 18. 2 (n. 211).

"circumscribed in space": literally "in lesser space"; cf. ἐν ἐλαχίστῳ μέρει γῆς in the parallel passage in Justin, *Dial.* 127. 3, and ἐν ὀλίγῳ γῆς μορίῳ, *ibid.* 60. 2. Cf. also Theophilus of Antioch, *Ad Autol.* 2. 22 (on the Word as speaking with Adam in Paradise – cf. c. 12; Theophilus says that theophanies are of the Son because the Father is not to be circumscribed in space, and adds, echoing Isa. 66. 2 as above, "for there is no place of His rest").

"who was always with mankind . . .": cf. not only the Word in Paradise (c. 12) but also the descriptions of Wisdom, e. g. Prov. 8. 31: *my delights were to be with the children of men*; and the interesting quasi-identification of the Word with the just throughout history in Melito of Sardis (fragment from the *Tractatus de fide*).

[220] Exod. 3. 7 f. (with omissions).

"He it was who spoke with Moses" — because theophanies are of the Son; cf. end of preceding chapter.

[221] "was mounting and descending": imperfect tense, giving the sense of repeated or progressive action, or "aimed" as distinct from accomplished action; there is here probably the nuance that He was already preluding the definitive ascent-and-descent. The verb rendered "was mounting" (*elanēr*) can also mean "was going forth," and some versions adopt this "versio facilior"; but cf. A.H. 3. 6. 2: "qui ascendit et descendit propter salutem hominum" (and in Jacob's dream the angels "ascending and descending" by the ladder).

"deadly turbulence of the Gentiles": cf. Ps. 2. 1 (*Why have the Gentiles raged . . . ?*); "deadly" = causing death; the comparison is with the (Red Sea's) waves that drown.

"bitter current": "bitter" referring to the saltness of the sea, and "current" to its "drag" or surge; "current" is not a literal rendering of the text, but an attempt to convey the metaphor in English. The text uses the word *sahet'umn*, which means etymologically "slipperiness" or "slide," and has the sense "attraction" or the like (cf. "scandal," etymologically "stumbling block").

For the comparison between the Exodus and being led forth from paganism, cf. A.H. 4. 28-30.

[222] "rehearsed": *yar̄ajagoyn krt'eal varžiwr*, "exercised beforehand by practice."

"the Word of God . . . prefiguring": *Banin Astucoy . . . gałap'arawrēn c'uc'eloy yar̄ajagoyn*, a "genitive absolute"? If so, *c'uc'elov* would be more in accordance with the practice of our version, for the active voice; moreover the text punctuates after *Astucoy*. Are we to understand a dative-of-agent, "rehearsed by the Word of God, [who was] prefiguring. . ."?

Water from rock, cf. Exod. 17. 6; "the rock is Himself," cf. 1 Cor. 10. 4. (The "bitter" servitude so called no doubt in contrast to the "sweet" spring water.)

Twelve springs, cf. Exod. 15. 27; Num. 33. 9; "teaching of the twelve apostles," hardly an allusion to the title of the *Didache*.

"let the recalcitrant . . . die out . . . but brought those who believed in Him . . . into the heritage of the patriarchs": cf. c. 27; that is, transferred His call from Israel to the Gentiles.

"children in malice": cf. c. 27 (only those who knew not right from left at time of spies episode allowed to enter the Promised Land), and c. 96, the faithful are "become infants in malice"; cf. 1 Cor. 14. 20: *in malice be children*.

"not Moses but Jesus" distributed the heritage: cf. c. 27; "Jesus" (= Josue, cf. n. 144) son of Nun, in the type; in the reality, Christ; "Moses" as a type of the Law.

Moses frees from Amalec by stretching out his hands, Exod. 17. 11; here a type of the crucifixion. So also in Barnabas, *Epist.* 12. 2; Justin, *Dial.* 91; 112; 131.

[223] "the Son is God; for He who is born of God is God": for the Fathers the proof of the divinity of Son and Holy Spirit was their procession from the Father. Though Irenaeus does not assert the divinity of the Holy Spirit, it may be inferred from this assertion of the divinity of the Son (cf. Introd. § 32).

[224] Note the assertion that the distinction between Father and Son is shown in the economy of redemption, and that the Son is the Father's link with creatures (cf. Introd. § 35).

"those who are to approach . . . must have": *part ē unel . . . handerjealk'n merjenal*; the syntax demands *handerjeloc'n*. "access": *nuac̆umn ar̄ajacut'eann*, literally ὑπόταξις προαγωγῆς, which suggests a military metaphor, "formation for advance," cf. ὑπόταξις for the drawing up of light-armed troops behind the phalanx; but the expression is probably simply a doublet for προσαγωγή (*nuačut'iwn* in the Armenian version of the following quotations) " access."

Cf. Eph. 2. 18: *for by Him we have access both in one spirit to the Father*, and 3. 12: *in whom we have boldness and access with confidence by the faith in Him.*

[225] Ps. 44. 7 f. (with omissions) .

[226] Cf. A.H. 3. 6. 1, 3. 18. 3; contrast c. 53 (n. 242).

[227] Ps. 109.

saith: Armenian *asē*, but may stand for Greek " said " as in LXX; similarly in the following chapter, but c. 85 has " said."

With thee in the beginning: sic! (ἐν ἀρχῇ· LXX ἡ ἀρχή).

in the day: sic! (not " of days," as PO*).

daystar: emending the manuscript's *useak* into *aruseak*.

ruins: Douay's word. Armenian *korcaneals*, LXX πτώματα.

[228] " and (judged) the kings ": emending the manuscript's *t'aga-wornn* to *t'agaworsn.*

" who now . . . persecute His name ": not necessarily referring to Septimius Severus, as Hitchcock maintained (*Journal of Theological Studies* 9 [1908] 286), and so not indicating that the *Proof* was composed at the end of Irenaeus's life (about 202).

" when God called Him a priest for ever ": *k'ahanay asac'eal zna yawitenakan Astucoy.* If the genitive *Astucoy* be taken along with *k'ahanay*, the sense becomes " and in calling Him a priest of God for ever." But " of God " is not in the Psalm, whereas it is God who is represented as speaking; hence take *Astucoy* with *asac'eal* (this is not a " genitive absolute " but a regular Armenian construction, since " God " is the subject of the main verb to which the participle is added).

[229] " this is why ": referring ahead to the exegesis of the quotation.

" the exaltation with glory, after His human nature, and after humiliation and ingloriousness ": a literal version, in which " after " (*ĕst*) may be understood either temporally or as meaning " according to." The latter sense is not so readily understood in English, but in any case the sense is probably temporal. Cf. Justin, *Dial.* 33, where in the exegesis of the same verse we have " that He will first be lowly as man, and then be exalted." Weber L* however has " iuxta "; PO* has " His humanity and the glorious exaltation after . . . ," presumably taking " after his human nature " as τὰ κατὰ . . . , which seems highly unlikely. If " according to " be understood, then " humiliation and ingloriousness " must surely be taken as " lowly status " that is, " humanity " (cf. n. 304). Faldati has " per l'umanità di lui e per la sua abiezione."

[230] Isa. 45. 1, LXX, but with the variant Κυρίῳ instead of Κύρῳ ("to my anointed *Lord*" instead of "to my anointed, *Cyrus*"), a reading found before Irenaeus in Barnabas, *Epist.* 12. 11, and after him in other fathers (Tertullian, Cyprian, Lactantius); it has been suggested that this reading — though it is an error — was the original reading of the Septuagint, "Cyrus" being a correction made later.

Note, here and throughout the *Proof*, that the words "nations" and "Gentiles" are interchangeable, both being represented by the same word both in Greek (ἔθνη) and in Armenian (*het'anosk'*).

[231] The passage introducing the quotation is syntactically very obscure; of the possible clumsy renderings I have given one that seems to fit the argument, which seems to turn on the identification of the "anointed" of the previous quotation and the Son.

"the '*anointed*'": the Armenian has *K'ristosn* "(the) Christ," but the reference seems to be to the "anointed" of the previous quotation ("Christ" in Greek = χριστός = "Anointed"; the Greek cannot distinguish between the proper name and the common noun). Hence either render "Christ" in the quotation or "anointed" here; the latter is obviously the better course.

The Lord hath said . . . : Ps. 2. 7 f.

this day: emending the manuscript's *merk* to *serk*. *Merk* "naked," or "alone, only," would make sense, but the slip of the pen in the Armenian is more likely than the variant in the Greek.

[232] "to David": not "of David" (as rendered in AR*).

"the whole earth": here the *tiezerk' erkri* of the psalm text is represented by *tiezerk'* only, but "the whole earth" is the rendering called for. *Tiezerk'* implies "totality" rather than "earth," in fact, and Weber's stricture — if it is to be taken as such — in saying (L* 76 note h) that EP* "adds" the word "ganze," is unjustified.

[233] "the '*anointed*'": again the Armenian has "Christ"; cf. n. 231.

The Lord saith . . . : Ps. 109. 1 ("saith," *asē*, may stand for past tense of the Greek, so agreeing with LXX); similarly in the preceding chapter, but c. 85 has "said."

"as we said before": in the preceding chapter.

[234] "Christ" = "Anointed," in Greek; here however the Armenian translator's interpretation of the word as the proper name may be followed.

[235] "taking form and shape in the likeness of the person concerned": does "the person concerned" (*aṙaǰikay dimac'n* = τοῦ προκειμένου προσώπου) mean the Person of the Trinity, or the prophet?

In either case "taking form and shape. . ." is difficult to account for.

Cf. Justin, *Apol.* 1. 36-38 (in 36 we have: "sometimes He speaks on the part of the Father . . . sometimes on that of Christ").

[236] "most properly . . . most properly": in the Armenian two doublets ("aptly and fitly . . . aptly and duly").

"report in the first person . . . the Father's speech with Him": cf. end of preceding chapter; the Armenian has literally "say that the Father spoke Himself with Himself."

"in the first person" (second occurrence): literally "Himself concerning Himself."

[237] Isa. 49. 5 f.

[238] "first to be called 'Israel'": cf. Gen. 32. 28.

"every son being a servant of his father": cf. Gal. 4. 1, but there with the reservation *so long as the heir is a child.* Hermas (*Sim.* 5. 5 f.) also regards the Son's being called a servant of the Father as requiring explanation.

[239] "was to take flesh": the text has *darjeal ēr marmnanal* = " again was" + "to take flesh"; but the infinitive cannot be used, as it can in English, as a future participle, in Armenian, nor can the form be explained as an imitation of the Greek. If "again" is to be retained, it will have to be understood "moreover," but it is an awkward expression (it cannot be put between commas as "again" can in English, because *darjeal* must be taken with the verb; the proper sense would be "to become reincarnate"). Hence I propose the emendation of *darjeal* to *handerjeal*, which also rights the syntax (*handerjeal ēr = ἔμελλε*).

"the Father of all effecting also His incarnation": *Hawrn bolorec'un ew gorcelov zmarmnaworut'iwnn nora*, a "genitive absolute."

Therefore . . .: Isa. 7. 14-16 ("even distinguish" for LXX: "choose *or* prefer").

the virgin: *koysd*, that is, "*ista* virgo," "this virgin of thine" or the like.

[240] "For this is an error even of the one that is born": a literal version of the text's *k'anzi ays molorut'iwn ē ew cnic'eloyn.* The text is surely corrupt, but I do not know how to restore it. Weber (*Theologische Quartalschrift* 91 [1909] 563 f., 93 [1911] 162; and L* 79 note p) sees a reference to the inability of the child to distinguish good and evil. Conybeare proposed to read *soworut'iwn* "custom" instead of *molorut'iwn* "error" (*s* > *m*, *w* > *l* are very easy corruptions in Armenian script). Neither explanation seems to me satisfactory. The problem is complicated by what follows: "and He has a double

name . . ." and the discussion first of "Christ Jesus" and then of the name here in question ("Emmanuel") which, as it means "God with us," seems hardly the best proof of genuine humanity. Does Irenaeus mean that the name is an error, the true name being "Christ Jesus," and "Emmanuel" merely being "an expression of desire uttered by the prophet" (next chapter)? PO* renders "for this seems to us an error regarding the one who is born," but the text has "this *is* an error (*even*) *of* the one who is born" (or ". . . also of the one that is born"). The parallel passage A.H. 3. 21. 4 complicates the matter by regarding the name as the proof not of humanity but of divinity: "The Holy Spirit pointed out . . . that He is God — for the name Emmanuel means this — and He makes clear that He is man by saying *He shall eat butter and honey*, and by calling Him a child, and *before He know good and evil*; for all these things are characteristic of a human baby." This last clause, "haec enim omnia signa sunt hominis infantis," resembles the sentence under discussion not only by its position in the argument but also in its form; but now we have "hoc enim est *error et* infantis," or, with Conybeare's emendation (very slight, in Armenian script) "hoc enim est *consuetudo et* infantis." Conybeare understood this to refer to the "custom" of giving a name; but can the expression be understood as "(all) this is normal for a child"? This would be a good solution, but it seems better to admit that the text is corrupt, and has probably suffered omission, and translate it as it stands; there is no way of telling what Irenaeus wrote.

[241] "He has a double name in the Hebrew tongue, Messias — Christ (Anointed) — and Jesus — Saviour": the text gives: "He has a double name in the Hebrew tongue, Messias Christ, and in Armenian, Jesus Saviour." I have suppressed "and in Armenian" and added "(Anointed)," since in the Greek the name "Christ" is simply the translation of the Hebrew "Messias," that is, "Anointed," Greek χριστός.

[242] "anointed and arrayed": *awc ew zardareac′* = ἔχρισε καὶ ἐκόσμησε. "Array" means both "set in order" and "adorn"; in the former sense it is applicable to the Word's activity in creation, while in the latter it was associated with anointing (the preliminary to bodily "adornment").

Cf. Justin, *Apol.* 2. 6 (and note that Irenaeus's explanation supports Scaliger's emendation καὶ χρῖσαι for the κεχρῖσθαι of that passage).

"He was the Anointed by the Spirit of God His Father": in the

text there is the same ambiguity as in the English ("the Anointed
. . . of God" or "Spirit of God"?; contrast c. 47. "He was": more
literally "He became," "He was made" (*elew* = ἐγένετο).

The Spirit . . . : Isa. 61. 1.

²⁴³ With the reference to Christ's miracles of healing in connection with the name "Jesus" = "Saviour" cf. Justin *Apol.* 2. 6 (as
for "Christ" of last note); there seems to have been an association
of the name Ἰησοῦς with the word ἴασις "healing" in Greek.

²⁴⁴ Emmanuel: Hebrew *'immānû'ēl* = "with us God."

"God with *us*": the text has "God with you," presumably a
scribal error, as the correct pronoun is used in "God be with us."

"good tidings": referring to Isa. 61. 1 just quoted, *to bring good
tidings to the poor.*

²⁴⁵ "'behold . . . the virgin . . .'": exegetic paraphrase of Isa. 7. 14,
quoted in the preceding chapter.

"while as it were marvelling . . . he at the same time tells": cf.
c. 71: "Scripture both tells . . . and as it were is struck with astonishment," and similar expressions in Justin, *Apol.* 1. 47, and *Dial.* 118.

²⁴⁶ Isa. 66. 7.

there came forth delivered a man child: Armenian *čołopreac'
p'rcaw aru*; the apposition *čołopreac' p'rcaw* seems to be a doublet for
ἐξέφυγεν in LXX ἐξέφυγεν καὶ ἔτεκεν ἄρσεν, the words καὶ ἔτεκεν being
omitted.

²⁴⁷ Isa. 9. 6 (LXX 9. 5). See foot of p. 33.

Wonderful Counsellor, God the Mighty: obelised by Origen, but
both quoted and commented here and in c. 40. On the other hand,
Irenaeus here omits "whose government is set upon his shoulders."

²⁴⁸ "even of the Father": "even" for Armenian *kam* "or."

And God said: Gen. 1. 26.

²⁴⁹ "He is here seen clearly, the Father addressing the Son, as
Wonderful Counsellor of the Father": reproducing the ambiguity
of the original *erewi astanawr Hayr aṙ Ordin aselov sk'anč'eli xorhrdakic' Hawrn.* In normal Armenian *Hayr* would be the subject
("The Father is seen addressing the Son"), an interpretation also
possible in the English version. On the other hand, it is more likely
that *Hayr . . . aselov* renders a genitive absolute ("as the Father is
addressing the Son") which is also the natural interpretation of the
English version. Weber is therefore probably correct in emending
Hayr to *Hawr* (L* 81 note k), though there is in the *Proof* another
case of "nominative absolute" with "gerund" (cf. n. 281; and for
"nominative absolute" with participle, n. 200).

For the view that "Let us make . . ." is addressed to the Son, cf. before Irenaeus, Theophilus of Antioch, *Ad Autol.* 2. 18 (addressed to Word and Wisdom), and Barnabas, *Epist.* 5. 5 (to our Lord), 6. 12 ("the Scripture speaks of us when He says to the Son: Let us make . . ."); similarly in A.H. 5. 15. 4.

250 "Now He is also our Counsellor, giving counsel": *ti na ē ew mer xorhrdakic' linelov ew xrat talov.* The syntax is not clear; *ē ew mer xorhrdakic'* = "He is also our Counsellor" or *(mer) xorhrdakic' . . .talov* = "having become (our) Counsellor and giving counsel"; but how combine the two? The interpretation of *linelov* as "being (with us)" (". . . our Counsellor, being [with us] and giving counsel") seems to me unlikely. Perhaps there was no verb in the original, the sense being, along with the preceding sentence: "Here He is seen . . . as wonderful Counsellor of the Father; but now also (sc. He is seen as) having become our Counsellor. . . ." The verb "is" would then be a scribal "correction."

"not constraining, as God, and nonetheless being 'God the Mighty,' he says": the added "he says" and the repetition "and giving counsel" suggest that perhaps the text had simply "our Counsellor, and giving counsel to leave off" ("and" in the Armenian, cf. preceding paragraph of this note), and assumed its present form by the incorporation of a gloss "and giving counsel: not constraining . . . God the Mighty, he means." More likely, however, the text is correct. Cf. A.H. 5. 1. 1 (non cum vi . . . sed secundum suadelam suadentem, non vim inferentem), and 4. 37. 1: man was made free "ad utendum sententia Dei voluntarie et non coactum a Deo. Βία Θεῷ οὐ πρόσεστιν· ἀγαθὴ δὲ γνώμη πάντοτε συμπάρεστιν αὐτῷ," which seems, in spite of the prosaic συμπάρεστιν, to have a lyric origin; and *Epist. ad Diognetum* 7: ὡς πείθων, οὐ βιαζόμενος· βία γὰρ οὐ πρόσεστι τῷ Θεῷ, where the beginning of the passage quoted in *Adversus haereses* appears in pure iambic form.

251 Isa. 9. 5-7. See foot of p. 33.

Messenger of Great Counsel: I render "Messenger" instead of "Angel" (the same word in Greek, and also in Armenian) because the exegesis which follows demands this rendering in English.

Great is His empire: emending the manuscript's *meci* (genitive-dative) to *mec* (nominative) "great."

to guide: in the Armenian a doublet, *yaǰołel ew včarel* = LXX κατορθῶσαι.

to uphold: another doublet, *i koys linel ew buṙn harkanel* = LXX ἀντιλαβέσθαι. PO*'s strange "set it aside" seems due to a misunderstanding of *i koys linel*, literally "be(come) at the side" (that is "stand by," support, assist).

²⁵² "of the risen Christ": I have supplied "Christ" to make the text's *yaruc'eloyn* = τοῦ ἀναστάντος intelligible in English.

²⁵³ "on which He held His back when crucified": *yorum zt'ikunsn uner bewereal*. Cf. parallel in Justin, *Apol.* 1. 35: "to which He set His back when crucified"; there is no need to see an idiom of the type "He *had* His back *nailed*" (*zt'ikunsn uner* = τοὺς ὤμους εἶχε; case of *bewereal* "nailed, crucified" is uncertain).

Cross an ignominy: crucifixion, as the most ignominious form of execution, was still in force in the time of Irenaeus, and the "ignominy of the Cross" was a very real thing. Cf. Justin, *Dial.* 101, on Ps. 21. 7 (*the reproach of man*); and cf. Deut. 21. 23 (*he is accursed of God that hangeth on a tree* — though the reference is not there to crucifixion) — and 1 Cor. 1. 23 (*Christ crucified . . . unto the Gentiles foolishness*) etc.

²⁵⁴ "as Christ": that is, as "the Anointed" (Greek χριστός), as the Messianic King (cf. c. 47, 49, 53).

²⁵⁵ "Thus": *i jern ayspiseanc'* = διὰ τοιούτων, "by means of such" ("prophecies," adds PO*); EP* "unter anderem." Hence Barthoulot's curious interpretation ("Voici les paroles que Moïse mit sur les lèvres *de ces prophètes*" — my italics).

There shall not lack . . . : Gen. 49. 10 f.

till he come, for whom it lies in store, and he shall be the expectation of the nations: ("nations" and "Gentiles" interchangeable, being the same word in Greek and also in Armenian); LXX: *till that come which lies in store for him, and the expectation of the nations.* The reading ᾧ ἀπόκειται "for whom it lies in store," a corruption, in favour among Christian apologetes, of the true reading τὰ ἀποκείμενα αὐτῷ, "what lies in store for him" is also followed in A.H. 4. 10. 2, and Justin, *Dial.* 120, maintains that it was the original reading of the Septuagint, the other being, he says, a Jewish corruption.

washing his robe: Irenaeus here omits "tying his foal . . ." (which he does not omit in A.H. 4. 10. 2), and has "washing" instead of "he shall wash."

²⁵⁶ Jews take their name from Juda: in Greek, "Jew" = Ἰουδαῖος, "of-Juda," as it were "Judan." ("Judaea" is simply the feminine of the same word, meaning "[land] of Juda.")

In the parallel A.H. 4. 10. 2 the argument from the Jewish loss of independence when Christ came is not developed in the manner in which it here is.

[257] "the forces of the quiver were taken": The text has *korovk' kaparčic' zinu ařan*. Here *korovk'* is the plural of *korov*, which means "force, strength, vigour"; but it also means "dexterity," and may be used for *korovi* "skilful," and in particular, "marksman." Hence "the marksmen . . ." is just possible (hence L* "sollertes"). *Kaparčic'* is a genitive (-dative) "of the quiver" and *zinu* is genitive (-dative) or instrumental of *zēn* "weapon, armour." As genitive, it gives "quiver-armour" or the like, cf. EP*: sind die Kräfte seines Schützenbogens erlahmt ("the forces of his bow are [become] crippled"); or L*: sollertes pharetrae telorum ("the skilful in the quiver of darts" or "in the darts of the quiver"), which takes the word as (collective) plural in sense; so also F*. As instrumental, it gives "were taken by force of arms" (literally "by-weapon"), that is, "were captured," cf. AR*: "the might of the quiver was captured." This seems to me the most likely interpretation, but I have rendered "the forces of the quiver were taken" in order to allow so far as possible the different interpretations (for different senses attributed to *ařan* "were taken": cf. the versions quoted above, which derive "destroy" or the like from "take [away]"). One might suspect that *zinu* stood for αἰχμα- in a doublet *zinu ařnum* = αἰχμαλωτεύω, but that this word is elsewhere rendered normally (that is, by *gerem*; so e.g. in Ps. 67 (c. 83); but there the familiar quotation may account for the normal rendering, leaving it possible that the translator of the *Proof*, left to himself, might render *zinu ařnum*). Can we perhaps understand "the marksmen of the quiver were taken by the *blade*" or the like, that is, the Biblical bow by the Roman sword?

The whole expression seems as if it might be a quotation, perhaps from an apocryphal psalm or prophetic passage. EP* refers to Gen. 49. 8 f. and 23 f.; 8 f. does not seem helpful, but in 23 f. we have (LXX) *and the lords of bolts contained him; and he shattered with force their bows*. Here "lords of bolts," κύριοι τοξευμάτων, which might not unfairly be taken as "masters of the bow's-shaft," bears a distinct resemblance to "marksmen of the quiver's-*zēn*." Weber (L* 84 note b) to his other criticisms of EP* adds ("reasonably enough" comments Faldati, F* 120 n. 5) that the above references contribute scarcely anything; but perhaps it did not occur to the Latins that they were, of course, to the LXX. Weber himself refers to Ps. 77. 9 (*the sons of Ephraim, who bend and shoot with the bow: they have turned back in the day of battle*), which is not very apposite. Better would have been Ps. 75. 4: *there hath he broken the powers of bows*.

²⁵⁸ " He had come to His destination ": literally " He had come and arrived."

²⁵⁹ For this argument especially, but also 'for the whole of this section, cf. Justin, *Apol.* 1. 32 (AR* Introd. 6 f. points out the parallels); and for this argument cf. also Justin, *Dial.* 54. Cf. Ps. 103. 13-15: *Thou waterest the hills . . . the earth shall be filled with the fruit of Thy works . . . that Thou mayst bring bread out of the earth, and that wine may cheer the heart of man.*

²⁶⁰ *the Lord Himself:* cf. Isa. 7. 14, quoted in c. 53 (*the Lord Himself shall give thee a sign*).

" who also gladdens those who drink Him ": cf. Ps. 103. 15, end of preceding note, and the continuation (LXX) of the passage just commented on by Irenaeus (Gen. 49. 12: *His eyes are more glad- dening than wine*).

" an everlasting gladness ": apposition to " Spirit," or internal accusative, " gladdens . . . *with* everlasting gladness." Cf. the *ever- lasting joy* of Isa. 35. 10, also in a description of the Kingdom, and perhaps in Irenaeus's source (cf. next note) close to the text com- mented.

²⁶¹ " of those who hope in Him ": as exegesis of " the nations," (or " the Gentiles," identical in Greek as also in Armenian); from Isa. 11. 10, quoted also by Justin, *Apol.* 1. 32, in the same connec- tion (LXX: *in Him the nations shall hope*; Justin: *and in His arm the nations shall hope*). Harris suggested that the two texts so asso- ciated in the parallel passages of Justin and the *Proof* were taken from a common source which so associated them (*Expositor* 7. 3 [1907] 255, reprinted in *Testimonies* 1. 68 f.); cf. Introd. § 37.

²⁶² Num. 24. 17.

leader: LXX " man " (ἄνθρωπος); Irenaeus's version agrees better with Massoretic *šēbeṭ* " sceptre," and is found also in A.H. 3. 9. 2 (dux) and in Justin, *Dial.* 106 (ἡγούμενος).

²⁶³ " dispensation ": *tnawrēnut'iwn* = οἰκονομία.

²⁶⁴ Cf. Matt. 2. 1-12.

With Irenaeus's account of the entry of the star and its standing above the Boy's head cf. *Protevangelium Iacobi* (cod. D) " until it entered . . . and stood over the head of the child," and *Opus imper- fectum in Matthaeum* p. 30; also the readings of Codex Bezae, with which also the Old Latin version agrees, in Matt. 2. 9 (*the star . . . went before them, until it came and stood over the child,* instead of . . . *over where the child was*).

²⁶⁵ Isa. 11. 1-10.

according to appearances: ĕst karceanc' = κατὰ τὰ δοκοῦντα, but may well render LXX κατὰ τὴν δόξαν. Or "according to opinion," but "appearances" agrees with context and Massoretic lᵉmar'ēh 'ēnāw ("according to the seeing of his eyes"; parallel: "hearing of his ears" rendered "report").

shall have pity on the lowly: reading therefore ἐλεήσει for ἐλέγξει, a confusion also found in Jude 22. In A.H. 3. 9. 3 we have "arguet gloriosos terrae."

And a little child shall thrust: omitting "and a little child shall lead them" and all v. 7 (homoeoteleuton? *manuk tłay* may represent either παιδίον μικρόν of v. 6 or π. νήπιον of v. 8).

His rising shall be honour: reading therefore ἀνάστασις instead of ἀνάπαυσις in "His resting shall be honour." Hitchcock (*Journal of Theological Studies* 9 [1908] 288) tries to account for this corruption by a misreading of the Hebrew, but this does not seem very likely.

²⁶⁶ "the descendant who conceived Christ, the Virgin, is thus become the rod": The text reads: (*ew hayr Dawt'ay*), *cnund* or *yłac'awn zK'ristos. Koysn ełew ard gawazann.* Robinson renders "(and David's) descendant the virgin was who conceived Christ. Now (as to) the *rod*": a version which supposes *ew Dawt'ay* to have dropped out before *cnund* — and punctuates after instead of before *koysn ełew*; the emendations are reasonable, but leave *Ard gawazann* in the air. On the other hand, the use of the article does not favour my version. Should one keep the text's punctuation, and emend *cnund or* to *oroy cnund*: "of whom a descendant conceived Christ. The Virgin is thus. . ."? The "rod" might be expected to be identified with Christ rather than with the Virgin — cf. Justin, *Dial.* 86 (also 100. 4 and 126. 1); but Irenaeus does seem to have meant to identify it with the Virgin, since he goes on to identify the "flower" with "His body," and speaks of the rod with which Moses worked his miracles (but see the following note; and how does "the rod is a sign of empire" fit in?).

²⁶⁷ "with a rod": the text's *handerj gawazanaw* means not simply "by means of a rod," but "along with a rod," corresponding to μετὰ ῥάβδου, as in Justin, *Dial.* 86. 1: "Moses was sent along with a rod for the redemption of the people"; here however the "rod" is identified with Christ.

²⁶⁸ Isa. 11. 3, from the passage quoted in the preceding chapter.

have pity on the lowly of the earth: cf. n. 265. Here "lowly" is singular, whereas in c. 59 it was plural, as in the LXX; and "in the earth" is substituted for "of the earth" of c. 59, which agrees with

LXX. Hence probably a scribal error, as the corruption is easy (*nuastic' erkri* corrupted to *nuasti yerkri*; letters *c'* and *y* are similar in form); hence emend to agreement with c. 59: Akinean's emendation, *HAm.* 24 (1910) 207 n. 2.

[269] *he shall strike . . .* and *his loins . . .* : Isa. 11.4 and 5 respectively, from the passage quoted in the preceding chapter. Is " by a word alone " to be taken as attributed to the quotation?

[270] " the elders say . . .": " the elders," cf. Introd. § 40. Here Irenaeus's source was Papias (cf. A.H. 5. 33. 4; and Eusebius, *Hist. eccles.* 3. 39).

Chiliasm (Greek χιλιάς = " thousand ") or Millenarianism is the name given to belief in the Millennium or thousand-year reign of Christ at the end of the world, before the final destruction of the world and the general judgement, a period in which the forces of evil will be enchained, and Christ will reign with the martyrs in peace and temporal felicity. The belief was founded not only on literal interpretation of the Apocalypse (ch. 20, etc.), but also on such passages as that here commented. It is found not only in Papias, but also in Irenaeus's master, Justin (especially *Dial.* 80 f.); and in *Adversus haereses* (5. 32 f.) Irenaeus explains the Isaias passage in the Millenarian sense, rejecting (5. 35) the suggestion that it might be explained simply of the peace in the Church. He did not however, reject the latter interpretation as in itself incorrect, just as here he mentions the Millenaristic one; and Tixeront (PO* 786 n. 1) points out that though Irenaeus has changed his opinion, he does not exactly contradict himself. Nevertheless the change of opinion is noteworthy, though I hesitate to agree with Faldati (F* 44) that it constitutes such a " profound change " that it must have been the work of many years. See however second paragraph of n. 107 to Introd.

[271] " men of different nations and like character ": (emend, with Akinean, *HAm.* 24 [1910] 207 n. 2, *zannman azgeac'n* to *zannmanazgeac'n*); the expression is curious.

" selfish pride": an attempt at rendering *awelastac'ut'iwn* = πλεονεξία.

" the women took on the likeness ": " took on the likeness " is not in the text; I have repeated it for clarity.

" as like as not": *t'erews ardewk'* = τάχα πάντως, of which " quite capable (of . . . -ing) " would also be a fair rendering; one need not quarrel, as Weber does (L* 88 note h), with EP*'s " imstande waren "; L* has, accurately, " nimirum," Faldati less happily " (uccidevano) in realtà."

"out of cupidity . . .": here there is either a lacuna or an aposiopesis.

"in one name": the text has "in my name"; I suppose (with AR* 125 n. 1) emendation of *im* "my" to *mi* "one."

"will be possessed by the grace of God in justice of conduct": *i bars arders stasc'in i šnorhēn Astucoy*. Or "will be kept . . ." (*stanam* = περιποιοῦμαι). AR* has "have acquired righteous habits by the grace of God" (reading *bars* [not *i bars*] *arders stac'an i jeřn šnorhin Astucoy*, or simply paraphrasing, with change of tense?). The tense is future, of course, because it is the exegesis of a prophecy.

[272] Isa. 11. 10, from the passage quoted in c. 59.

[273] *Ibid*. For the reading, cf. n. 265.

[274] Amos 9. 11, quoted in Acts 15. 16; also quoted in c. 38.

[275] "clearly he is declaring . . .": AR* "he plainly declares" is ambiguous; "clearly" qualifies not "declare" but the sentence.

Body called "tabernacle": cf. Wisd. 9. 15, *the earthly habitation* (σκῆνος however in the Greek); 2 Cor. 5. 1, *the earthly house of our habitation* (σκῆνος); 2 Peter 1. 13 and 14, *as long as I am in this tabernacle . . . the laying away of my tabernacle is at hand*.

[276] "the *anointed": *K'ristosi* = ΧΡΙΣΤΟΥ. If the genitive is correct, one must render "the anointed," referring to David, and suppose that the translator erred in using the proper name *K'ristos* "Christ"; alternatively one might suppose the reference was to Christ, and emend to *K'ristos*, nominative: "He who . . . was of the seed of David, Christ, would be Son of God" (in Greek Χριστός = "Anointed," the translation of the Hebrew *Māšîăḥ*, "Messias").

[277] Mich. 5. 2, quoted however as in Matt. 2. 6 according to the readings of Codex Bezae (and the Old Latin versions).

of Judaea: that is, reading τῆς Ἰουδαίας with Codex Bezae and the Old Latin, instead of the received γῇ Ἰούδα.

art not the least: "not" is here *mi* = μή, as in Codex Bezae instead of the received οὐδαμῶς, the literal sense of the Greek being the rhetorical question "art thou the least . . . ?" = implying the answer "no." As *mi* is so explained as a servile rendering of the unusual reading, there is no need to have recourse to the suggestion (L* 90 note g) that *mi* is here the adjective "one, only" ("thou alone art a little one" or the like, L* "sola exigua").

Justin also (*Apol*. 1. 34; *Dial*. 78. 1) quotes this passage in the Gospel form, but with the received readings.

[278] "David's country": "country" is *gawař*, "province, region," and "(native) land" in the sense of "place of origin" (used for πατρίς in Matt. 13. 54, 57); cf. French use of "pays" in this sense.

[279] Ps. 131. 10-12.

Thy servant: the text has "my," presumably a slip of the pen.
(A.H. 3. 9. 2 has "Thy.")

Thy *anointed: the Armenian has "Thy Christ" (Greek χριστός
"anointed").

of the fruit of thy bowels: the text has *i ptłoy orovaynē k'ummē*,
"de fructūs ventre tuo," for which inversion cf. n. 180. Emend to
i ptłoy orovayni k'oyoy.

and their son for evermore: nominative, so in apposition to "thy
children," not to "with them," if the text is to be taken as it stands;
in fact these words give the subject of the following sentence: LXX
and their sons for evermore will sit on thy throne. The singular
"son" is of course required by the exegesis, but it is strange if
Irenaeus omitted the rest of the sentence.

[280] Not Isaias, but Zach. 9. 9, quoted in Matt. 21. 5 (but cf. Isa.
62. 11: *tell the daughter of Sion: behold thy Saviour cometh*). The
text is quoted as in the gospel, save that for the gospel's *thy king*
Irenaeus has *a king* (that is, omits σου — perhaps the omission is only
a scribal oversight) and the words "and upon" are omitted before
a colt. In omitting "upon" our text agrees both with some readings
of the gospel, notably Tatian's and that rendered by the Sinaitic
Syriac, and with the Old Testament reading; but Irenaeus also omits
the "and"; and he agrees with the gospel, as against the LXX in
reading *the foal of an ass* (LXX "a young foal"), and in omitting
"righteous, saviour."

So also Justin, *Apol.* 1. 35. 11, omits "righteous, saviour," with the
gospel; but he has "Rejoice greatly . . . ," as in Zachary, and attributes the prophecy to Sophonias; in *Dial.* 53. 3 he includes
"righteous, saviour." All these variants suggest that the immediate
source was neither a copy of the Old Testament, nor the gospel (cf.
Introd. § 37).

[281] "the multitudes spreading their garments for Him to ride
upon": this version is an attempt to compromise between the possible interpretations of the corrupt text, which reads: *st'aranalovn ew
nstelov nma žołovurdk'n zhanderjs iwreanc'*. This seems to be a
"nominative absolute" with the "gerund," meaning "the multitudes
?-ing and ?-ing for Him their garments." *St'aranal* (a hapax legomenon) seems to mean "spread as a cover" (cf. *st'ar* "caparison"
etc.); the second verb as it stands is the verb "sit." Lüdtke (*Zeitschrift für Kirchengeschichte* 35 [1914] 258 f.) proposed to emend
nstelov to *nsteloy*, and render "spreading their garments for Him

(even) as He sat." Weber (L* 92 note a) proposed to emend it to *nstuc'elov* (sic!) and rendered "cum prosternerent et submitterent ei"; this is surely to add another hapax legomenon: I know of no word *nstuc'el* "submittere," and the causative *nstuc'anel* means "seat," "set down," and governs the accusative. Vardanian (*HAm.* 24 [1910] 305) emends *nma* to *i nma* and changes the order of words: *st'aranelovn žołovurdk'n zhanderjs iwreanc' ew nstelov i nma* (word for word "the multitudes spreading [?] their garments and sitting on it), cf. PO*: "when the people spread their garments and He sat upon them." Of these emendations the simplest and at the same time the least unsatisfactory is in my opinion that of Lüdtke.

Cf. Matt. 21. 6-8: *and the disciples . . . brought the ass and the colt, and they laid their garments upon them, and made Him sit thereon. And a very great multitude spread their garments in the way.* Our text seems to mean that "the multitudes" spread their garments for Him to sit on (understanding "they" of the gospel in a generic sense?), but it may mean that they spread them "in the way." "For Him to ride upon" is a compromise between the two senses.

[282] "when He came He would heal men": Text: *i mardkanē ełeal bžškel.* Here *i mardkanē ełeal* seems to mean "sprung from mankind" (so AR*) or rather "having become a man" (τῶν ἀνθρώπων γενόμενος: ἐξ ἀνθρώπων . . . or ἀπ' ἀνθρώπων . . . would be rather "having quitted mankind," "having been absent from mankind"). I have understood the participle absolutely, and taken *i mardkanē* as partitive, so improving the sense; but the possibility of this interpretation is doubtful. Alternatively, therefore: "having become a man, He would heal those whom He healed, and raise the dead, whom He raised. . . ."

[283] Isa. 53. 4, but as quoted in Matt. 8. 17 (agreeing neither with LXX nor with Massoretic text); in the next chapter Irenaeus quotes this verse, in a longer passage, as in the LXX (n. 288).

[284] "sometimes": *ē urek' zi,* literally "it is (= happens) elsewhere that." Cf. Justin, *Dial.* 114. 1, for a parallel to the whole sentence. There the expression corresponding to our *ē urek' zi* is ἔσθ' ὅτε.

[285] "he *recorded": the text has *yišesc'ē* "he will record." I render "recorded" (*yišeac'*), but the parallel in Justin (*loc. cit.*) has "for the sake of example, I might quote (εἴποιμ' ἄν) certain prophetic words. . . ." Hence it is possible that the sense is "he would record," or that Irenaeus had "I might quote," and the verb was "corrected" to third person.

In that day . . . : Isa. 29. 18.

in darkness . . . the eyes: LXX οἱ ἐν τῷ σκότει . . . ὀφθαλμοί, which might be rendered " the eyes . . . that are in darkness. . . ." I have rendered according to the Armenian, which, like the English, is incapable of reproducing the Greek use of the article.

[286] " the same prophet ": I have supplied the word " prophet."

Be strengthened . . . : Isa. 35. 3-6.

palsied: the text's *lucealk' ew kt'otealk'* is simply a doublet for LXX παραλελυμένα.

dispirited: another doublet, *karčogi vahotk'* = LXX ὀλιγόψυχοι.

will render judgement: LXX κρίσιν ἀνταποδίδωσιν καὶ ἀνταποδώσει (rare variant κρίσιν ἀνταποδώσει καὶ ἀνταποδώσει); Irenaeus's reading corresponds to Hilary's " iudicium reddet " (doublet *p'oxanak hatusc'ē* = ἀνταποδώσει LXX's ἀνταποδίδωσιν καὶ being omitted).

Cf. Justin, *Apol.* 1. 48. 2, for the same passage applied in the same manner.

[287] *So shall* . . . : Isa. 26. 19.

" He will be believed ": the future tense attributes to the prophet the realisation that the miracles were proofs of Christ's divinity.

[288] Isa. 52. 13-53. 5.

*shall *understand*: emending the text's passive *imasc'i* to the corresponding active *imasc'ē* (= LXX συνήσει: AR*'s emendation, 129 n. 1). The passive (" shall be recognised " or the like) was induced by the following passives.

He had no comeliness (first occurrence): LXX has present tense.

He beareth . . . pains: 53. 4, quoted in the preceding chapter as " Isaias," but in the different form found in Matt. 8. 17.

Cf. Justin, *Apol.* 1. 50, for the same passage applied in the same manner.

[289] Not in the Psalms; perhaps a heading or gloss from a collection of texts used as a source has been mistaken for a quotation (cf. Introd. § 37). Cf. however Ps. 37. 9: *I am afflicted and humbled.*

[290] For the same argument, cf. Justin, *Apol.* 1. 35. 6.

[291] " *the Word ": the text has " His Word." Perhaps Irenaeus wrote " the Word Himself," and αὐτός became corrupted into αὐτοῦ. In c. 94 John 1. 14 is quoted in the form " And *His* Word was made flesh," where the above suggestion would not apply; but there the " His " is made possible by a preceding " the Word of God."

I have given . . . : Isa. 50. 6. Quoted also in c. 34, but there with " them that spat " in place of " spitting." The present reading agrees with the LXX.

[292] Lam. 3. 30.

[293] Isa. 53. 5 f. I have restored the usual punctuation in place of that of the text, which would give: ". . . we are healed, all of us. Like sheep we have gone astray. . . ."

[294] Isa. 53. 7.

[295] The words *He was offered because it was His own will*, which occur in Isaias between the two preceding quotations, would of course have been still more to the point for this argument; but they do not occur in the Septuagint, hence their omission here.

[296] Isa. 53. 8.

[297] The meaning of this obscure expression seems to be, that Christ's abasement, that is, His Passion, is in fact the form in which "judgement is taken" away from the saved, and on the reprobate (cf. what follows).

[298] " there is taking *to* a person, and there is taking *from* a person ": reading *aᵲeal lini ē* or *umek' ew ē* or *yumek'ē*, " there is what is taken to (or for) someone, and there is what is taken from (or by!) someone." The text has the impossible ablative *umek'ē* instead of the dative *umek'*, but the latter is clearly called for, to correspond to the datives which follow (rendered " on "). Perhaps the translator rendered an original τινι, ἔστιν καὶ as *umek' ē ew*, and then emended the order of words by putting *ē* after *ew*, but without striking out the first *ē*. Barthoulot's free rendering " on peut être reçu d'une façon par les uns et d'une autre par les autres " both gives the impression that the reference is to the manner in which Christ was received by different classes of men, instead of the manner in which " judgement was taken," and suggests that he emended *umek'ē* to *yumek'ē*, and understood this as meaning " by someone " instead of " from someone " (cf. following note). From what follows, however, the sense must be as I have rendered it; it is not easy to reproduce the original expressions in idiomatic English: in what follows I have rendered the dative by " on " because the sense is that of the English " take judgement on," and have used " off " instead of " from," the expression " take judgement off " having here to be understood in the sense " acquit."

[299] " by them ": *i noc'anēn*. The construction (*i* with the ablative, like Latin " ab " with the ablative) means also, and indeed primarily, " from . . ." (as in the " taking from " above). The context here demands the opposite sense, but instead of emending to the dative (as suggested by Weber, L* 96 note f) and rendering " on them," I have understood " by them," since " they took judgement on themselves."

[300] Isa. 53. 8.

[301] " He who underwent all these things has a generation that cannot be declared ": parallelled word for word, save that " all " is there lacking, in Justin, *Apol.* 1. 51. 1.

" lineage ": (*azg* = γένος), in the sense of " high birth," as an object of awe, though in this sense *azn* might rather have been expected in Armenian.

" and that is, His Father is . . .": or *ē Hayrn nora . . . ē. Hayrn* surely is subject of the second verb rather than complement of the first one, so not " which is His Father: He is . . ." or the like. In A.H. 2. 28. 5 Irenaeus quotes the verse here commented as a proof that the divine procession itself is ineffable.

[302] " Jeremias ": an interpolation? Cf. n. 307.

The spirit . . . Gentiles: Lam. 4. 20; " and how " is not there read, but here seems to form part of the quotation (cf. end of next note). The meaning is of course " the breath of our mouth (= ' our life ') is the Lord's anointed," but the exegesis demands " spirit " and " Christ."

the Lord Christ: " Lord " precedes " Christ," whereas LXX, and the quotation in A.H. 3. 10. 3 (and Justin, *Apol.* 1. 55. 5, which also reads " before our face ") have the order Christ–Lord. Greek Χριστός = " Anointed," but here taken as the proper name. Rahlfs proposes the excellent emendation Κυρίου for LXX Κύριος (explained as an expansion of the abbreviation κ̄ν̄) so giving " the Lord's Anointed." It may well be that Irenaeus also had the genitive; with the altered order Lord–Christ it would then be possible to understand " the spirit of *our Lord's* face " (though the position of ἡμῶν would be strange), and this may perhaps account for the following " Christ, being Spirit of God." The nominative is of course read in our texts of Irenaeus and Justin.

[303] " Christ, being Spirit of God ": for a possible explanation of this strange expression cf. end of preceding note. Identifications of Christ with the Holy Spirit are found in early writers (cf. Hermas; and Justin, *Apol.* 1. 33. 6: " by ' Spirit ' . . . one can understand none other than the Word," on Luke 1. 35: *the Holy Spirit shall come upon thee*), but they are eschewed by Irenaeus. " Spirit " must be understood not in the personal sense, but as meaning " of spiritual nature " (" Spirit of God " = " divine and spiritual "), by contrast with the bodily sufferings. So in the " Second Epistle " attributed to Clement of Rome we have (9. 5): " Christ the Lord, being first Spirit, then became flesh."

" as it were is struck with astonishment and wonder ": this expression might be accounted for by taking the words "and how," which seem to be intended as part of the quotation, in the exclamatory sense; but there is no need for any such explanation; cf. n. 245.

[304] "lowliness and abjection": cf. Justin's references to Christ's human nature as "ignoble and unsightly" (ἄτιμος καὶ ἀειδής, *Dial.* 14. 8; less emphatically *Apol.* 1. 52. 3), and his frequent references to Christ as "unsightly" (ἀειδής) in body (*Dial.* 49, 85, 88, 100, 110, 121), and Isa. 53. 2 f., quoted in c. 68; and cf. n. 229.

"the shadow even of bodies . . .": here "shadow" is *stuer*, whereas in the Scriptural passage and elsewhere in this chapter the word *hovani* is used; I can see no reason for the change of word, nor can I see to what it can have corresponded in the Greek.

"was cast to the ground and trodden underfoot by His Passion": or "cast to the ground by His Passion, was trodden underfoot," as EP* takes it.

"as it were": *t'erews*. The word would make better sense with a change of punctuation, giving: ". . . trodden underfoot by the Passion. *Perhaps*, too, he named. . . ." I have, however, kept the punctuation of the text, and rendered "as it were," because some such qualification seems to be called for, and also because it is not Irenaeus's way to qualify his exegesis with "perhaps."

[305] "as having become a shade of the glory of the Spirit, covering Him": *ibru hovani eṫeal Hogwoyn p'aṙawk' ew cackeal zna*. Other translators have taken *Hogwoyn* as the subject of the two participles, and rendered "in that the Spirit overshadowed and covered it (or Him) with glory" or the like. But the literal sense would be "in that the Spirit has become a shadow with glory and covered it (or Him)," which is clumsy and identifies not the body but the Spirit with the shadow. I do not think *hovani eṫeal* is a doublet "overshadowing"; and *p'aṙawk'* may be a misinterpretation of the Greek (instrumental for dative). The sense may then be: "as having become a shade for the glory of the Spirit, and covering Him (*or* it)." *Hovani* means also "shade" in the sense "cloak," and Weber (L* 98 note f) thinks it here renders σκενή (sic! = σκέπη? or σκηνή?), but it seems unlikely that the Greek would have changed from the σκιά of the rest of the chapter, which makes good sense. The rendering I have given is an attempt to allow both of the interpretations discussed in this note, while rendering rather the latter one.

[306] It is not said of Christ in the New Testament that His shadow cured the sick; but it is said of St. Peter (Acts 5. 15).

[307] Not "the same prophet" (that is, Jeremias) but Isa. 57. 1-4.

Quoted also (in variant form, cf. below) by Justin, *Apol.* 1. 48. 4, *Dial.* 16. 5, and — partially — *Dial.* 97. 2 and 110. 6, and in all these places attributed correctly to Isaias. The fact that the last quotation but one was from Isaias (Isa. 53. 8, in c. 70), and that the last quotation (Lam. 4. 20, in c. 71) was introduced by the words " And in another place Jeremias says," in which " in another place " is superfluous alongside the attribution to Jeremias (although the expression is perfectly normal) suggest that perhaps " Jeremias " is there an interpolated correction, and that the text originally was " And in another place he says," so giving attribution of Lam. 4. 20 to Isaias instead of that of the present quotation to Jeremias. In A.H. 3. 10. 3, where he quotes Lam. 4. 20, and in 4. 34. 5, where he quotes Isa. 57. 1, Irenaeus does not identify the prophets.

His burial shall be peace; he hath been taken away from the midst: LXX " in peace," and Irenaeus in his exegesis uses the expression " in peace "; but as the text has simply " peace " both here and when it is repeated below for exegesis, I do not emend " peace " to " in peace."

[308] " those who believe in Him, who, like Him, are persecuted and slain ": from a source common to Irenaeus and Justin (cf. Introd. § 37)? Justin, *Apol.* 1. 48. 4, has a similar expression (" along with the men who hope in Him ") in reference to the text here commented; and in *Dial.* 110. 6 he applies the same text to the persecution of Christians.

[309] " for ' in peace ' means, in that of salvation ": *k'anzi i xalalut'ean ē p'rkut'ean* = word for word ἐπεὶ ἐν εἰρήνῃ ἐστὶ σωτηρίας. AR* " it is in the peace of redemption " is a fair rendering of the words, but the sense seems to be more than that. PO* " in peace is salvation " gives a better sense but supposes emendation to *p'rkut'iwn*, unless it is to be taken as a mere paraphrase. As the text stands, " in peace " seems to be a quotation (though Irenaeus does not seem to have read " *in* peace " in the text commented, the original source of the exegesis probably did), and the expression " ' in peace ' is ' of salvation ' " may well be a reference to the Christian epitaph ἐν εἰρήνῃ, " in peace."

[310] " He was no more seen as one dead, after His burial ": *oč' ews erewec'aw yet t'alelwoyn mereal*; not " He appeared no more after His death and burial " (AR*), which both mistranslates the Armenian and is untrue in fact. The text punctuates before " for He was no more seen," thus giving: ". . . from the dead. Because He was no more seen . . . , for by dying and rising again . . . , the prophet says . . . ," but surely " He was no more seen . . ." is the explanation of what precedes. Doubtless the original source of the exegesis

understood " *His burial* hath been taken away," as Justin did (*Apol.* 1. 48, *Dial.* 16); this would make the explanation more fitting.

[311] Ps. 20. 5.

[312] Ps. 3. 6.

[313] Ps. 2. 1 f.

anointed one: Greek χριστός = " anointed," here so rendered by the Armenian (*awceal*) instead of as the proper name " Christ."

[314] Pontius Pilate was in fact governor from 27 to 37 A. D., under Tiberius, and so was recalled before the accession of Claudius (41 A. D.). Irenaeus, however, maintained that Christ died at the beginning of the reign of Claudius, and so makes Pilate " the procurator of Claudius." In A.H. 2. 22. 5 Irenaeus says that this dating of Christ's death was the witness of all the " elders " who knew John in Asia, as being St. John's own account, and that others gave the same account as being that of other apostles; and in the following section (2. 22. 6) alleges as confirmation John 8. 57: *the Jews therefore said to Him: thou art not yet fifty years old*; from this Irenaeus concludes that He must have been at least forty. He supposed, therefore, that about ten years of teaching elapsed between Christ's death and His baptism (in the fifteenth year of the reign of Tiberius, at the age of about thirty, cf. Luke 3. 1 and 23). As Irenaeus had had personal knowledge of at least one " elder " who had known John in Asia — namely, Polycarp — his evidence is not without weight, and it is not easy to explain how he could have fallen into this error of dating; for error it certainly is, though supported by a " proof from tradition " of greater weight than most such proofs.

[315] " Pilate . . . by Herod ": emending *Pilatosi Herovdea* to *Pilatos i Herovdea* (Akinean, *HAm.* 24 [1910] 207 n. 2).

" on the grounds that not to do so would be to go against Caesar ": *or zi t'ē oč' or zays arasc'ē k'an zhakaraksn Kayser gorcel.* The general sense is clear enough but the syntax is far from clear. Weber renders " qui enim nisi [is esset] qui [potius] hoc faceret quam opposita Caesari operaretur" ("... operari" would have been more literal), "for unless he [was the man] who would do this [rather] than go against Caesar " (strictly "... to go ..."), and explains this protasis-without-apodosis by reference to the Jewish imprecatory idiom (L* 101 note a). If this rendering be adopted, the explanation is rather to be sought in the universal idiom of aposiopesis in threats (" if you don't . . . ! "), for here the Jewish idiom referred to would be an assurance, addressed by the Jews to Pilate, that he was in fact the man to do so rather than go against Caesar (" if not so-and-so " =

"I swear that so-and-so"). This interpretation, however, is not entirely satisfactory; and it seems not unlikely that the beginning of the expression is corrupt, and that *k'an* "than" is a misrendering of ἤ meaning not "than" but "or," or more probably of ἤ. If we take *k'an* = ἤ and omit the second *or*, we have "for (they said) if he did not do so (*or* one who would not do so) would surely be going against Caesar" ("they said" to render in English the sense of indirect speech conveyed in Greek by the infinitive corresponding to *gorcel*).

316 Ps. 88. 39-46.

317 Zach. 13. 7, cited also by Justin, *Dial.* 53. 6 (with different reading), with the same comment as that made below by Irenaeus, that the disciples did not believe until Christ was risen.

the sheep of the flock shall be scattered: agreeing with the form quoted in Matt. 26. 31, Mark 14. 27 (but not agreeing with their *I will strike*); LXX *you will scatter the sheep. . . .*

318 Cf. Osee 10. 6 (LXX: *him they bound and carried off among the Assyrians as a present to King Jarim*). Cited also by Justin, *Dial.* 103. 4, in a form nearer to the LXX, but still omitting the name "Jarim."

319 Cf. Luke 23. 6-12.

"bidding him ascertain by questioning whatever he wished concerning Him": *hraman tueal nma harc'anel, hastat gitel zinč' kami yałags nora*, literally "giving him command *or* leave to interrogate, to find out for sure whatever he wants concerning Him," which — if correct — is presumably to be understood as alluding to Herod's curiosity about Christ, cf. Luke 23. 8 f.: (Herod) *was desirous of a long time to see Him, because he had heard many things of Him; and he hoped to see some signs wrought by Him. And he questioned Him in many words.* AR* has however: "giving command to enquire of him, that he might know of a certainty what he should desire concerning Him," which seems to make better sense: Pilate enquires of Herod what the latter desires. In the text as it stands, however, it is Herod who is bidden to enquire. The dative *nma* must be taken with *hraman tueal*, "giving command (or leave)"; "to enquire of him" would require the accusative (*zna*) with *harc'anel* "interrogate."

320 An apocryphal quotation found also — with variants — in A.H. 3. 20. 4, 4. 22. 1, 4. 33. 12, 5. 31. 1, and in Justin, *Dial.* 72. 4. It is attributed, as here, to Jeremias in A.H. 4. 22. 1 and by Justin, who says the Jews have erased it from the text; in A.H. 3. 20. 4 however

it is attributed to Isaias; the other two places just cited do not mention the source of the quotation. In no two of the six occurrences in question does the text of the quotation exactly agree.

[321] Isa. 65. 2.

[322] Ps. 21. 17 f.
Hounds: literally "hunting dogs"; LXX however "many dogs" (and so too Justin, *Dial.* 104. 1).

[323] *Ibid.* 15, but with the order of the clauses inverted.

[324] *Deliver . . . sword*: *ibid.* 21.
for the council . . . : *ibid.* 17 (just quoted in its true form)?
and my body from the nailing: cf. Ps. 118. 120 (LXX: *pierce from thy fear my flesh*).
That this last-mentioned phrase (the middle phrase of the quotation) is founded on Ps. 118. 120 just quoted is confirmed by the occurrence of the same composite quotation, in a form which reproduces more closely the psalm, in Barnabas, *Epist.* 5. 13: "Spare my soul from the sword, *and pierce my flesh*, for the assemblies of the malignant are risen up over me."
The quotation is thus almost certainly a "composite" one, due most likely, in its original form, of which the one presented in our text seems to be a corruption, to the massing together into one quotation of isolated texts next to each other in a collection of texts (cf. Introd. § 37), and there is no need to seek a corruption, in the Armenian or elsewhere, to account for the origin of our reading from the rest of Ps. 21. 21, with which the quotation begins (that is, from *my only-begotten from the hand of the dog*, as in the LXX). That no such corruption is involved in the text of Irenaeus, and that there is no point in Harnack's remark (EP* 63) that Ps. 21. 21 seems to have had a peculiar reading in Armenian, is evident from the fact that the reading which we now have, or one like it, must have stood in the text as originally written by Irenaeus, since he sees in it a clear reference to *crucifixion*.

[325] Deut. 28. 66.

[326] Ps. 21. 19.

[327] Cf. John 19. 23 f.

[328] Quoted, and attributed to Jeremias, in Matt. 27. 9-10. The gospel, however, has *the price of Him that was prized, whom they prized of the children of Israel*, a difference of reading which doubtless accounts for Harris's statement (*Expositor* 7. 3 [1907] 254, reprinted in *Testimonies* 1. 68) that Irenaeus's source is evidently not the gospel (but a book of "testimonies against the Jews," cf. Introd.

§ 37; to this same source Harris attributes the quotation in the gospel itself: *Testimonies* 1. 56).

The words attributed to Jeremias do not occur in our Old Testament, and the only parallel that can be alleged from that prophet is Jer. 32. 6-9, where there is question of the buying of a field, but no other similarity. In Zach. 11. 12 f. there is question of thirty pieces of silver, weighed for the " wages " of the prophet: *And the Lord said to me: Cast it to the statuary, a handsome price, that I was prized at by them. And I took the thirty pieces of silver, and I cast them into the house of the Lord to the statuary.*

[329] " staters *of the Law ": the text has *zgawaȓin satersn*, " the provincial (*or* local) staters," but there was no " local stater " proper to Jerusalem, and Vardanian pointed out (*HAm.* 24 [1910] 327) that confusion between νομός (" province, region ") and νόμος (" law ") occurs elsewhere in Armenian translations from the Greek. He understands the expression " staters of the law " to mean the money spoken of in the Old Testament; so too Weber (L* 105 note g), and Faldati (F* 147 n. 4). If, however, the meaning was simply that, " staters of the law " would not be a great improvement on " local staters " meaning the money locally current; and Jeremias is not " the Law," but " the Prophets." Surely Irenaeus has taken the expression from a source for which it meant " shekels of the sanctuary," that is, the currency required by the Law (cf. Lev. 27. 25 etc.) for official payments, that is, in practice, in the time of Christ, Phoenician tetradrachms; the Jews not being able to coin their own money, payments in the currency of the Law were made, as the Talmud tells us, in Phoenician currency. This coin is called " stater " in Matt. 17. 27 (tribute money for Christ and Peter; as the tax was a didrachm, and the coin was paid for the two, it must have been a tetradrachm). In Codex Bezae and elsewhere the word " stater " is used of the coin in which Judas was paid, instead of the received " silver piece " (Matt. 26. 15).

[330] Cf. Matt. 26. 14-16, 27. 3-5.

[331] Cf. Matt. 27. 6 f.

[332] Cf. Matt. 27. 34 (*wine* mixed with gall) and 48 (vinegar), Mark 15. 23 (*wine* mixed with *myrrh*) and 36 (vinegar), John 19. 28 f. (vinegar). There is, for Matt. 27. 34, a variant " *vinegar mixed* with gall," and Irenaeus seems to follow this reading here, unless he is working from memory and has not noticed that though all three evangelists mention vinegar, they do not record it as " mixed with " gall; or he may have taken " vinegar mixed with gall " from a

source other than the gospel; cf. the association of " vinegar and gall
to drink " in Barnabas, *Epist.* 7. 3 and 7. 5, and *Evangelium Petri* 5.

[333] Ps. 68. 22.

[334] Ps. 67. 18 f.

The Lord . . . hath ascended: normal form (LXX): *The Lord
among them on Sina in the holy place. Thou hast ascended. . . .*
Our text has the normal punctuation, but third person instead of
second, and as Irenaeus in his exegesis quotes *the Lord in Sion hath
ascended on high,* I have punctuated in accordance with this reading,
though I have not changed " Sina " to Irenaeus's later " Sion " (cf.
following note).

He hath led captivity captive: again third person for LXX second.

He hath taken, hath given gifts to men: as with the other verbs,
the text has the third person; moreover it has combined with the
LXX " taken " the variant " given (*to* men)."

[335] *in Sion*: sic! and it is clear from what follows that Irenaeus
meant " Sion," that is, the hill of Jerusalem. Did he think that
" Sina " (= Sinai) in the psalm meant Sion? Or did he read " Sion "
in the psalm, instead of " Sina "? In the latter case the reading
" Sina " of our text is a scribal " correction " into conformity with
the received text.

[336] Cf. Acts 1. 9-12.

[337] Ps. 23. 7.

[338] Word not recognised by creatures in His descent: cf. *Ascensio
Isaiae* 10.

" the principalities ": that is, the angels so called (*išxanut'iwnk'n,
ai ἀρχαί*), an exegesis of the word " princes " (*išxank', ἄρχοντες*)
which has become intruded into the psalm thanks to a misreading
of Hebrew *ša'ar* " gate " as *sar* " prince."

" the angels underneath ": the text has " the angels *within*," that
is, inside the firmament; but as the latter is thought of as a spherical
dome surrounding the earth, " within " the firmament means below
it, whereas to an English reader, who would think instead of Christ's
entry *into* heaven, " within " would convey the opposite impression.
In the same way the following " *on* the firmament " puts the angels
" on " the sphere in the same way in which we are " on " the earth,
that is " outside " the sphere, and " inside " the zone to which Christ
was to be admitted.

[339] Ps. 23. 8.

[340] *Ibid.* 10.

[341] " when all His enemies are made subject to Him ": *hnazan-*

dec'eloc' nma amenayn t'šnameac' ὑποταχθέντων αὐτῷ πάντων ἐχθρῶν. As the style of our version makes use of " genitives absolute," I have so rendered, although in normal Armenian one would have to understand the genitive as dependent upon " judgement."

Cf. Jude 6: *And the angels who kept not their principality, but forsook their own habitations, He hath reserved under darkness in everlasting chains, until the judgement of the great day*; and 2 Peter 2. 4: *God spared not the angels that sinned, but delivered them . . . to be reserved unto judgement.*

Cf. also 2 Enoch 7. 1-3, 18. 1-6; with " those who are found in rebellion, angels . . . who spurned the truth " cf. 2 Enoch 7. 3: (angels) " who apostatised from the Lord, who obeyed not the commandments of God and took counsel of their own will." (The word rendered " rebellion " in our text is *apstambut'iwn* " apostasy," cf. the explanation of the name " Satan," n. 90.)

[342] " Indeed, the same prophet David ": *ew ink'n isk margarēn Dawit'*. I render " the same prophet David " instead of " the prophet David himself," supposing *ink'n* (" himself," αὐτός) to be an erroneous rendering of ὁ αὐτός (" the same," Armenian *noyn*); but the text seems to be corrupt.

The Lord said . . . : Ps. 109. 1, here " said " (the normal form) instead of " saith " as in c. 48 and 49.

[343] Ps. 18. 7.

from the ends of heaven: the text's *i cagac' erknē* is more likely to be an error for *i cagac' erkni* than an instance of the Armenian idiom whereby a genitive is replaced by an apposition. (Cf. the inversion in " fruit of . . . belly," n. 180.)

resting-place: that is, destination, stopping-place. The reference is of course to the sun.

[344] *Ibid.*

there is none: Hitchcock, *Journal of Theological Studies* 9 (1908) 289, says that Irenaeus here follows the Hebrew against the LXX by reading " nothing "; he was misled by the rendering " nichts " in EP*. The text has *oč' ē* or . . . , which agrees with LXX οὐκ ἔστιν ὅς, though Armenian does not distinguish the gender.

[345] " and as what manner of man He should appear ": the text has *ew orpisi patmē erewel* = καὶ ὁποῖ- ἀγγέλλει φαίνεσθαι (case of ὁποῖ- uncertain). AR*: " in what manner He should make known His appearance," so agreeing with BK*; but *orpisi* is an adjective, so that " in what manner " should be " as what manner of man," and *patmel* is hardly a suitable verb for such a sense. The reference can hardly

be, for instance, to the star of Bethlehem, which in any case has received only passing mention in connection with prophecy. As the text stands it should mean "and what manner of man announces [His] appearance," and Faldati so takes it; so already L* "et quis narret [eum] apparere," taken (L* 108 note k) as a reference to John the Baptist; but no *prophecy* about the latter has been mentioned, not even in c. 41, referred to by L*, where Irenaeus mentions the Precursor. EP* takes *orpisi* as a mere expansion of the preceding *orpēs* "how," rendering "in welcher Weise er erscheinen sollte" ("in welcher Weise" for *orpēs ew orpisi*); Barthoulot renders *orpisi* "dans quelles conditions"; PO* "as what kind of a one"; and all three neglect *patmē*, taking the sense to be simply ". . . he should appear." This seems to me correct; one might suppose corruption to have arisen in the transmission of the Armenian text, for example of *pateh ē* to *patmē* ("He should appear" to "announces [Him] to appear"); more likely is the corruption ΜΕΛΛΕΙ to ΑΓΓΕΛΛΕΙ (same change of sense) in the Greek. This solution seems to me preferable to the emendation *patmec'in* for *patmē* (giving "and have announced as what manner of man He appears").

[346] Isa. 52. 7 (cf. Nah. 1. 15), but as quoted in Rom. 10. 15. The reading here agrees, against the LXX, with that of the epistle (but with the "Western" text thereof, in including *that bring good tidings of peace*, our text also adding *and*).

[347] Isa. 2. 3.

[348] Ps. 18. 5 (quoted Rom. 10. 18).

[349] Isa. 10. 23 (LXX), quoted in Rom. 9. 28.

[350] Rom. 13. 10.

[351] Matt. 22. 37-40.

[352] Cf. Isa. 50. 8 f. for the first part of the quotation (up to *eat you up*), and 2. 17 (rather than 11) for the rest; but the reading differs somewhat from that of the LXX.

is judged . . . is justified: LXX in both cases κρινόμενός μοι. Armenian *datin . . . ardaranin*. The former verb may also be a deponent, "judges" instead of passive, and is so taken by all save Barthoulot. PO* even renders the other verb in the active.

[353] Isa. 65. 15-16.

[354] Isa. 63. 9. Cf. c. 94 for an exegesis of this quotation.

[355] "The law has been fulfilled by Christ": the verb is *lnul* = πληροῦν, not *katarel* which might be ambiguous (cf. n. 360); hence "has been fulfilled," not "a été abrogée" (Barthoulot). Cf. Matt. 5. 17: *do not think I am come to destroy the law . . . I am come not to destroy, but to fulfil.*

"go free": or "live" in the sense "save their lives" (april = σώζεσθαι); "go free" better than "be saved."

"through faith and love towards the Son of God": or "through faith in the Son of God and charity" (i jeřn yOrdwoyn Astucoy hawatoy ew siroy).

356 Isa. 43. 18-21.

*in the desert: (so LXX) reading yanapati instead of the text's zanapati, which would give the sense "I will make the desert a way."

in dry land: after these words, the end of verse 19, Irenaeus — or his scribe, misled by homoeoteleuton, though the order of the words in the two like expressions differs in the LXX — omits "the beasts of the field shall bless me . . . because I have given . . . rivers in the dry land" and continues from there "go give drink. . . ."

357 "nor gave them to drink the Holy Spirit": ew oč' Hogin Surb arbuc'anēr znosa, which would be "nor was the Holy Spirit giving them to drink" (arbuc'anēr hardly passive), but I agree with Armitage Robinson (AR* 143 n. 2) that one should read zHogin Surb, accusative (in Greek nominative and accusative formally identical, πνεῦμα being neuter, which would account for the error). To the following relative "who" PO* add a note "(the Word)," but in the Armenian text it is impossible to identify the antecedent, and it seems more natural to refer "who" to the Spirit, though that is not so clear in the Armenian (cf. order of words in Armenian text cited above).

358 "And He has poured": so the text. Some suppose a negative and render "nor had He poured"; but the tense is aorist, as for the preceding affirmation, not imperfect, as for the negations.

"as He had promised through the prophets": cf. Joel 2. 26-29, quoted in Acts 2. 17 f.; and Isa. 44. 3.

"in the end of days": or ". . . of these days" (i vaxčan awurc's); cf. n. 41.

359 Rom. 7. 6.

in the oldness *of the letter: the text has i hnut'ean meroy = "in our oldness"; emendation of meroy to groyn gives the Pauline text.

360 I will perfect . . . a new covenant, not according to the covenant which . . . : the text has I will (perfect; but see below) the covenant which . . . ; I have restored the missing words, supposing the omission to be a scribal error due to homoeoteleuton (in the Greek "covenant" precedes "new"), a corruption more likely to have occurred in the transmission or translation of the Greek than in the Armenian, since the article appended to "covenant" in Armenian would be found at the end of the second occurrence, but not of the first, and "new"

would precede " covenant." If Irenaeus himself *did* read the text as we have it, he must presumably have understood συντελέσω " I will conclude " not as " I will perfect " but as " I will bring to an end."

[361] Jer. 31. 31-34, quoted in Heb. 8. 8-12 (LXX reference 38. 31-34).

covenant: first and third occurrence doublets (*uxt ktakarani* = διαθήκη; second occurrence *uxt* alone.

which I *will covenant: so LXX and Hebrews; the text has again " which I covenanted," but emendation of *uxtec'i* to *uxtec'ic'* gives the future tense.

I will be propitious: a doublet, *nerec'ic' ew k'awič' elēc'* = ἵλεως ἔσομαι.

to their iniquities: " iniquities " a doublet, *melac' anawrēnut'eanc'* = ἀδικίαις.

[362] " in whom ": *yors* = ἐν οἷς or εἰς οὕς. Hardly simply " to whom "; but may perhaps be for ἐν ᾧ " when."

" opened," that is, revealed, realised, as in c. 8.

[363] Isa. 17. 7 f.

[364] " the Word Himself says ": because the statement attributed to Him is in the first person, the Holy Spirit so speaking on the Word's behalf in the prophet (cf. n. 65 to Introd.).

I have been manifested . . . : Isa. 65. 1, of which the beginning (to *sought me not*) is quoted in Rom. 10. 20. The two clauses of this first part of the quotation are however in the opposite order to that of our text, both in Romans and in the LXX, except Codex Vaticanus and the " recension of Lucian," which have Irenaeus's order.

[365] Cf. Osee 2. 23 f. (LXX 2. 25) and 1. 10 (LXX 2. 1), but the quotation is given as in Rom. 9. 25 f.

The gender (" her ") of the " not-beloved " is taken from the Greek; Armenian does not distinguish gender. The text punctuates: " her that was not beloved, beloved shall be. In the place "; as the Scripture has " her that was not beloved, beloved. And it shall be," it is better to emend the punctuation as I have done, than to emend the grammar to " she . . . shall be beloved." Perhaps the text originally had also the " And " of the Scripture, and this was dropped when the punctuation was altered.

[366] Matt. 3. 9.

[367] " our hearts, taken away from stony services through faith see God ": " through faith " may be taken with " taken away " or " see God," occurring in the text as in the English between the two verbs. It would be more natural however to take them with " taken away."

The sense is not " delivered from stony services *and drawn* through faith " or the like, as PO* or F* ("lifted up [sollevati] through faith ") take it. The expression *i bac' korzeal hanealk'* is simply a doublet corresponding to ἀφαιρεθεῖσαι, as is seen from the following quotation (cf. following note, on " take away ").

" stony services ": cf. the " stony heart " of the quotation which follows. Irenaeus alludes to "worship of stones," cf. A.H. 3. 9. 1, " a lapidum cultura," in exegesis, as here, of the Osee quotation; and 4. 7. 2 " a lapidum religione."

368 Ezech. 36. 26 f., with an omission.

them, their, they: LXX has second person plural.

take away: a doublet, *i bac' korzeal hanic'* = ἀφελῶ.

another heart of flesh, so that: " another " not in LXX; between " flesh " and " so that " our text omits the beginning of verse 27.

369 John 1. 14 (" *His* Word ": sic!).

370 " Elias's angel ": *hreštak Ełiay*. Or, taking *Ełiay* as in apposition to *hreštak* (nominative), so giving " Elias as a messenger " (" angel," Greek ἄγγελος = " messenger "). This may perhaps be the sense intended, that is, not through the Law (" Moses ") nor through the prophets (" Elias "); but L* may well be right, in spite of the indefinite *hreštak*, in understanding the genitive (= *Ełiayi*), so giving " Elias's angel," the sense thus being, not through a mere man as intercessor (as Moses was instrumental in saving the Hebrews from Egypt) nor even through an angel (as Elias was succoured by an angel, cf. 3 Kings 19. 5-7); a sense which seems to me more likely.

Cf. Isa. 63. 9, quoted in c. 88; *not an intercessor, nor an angel, but the Lord Himself hath given them life.*

371 " than to the Synagogue of the past ": *zařajnoc' žołovanin*, without " than," so apparently in apposition with " Church "; PO* " (the Church) the company of the first-born " — but *zařajin* is not " first-born "; F* " all'adunanza dei primi," whatever that means. L* " quam priorum synagogae," supposing (L* 115 note c) *k'an* " than " to have dropped out — cf. end of chapter, where " the former Synagogue " is *ařajin žołovarann*, and supporting this contention by taking *z-* of *zařajnoc'* as the sign of the accusative usual after *k'an*. This would require emendation of *žołovanin* to the accusative; but it is simpler to suppose that *zařajnoc'* is from *zařajin* and that *k'an* was here followed by the dative, balancing the dative of the preceding term, a comparatively rare but perfectly regular construction,

which in instances such as the present one is even preferable to the more usual use of the accusative.

Even before the first publication of the new-found *Proof* Rendel Harris had remarked that the greater fruitfulness of the Church as compared with the synagogue seemed to have been a feature of the Catena against the Jews which may well have been the source of much of the *Proof* (*Expositor* 7. 2 [1906] 406 f.; reprinted in *Testimonies* 1. 16 f. Cf. Introd. § 37). For this argument, cf. *Epistola* 2. 2 attributed to Clement of Rome.

[372] Isa. 54. 1 (quoted in Gal. 4. 27).

didst not bear . . . wast not in travail: LXX and Gal. have present tense. With the statement that the former Synagogue had the law for husband, and the implication that the Church is " desolate," contrast A.H. 4. 31. 2, where Irenaeus, seeking edification in the story of Lot's daughters' incest with their father, says that it shows " that there is no other that can give generation of children to the elder and the younger synagogue, but our Father," meaning the Word.

[373] Deut. 28. 44.

[374] Deut. 32. 21, but with " ye, you " for LXX " they, them." The latter portion (*I will make* onwards) is quoted in Rom. 10. 19, which also has the second person.

[375] " prophesying for Baal ": cf. Jer. 2. 8.

" God's citizens ": *i k'ałak'avarut'eann Astucoy* = ἐν τῷ πολιτεύματι Θεοῦ.

[376] Cf. Polycarp, *Ad Phil.* 3. 3: " He who has charity is far from all sin "; Rom. 13. 10: *the love of our neighbour worketh no evil*; and 1 John *passim*.

[377] Cf. Gal. 3. 24 f.: *the law was our pedagogue in Christ, that we might be justified by faith; but after the faith is come, we are no longer under a pedagogue.* " Pedagogue " does not mean " schoolmaster "; if there is any " schoolmaster " in the metaphor, it is Christ, to whom men were led by the law that they might learn the faith. A " pedagogue " in ancient times was a slave attendant upon a child, his chief duty being to conduct him to school.

[378] Cf. 1 Cor. 14. 20: *in malice be children, and in sense be perfect* (and the explanation of man's primal innocence as that of childhood, c. 14).

[379] Exod. 20. 14; and Matt. 5. 27.

[380] Cf. Matt. 5. 28: *whosoever shall look on a woman to lust after her hath already committed adultery with her in his heart.*

" who has not *even conceived the desire ": *or oč' ē c'ankut'iwn ankam oč' ekeal.* In this and in the parallel phrases later in the chapter the syntax is curious, but the sense clear enough. Here however the sense would be " who has not conceived involuntary desire," but the parallel expression below ("cannot even put forth his hand to revenge ") supports the emendation of *ankam* to *angam,* so giving the version I have adopted.

[381] Exod. 20. 13; and Matt. 5. 21.

[382] Cf. Matt. 5. 22: *whosoever is angry with his brother, shall be in danger of the judgement.*

[383] Exod. 20. 17 (LXX, with omissions).

[384] Cf. Matt. 6. 19 f.; Luke 12. 33.

[385] So in Matt. 5. 38; cf. Exod. 21. 24 = Lev. 24. 20 = Deut. 19. 21.

[386] Tithes: cf. e. g. Exod. 22. 29.

" who leaves father and mother . . .": cf. Matt. 19. 29.

[387] " constantly keeping sabbath ": cf. Justin, *Dial.* 12. 3 ("the new law would have you celebrate a perpetual sabbath ").

Christians are God's temple: cf. 1 Cor. 3. 16 f.

[388] Osee 6. 6 (*I desire mercy and not sacrifice* also Matt. 9. 13 and 12. 7).

[389] Isa. 66. 3.

immolate: Armenian *spananic'ē* " slay," so corresponding to the LXX ἀποκτέννων. In saying that Irenaeus here quotes in accordance with the Massoretic text rather than with the LXX, Hitchcock, *Journal of Theological Studies* 9 (1908) 289, is misled by EP* " würge " ("strangle ").

[390] Joel 2. 32 (LXX 3. 5), quoted Acts 2. 21 and Rom. 10. 13.

[391] A free quotation adapted from Acts 4. 12.

[392] Cf. Mark 1. 27.

[393] " *Satan is cast out from men ": the text has *mekneal zatani i mardkanē,* which may be represented literally by " being-sundered departs from men," with no subject expressed. Attempts to take the verb impersonally (EP* " findet eine Schneidung in der Menschheit statt "; AR* " there is a separation and division among mankind ") do not do justice to the expression, and PO* " He upon whom is called the name of Jesus Christ . . . is separated from men " involves also distortion of the preceding words. As Weber points out

(L* 118 note c), the context does not suggest any reference to the separation of saved from reprobate or the like. On the other hand, the previous sentence referred to the devils and evil spirits as obeying Christ, and there is abundant evidence for the use of the expression " in the name of Jesus Christ, crucified under Pontius Pilate " (note the addition, pointless if the reference is simply to a " separation " of mankind) in the formula of exorcism. So e. g. Justin, *Apol.* 2. 6. 6; *Dial.* 30. 3, 76. 6, 85. 2. Hence the missing subject must be "the devil " or the like. One might simply emend the verb to a plural: " they are cast forth " (" they," that is, the " devils " etc. just mentioned), but it is better to supply a subject; L* supplies " daemonium," F* " lo spirito del male." I propose the emendation of *mekneal zatani i mardkanē* to *mekneal zatani Satanay i mardkanē*, where the similarity *zatani: Satanay i* is sufficient to account for the corruption (*zatani* to *Satani* would be a smaller change, and the insertion of *Satani* after *zatani* would give a more easily explained corruption, and be from the point of view of textual criticism the obvious emendation, but the translator of the *Proof* surely wrote — or meant to write — *mekneal zatani Satanay*). I find that this emendation has occurred independently to L.-M. Froidevaux.

³⁹⁴ " and do His will ": the verbal form is the " gerund " (*aṝnelov*), like that of the preceding " by invoking," while " believe in him " uses the participle. The distinction is probably due to the fact that " invoke " and " do " are active, whereas " believe " governs the dative. In any case, all three forms were most likely genitive participles in the Greek, and the sense is surely as I have rendered, not " by invoking Him — of those who believe in Him — and *by doing His will*."

³⁹⁵ " rendering thanks ": or " giving praise "; *gohanamk'* = εὐχαριστοῦμεν or ἐξομολογοῦμεν or the like.

" His human career ": *mardoyn k'alak'avarut'iwnn nora* = " His πολίτευμα as man."

the things . . . : Luke 18. 27.

³⁹⁶ Not Jeremias but Bar. 3. 29-4. 1. Harnack remarks (EP* 64) that this is important as one of the earliest citations of Baruch, and that Athenagoras cited him first. The verse *he was seen upon earth and conversed with men* (= 3. 38) is echoed in A.H. 4. 20. 4, without mention of any prophet's name, and not, indeed, expressly as a quotation; and similarly without attribution in Athenagoras, *Suppl.* 9, we have " the Lord is our God, none other shall be accounted with Him," which corresponds well enough with 3. 35. It is noteworthy that both of these echoes are from the passage here quoted.

her: in Baruch the feminine is used, and I have accordingly so translated, though Armenian does not distinguish gender. In Baruch the pronoun refers to Wisdom (Greek Σοφία, feminine); here it seems to be applied to " redemption " (ἀπολύτρωσις or σωτηρία " salvation," both words feminine in Greek) rather than to "Wisdom." PO* uses the masculine, as if the reference were to Christ; this is of course possible as a rendering of the Armenian, but the Greek original presumably had the feminine, as in the LXX.

knoweth her with His wisdom: LXX " knoweth her and hath found her with His wisdom ": scribal error, homoeoteleuton?

fat cattle: literally " with fat-things, with-quadrupeds," *čarpovk' č'ork'otaneawk'*.

that is for ever: as LXX, qualifying " law "; the verb is plural in Armenian because *awrēnk'* " law " is plural in form.

[397] Cf. the account of creation, c. 11 (and Introd. § 33).

[398] " This, beloved, is the preaching of the truth ": taking " beloved " as a vocative, rather than the grammatically possible " This is the beloved preaching of the truth."

[399] " way of life ": cf. c. 1.

" the Church in the whole world ": that is, the ecumenical or " Catholic " Church; an expression frequent in *Adversus haereses*.

" sound moral character ": *aŕołj kamawk' baruc'n*, more literally " healthy will of behaviour."

[400] " And now ": the text has *yoržam* = " when," probably a corruption. Marcion and the Gnostics opposed the Creator, regarded as a subordinate demiurge, to the Father-God of the New Testament, cf. Introd. § 29, 30. With the expression " think they have found on their own account something greater than the truth " cf. similar expressions in the same connection in *Adversus haereses*, e. g. A.H. 3. 12. 12: " putaverunt semetipsos plus invenisse quam apostoli, alterum deum adinvenientes."

[401] That is, in *Adversus haereses*; cf. n. 51 to Introd.

[402] " the dispensation of His incarnation ": I have rendered as " dispensation " the word *tnawrēnut'iwn* = οἰκονομία, although in such expressions as the present one it is more usually rendered " Mystery," since Latins are accustomed to speak of " the Mystery of the Incarnation." Here such a rendering would blunt the point of the expression, since what the heretics referred to had " despised " was more precisely the manner and genuineness of the Incarnation. The reference is to docetic and similar views, denying the true human birth of Christ; cf. Introd. § 31.

[403] Marcion and others denied the gifts of the Holy Spirit in general (rejecting the gospel of St. John and the sending of the Holy Spirit), and in particular denied prophecy.

"do not admit": Faldati by an oversight omits the negative.

[404] Isa. 1. 30.

[405] "three articles of our seal": that is, the Persons of the Trinity (cf. c. 6, and for "article," end of n. 39), "our seal" being baptism (cf. n. 22).

[406] Cf. Introd. § 7.

INDEX

INDEX

Aaron, 64 f., 161
Abeghian, M., 119 f.
Abel, 58
Abimelech, 161
Abraham, and Sem's blessing, 60, 62 f.; God's promises, 63, 65, 70; search for God, 35, 62, 160 f.; theophany, 26, 62 f., 76 f., 183; faith, 43, 62 f., 70, 104 f.; " God of A.," 34, 53, 63 f.; Christ's ancestor, 67, 70 f., 73, 87, 90; genealogy, (60), 158; other refs., 76, 157, 160 f. See *Apocalypsis Abrahami*
absolute, 23 f., 136 ff., 146
ἀχώρητος, 138, 141
Acts of Apostles, 34; cited (?) in *Proof*, 106; (in Notes) 158, 161 f., 176, 184, 197, 216
Adam, creation, 42, 54, 68; original privilege, 26 f., 30 f., 41, 54 ff., 150; theophany, 26, 55, 184; and human race, 68 f., 166 f.; and Christ, 30, 42, 68 f., 167-71; other refs., 61, 148, 150
Adam and Eve, children, 38, 42, 55 f., 150; fall and after, 56 ff.
Adontz, 119
adoption, of man by God, 30, 52
" Adversary " (Satan), 153
Adversus haereses: mention in *Proof*, 108; title, 22, 124; and *Proof*, 6, 14 f., 22, 35 ff., 44, 117, 181, 196 and parallels in Notes; Latin, 120, 127, 176, 178; other refs., 4, 14 f., 27, 34, 36, 38 f., 114, 121, 123-34, 136-44, 146-50, 153 f., 156, 165, 167-76, 181 183-86, 189, 191 f., 194 ff., 202, 204 ff., 214 f., 217 f.; and see Armenian Irenaeus
Aeon, 24, 26, 136, 146, 148
Africa, 158
Akinean, N., 9, 118 ff., 122, 135, 166, 196, 205

alchemy, 156
Alexandrian Fathers, 3, 21. See Clement, Origen
" Almighty " (παντοκράτωρ), 50, 52, 67, 69, 73, 145
Amalec, 78, 185
Ambrose of Milan, 163
Amorrhites, 59, 157
Amos, 9. 11 cited in *Proof*, 72, 89; cf. 128
ἀνακεφαλαίωσις, 127; cf. 142. See recapitulation
angel(s), fall(en), 57 f., 99 f., 106, 147, 149 f., 153, 155, 210 (see devil, Satan); unions with man, 58, 155; archangel of world, 54, 149 f.; other refs., 24, 27 f., 41, 52-55, 64, 76, 99, 102, 105, 120, 146-50, 191, 209, 214 (principal, 52-55, 146-50)
anger, 106
Anointed = " Christ," 82, 189, 192; for *K'ristos* of MS, 79 f., 89, (187, 197 f.); = King, 79 f., 192; by Spirit, 78, 82; other refs., 73, 95, 189, 202, 205
Apocalypse (canonical), 176 f., 196
Apocalypsis Abrahami, 161
Apocalypsis Petri, 150
Apocrypha, 34 f. See following entry, and *Apocalypsis (Abrahami, Petri)*, *Ascensio Isaiae*, Enoch, *Evangelium Petri*, Jubilees, *Protevangelium Iacobi*, *Testamentum Levi*
apocryphal quotations in *Proof*, 33 ff.; explicitly as Scripture, 75, 92, 97 f., (182, 200, 206 ff.); possible, 147, 157, 193
Apologists, 3, 20, 37 ff. (see individual names)
" apostate " (*apstamb*), 153, 210. See rebel
Apostles, and Irenaeus, 1, 19, 36,

223

character, sacramental, 135
charism(ata), 27, 40, 52 f., 109, 144 f., 147
charity, 43, 74, 88, 101 f., 105
Charles, R. H., 146
Cherubim, 54, 148
Chiliasm, 36, 42, 88, 129, 181, 196
childish innocence, 38, 55 f., 66, 78, 106, 150, 215
Christ, *passim*; in type & prophecy, 20, 51, 55, 60, 64 f., 67, 70, 72 f., 76-104, 107 f., 141, 151, 195; is Son of God, 25 f., 49, 51, 53, 61, 67-73, 75-86, 88-94, 100, 104-109; and the Spirit, 27, 29, 53, 67 f., 73 f., 78, 80, 82, 85 ff., 94 f., 108, 202 f. (Christ is "Spirit of God," 93, 202; Spirit of Christ, 94 f.; of Emmanuel, 85); and devils, 106 f., 150, 217; Gnostic "Christ," 26 (cf. heresy). See Abraham, Adam, Anointed, ascension, betrayal, birth, blood, body, burial, David, death, divinity, enemies, faith, glory, hell, heresy, Holy One, humanity, image, incarnation, king, life, man, manifestation, ministry, miracles, Moses, name, passion, primacy, race, resurrection, rock, shadow, triumph
Church, in type and prophecy, 42, 60, 65, 67, 74, 88, 101-105, 141, 159, 196, 214 f.; other refs., 21, 32, 44, 74, 104 f., 108, 218
Cineans, 157
circumcision, 63, 135
Claudius, 6, 36, 42, 95, 205
Clement of Alexandria, 21, 39, 140, 150
Clement of Rome (and Pseudo-Clement), 37, 135, 140, 163, 202, 215
Codex Bezae, 129, 194, 197, 208
Col. 1. 18 cited in *Proof*, 72 f.; cf. 177
Comitas, Catholicos, 118
communion, of God and man, 30 f., 51, 67 f., 73, 81, 127, 165 f., 177
concupiscence, 56, 151
Conybeare, C. F., 8, 118 f., 122, 188 f.

1. Cor., 28, 136, 176, 215
cosmetics, 58, 155 f.
convenants, of God with man, 56, 61, 63, 89, 103; cf. promises
creation, 26, 50, 75 f., 136-40, 180 f.; of man, 27, 54 ff.; parallel with incarnation, 26, 30 f., 41 f., 68 f., 169 ff.; and angels, 24, 52, 54, 148. See Son, Spirit
"Creative Word," 29, 71, 124, 175 f.
creed, 43, 131
Cremers, V., 129
Cross, crucifixion, and tree, 69; and universe, 70, 172; in type and prophecy, 77 f., 84, 90, 97 f., 185, 207; ignominy, 84, 192; Sign of Cross, 135, 172; other refs., 92 f., 95, 98
curses, 57-60, 62, 153 f., 156
Cyprian of Carthage, 187
Cyrus, 187

Dan. 11. 13 cited in *Proof*, 51 f.
David, Christ's ancestor, 67, 70-73, 87, 89 f.; speaks for Christ, 80, 92, 95; God's promise to, 70 f., 89 f.; *tabernacle of*, 72, 89; cited as source (for Ps.), 48, 78 ff., 89, 95-101; (for apocryphal quotation), 35, 92
death, comes into world, 56 ff., 68 f., 153; abolished by Christ, 51, 68 f., 71 f., 100; Christ's, 26, 49, 69 72 ff., 89 f., 92, 94-97, 204 f.
Decalogue, 42, 64, 106
"deification" of man, 135 f.
demiurge, 24 ff., 29, 124, 137 f., 145, 148, 175 f., 218
desert, 64 ff., 77 f., 102, 212
Deuteronomy, 32, 66 f., 128, 165; cited in *Proof*, 67, 98, 105 (named as source, 105)
devil(s), 24, 29, 57 f., 106 f., 149 f., 153 f., 217
διακονία, 145
Didache, 37, 132, 134, 185
Diekamp, F., 123
disobedience, primal, 57, 68 f., 71, 150; to God is evil, 69, 172
divinity, of Creator, 24 f., 40. 49-52,

ANCIENT CHRISTIAN WRITERS

The Works of the Fathers in Translation

Edited by

J. QUASTEN, S. T. D., and J. C. PLUMPE, Ph. D.

NO